MU123
Discovering mathematics

BOOK B
Units 5–7

This publication forms part of an Open University module. Details of this and other Open University modules can be obtained from the Student Registration and Enquiry Service, The Open University, PO Box 197, Milton Keynes MK7 6BJ, United Kingdom (tel. +44 (0)845 300 60 90; email general-enquiries@open.ac.uk).

Alternatively, you may visit the Open University website at www.open.ac.uk where you can learn more about the wide range of modules and packs offered at all levels by The Open University.

To purchase a selection of Open University materials visit www.ouw.co.uk, or contact Open University Worldwide, Walton Hall, Milton Keynes MK7 6AA, United Kingdom for a brochure (tel. +44 (0)1908 858779; fax +44 (0)1908 858787; email ouw-customer-services@open.ac.uk).

The Open University, Walton Hall, Milton Keynes MK7 6AA.

First published 2010. Second edition 2014.

Edited, designed and typeset by The Open University, using the Open University TeX System.

Printed in the United Kingdom by Henry Ling Limited, at the Dorset Press, Dorchester DT1 1HD.

ISBN 978 1 7800 7864 9

2.1

Contents

Contents

Algebra

Introduction

In Unit 2 you met the idea of using letters to represent numbers. In this unit you'll learn much more about this sort of mathematics, which is called **algebra**. You'll begin to see how useful it can be, and you'll begin to learn the techniques that will allow you to make the most of it.

You'll need to use the algebraic skills covered in this unit when you study some of the later units in the module, and they're essential for any further mathematics modules. So it's important that you become proficient in them. The only way to do that is to practise them! You'll have lots of opportunity for that in this unit.

Muḥammad ibn Mūsā al-Khwārizmī was a member of the House of Wisdom in Baghdad, a research centre established by the Caliph al-Ma'mūn. His name is the origin of the word 'algorithm'. As you saw in Unit 2, an algorithm is a procedure for solving a problem or doing a calculation.

The word 'algebra' is derived from the title of the treatise *Al-kitab-al mukhtasar fi hisab al-jabr* (Compendium on calculation by completion and reduction), written by the Central Asian mathematician Muḥammad ibn Mūsā al-Khwārizmī in around 825. This treatise deals with solving linear and quadratic equations, which you'll learn about in this module, starting with linear equations in this unit. The treatise doesn't use algebra in the modern sense, as no letters or other symbols are used to represent numbers. Modern algebra developed gradually over time, and it was not until the sixteenth and seventeenth centuries that it emerged in the forms that we recognise and use today.

1 Why learn algebra?

What's the point of learning algebra? Why is it useful? In this section you'll see some answers to these questions.

1.1 Proving mathematical facts

This first activity is about a number trick.

Activity 1 *Think of a number*

Try the following number trick.

Choose a fairly small number, so that the arithmetic is easy!

    Think of a number.
    Double it.
    Add 7.
    Double the result.
    Add 6.
    Divide by 4.
    Take away the number you first thought of.
    Find the corresponding letter of the alphabet.
    Name an animal beginning with that letter.

For example, if your number is 3, then your letter is C, the third letter of the alphabet.

Now look at the solution on page 51.

Activity 2   *Think of another number*

Try the trick in Activity 1 again, choosing a different number to start with. Look at the solution on page 51 and then read the discussion below.

In Activities 1 and 2 you probably found that with both your starting numbers you obtained the number 5 in the third-last step (the last step involving a mathematical calculation) and so each time you obtained the letter E. If you didn't, then check your arithmetic! When asked to name an animal beginning with the letter E, nearly everyone thinks of 'elephant'.

The idea behind the trick is that the number 5 is obtained in the last mathematical step, no matter what the starting number is. But how can you be sure that the trick works for *every possible* starting number? You can't test them all individually as there are infinitely many possibilities.

There's a way to check this – using algebra. In this unit you'll learn the algebraic techniques that are needed, and you'll see how to use them to check that the trick always works.

As you saw earlier in the module, a demonstration that a piece of mathematics *always* works is called a **proof**. Proofs of mathematical facts are needed in all sorts of contexts, and algebra is usually the way to construct them.

You might like to try the trick on a friend, or a child who's old enough to do the arithmetic. Write the word 'elephant' on a piece of paper beforehand, ready to reveal at the end of the trick.

1.2   Finding and simplifying formulas

Suppose that a baker makes a particular type of loaf. Each loaf costs 69p to make, and is sold for £1.24. The baker sells all the loaves that he makes.

On a particular day, the baker makes 30 loaves. Let's calculate the profit that he makes from them. The total cost, in £, of making the loaves is

$$30 \times 0.69 = 20.70.$$

The total amount of money, in £, paid for the loaves by customers is

$$30 \times 1.24 = 37.20.$$

So the profit in £ is given by

$$37.20 - 20.70 = 16.50.$$

That is, the profit is £16.50.

On a different day, the baker might make a different number of loaves. It would be useful for him to have a formula to help him calculate the profit made from *any* number of loaves. To obtain the formula, we represent the number of loaves by a letter, say n, and work through the same calculation as above, but using n in place of 30.

The total cost, in £, of making the loaves is

$$n \times 0.69 = 0.69n.$$

The total amount of money, in £, paid for the loaves by customers is

$$n \times 1.24 = 1.24n.$$

So if we represent the profit by £P, then we have the formula

$$P = 1.24n - 0.69n.$$

Remember that if a letter and a number are multiplied together, then we omit the multiplication sign, and we write the number first. So, for example, we write

$$n \times 0.69$$

as

$$0.69n.$$

Activity 3   *Using a formula*

Use the formula above to calculate the profit for 48 loaves.

You should have no further problems calculating your profit now, Mr Davies!

$$P = \frac{n^2(1.24^2 - \sqrt{n} - 0.69^2 + \sqrt{n})}{1.24n + 0.69n}$$

The formula makes it easy to calculate the profit, because you don't need to think through the details of the calculation. You just substitute in the number and do a numerical calculation. This is the advantage of using a formula.

In fact, the task of calculating the profit can be made even more straightforward. It's possible to find a *simpler* formula for P, by looking at the situation in a different way. The profit, in £, for each loaf of bread is

$1.24 - 0.69 = 0.55$.

So the profit, in £, for n loaves of bread is

$n \times 0.55 = 0.55n$.

So we have the alternative formula

$P = 0.55n$.

This formula, like the first one, can be used for any value of n.

Activity 4   *Using a better formula*

Use the new formula above to find the profit for 48 loaves of bread.

The alternative formula for the profit is better because it is simpler and using it involves less calculation.

In this case, a simpler formula was found by thinking about the situation in a different way. However, it is often easier to find whatever formula you can, and then use algebra to turn it into a simpler form. You'll begin to learn how to do this later in the unit.

Algebra can also help you to *find* formulas. The formula for the baker's profit was obtained directly from the situation that it describes, but it's often easier to obtain formulas by using other formulas that you know already. Algebra is needed for this process, and it's also needed to turn the new formula into a simpler form. You'll find out more about this in Unit 7.

1.3   Answering mathematical questions

Consider the following.

A school has stated that 30% of the children who applied for places at the school were successful. It allocated 150 places. How many children applied?

To help you to think clearly about questions like this, it helps to represent the number that you want to find by a letter. Let's use N to represent the number of children who applied.

The next step is to write down what you know about N in mathematical notation. We know that 30% of N is 150. That is,

$$\frac{30}{100} \times N = 150,$$

which can be written more concisely as

$$\tfrac{3}{10}N = 150. \tag{1}$$

This is an example of an *equation*. To answer the question about the school places, you have to find the value of N that makes the equation correct when it's substituted in. This is called *solving* the equation.

You'll learn exactly what 'equation' means in the next section.

One way to solve the equation is as follows:

> *Three*-tenths of N is 150,
>
> so *one*-tenth of N is $150 \div 3 = 50$,
>
> so N is $10 \times 50 = 500$.

You'll learn a different way to solve this equation in Section 5.

So the number of children who applied was 500.

You can confirm that this is the right answer by checking that equation (1) is correct when $N = 500$ is substituted in.

Activity 5 *Using an equation*

Two-fifths of the toddlers in a village attend the local playscheme. Twenty-four toddlers attend the playscheme. Let the total number of toddlers in the village be T.

(a) Write down an equation (similar to equation (1)) involving T.

(b) Find the value of T.

You could probably have answered the questions about the school places and the toddlers without using equations. But now read the following.

> Catherine wants to contribute to a charitable cause, using her credit card and a donations website. The donations company states that from each donation, first it will deduct a 2% charge for credit card use, then it will deduct a charge of £3 for use of its website, and then the remaining money will be increased by 22% due to tax payback. How much money (to the nearest penny) must Catherine pay if she wants the cause to receive £40?

This question is a bit harder! But it can be answered by writing the information in the question as an equation and using algebra, as you'll see at the end of the unit.

The advantage of writing the information in a question as an equation is that it reduces the problem of answering the question to the problem of solving an equation. The equation may be more complicated than the two that you've seen in this section, but there are standard algebraic techniques for solving many equations, even complicated ones. You'll learn some of these techniques in this unit.

So now you've seen just the beginnings of what algebra can do. Algebra is used in many different fields, including science, computer programming, medicine and finance. For example, it's used to create formulas so that computer programs can carry out many different tasks, from calculating utility bills to producing images on screens. And it's used in mathematical models, so that predictions, such as those about the economy and climate change, can be made by solving equations. Algebra allows us to describe, analyse and understand the world, to solve problems and to set up procedures. Our lives would be very different if algebra had not been invented!

You'll learn more about the power of algebra if you take further modules in mathematics.

1.4 How to learn algebra

Now that you've seen some reasons why algebra is useful, you should be ready to learn more about it.

Algebraic notation is 'the language of mathematics', and it takes time to learn, like any new language. So don't worry if you don't absorb some of the ideas immediately. Allow yourself time to get to grips with them, and keep practising the techniques. You learn a language by using it, not by reading about it! Remember that any difficulties will often be quickly sorted out if you call your tutor or post a question on the online forum.

The activities in this unit have been designed to teach you algebra in a step-by-step manner. They give you the opportunity to practise, and become familiar with, each new technique before you meet the next one – this is important, because most of the techniques build on techniques introduced previously. You should aim to do *all* the activities, and you should do them in the order in which they're presented.

Do the activities even if they look easy – many students find that there are small gaps or misunderstandings in their skills that they're unaware of until they attempt the activities or check their answers against the correct answers. This unit gives you the opportunity to identify and deal with such problems, and so prevent them causing difficulties later. You may even find that some activities throw new light on techniques with which you're familiar. Do *all* the parts of each activity – the parts are often different in subtle ways, and frequently the later parts are more challenging than the earlier ones.

Many activities are preceded by worked examples, which demonstrate the techniques needed. Before you attempt each activity, read through any relevant worked examples, or watch the associated tutorial clips if they're available, and try to make sure that you understand each step.

Tutorial clips are available for the more complex techniques. You will probably find that you learn more effectively by watching the tutorial clips rather than by just reading through the worked examples.

Set out your solutions in a similar way to those in the worked examples. Remember that any 💬 green text within the think bubble icons 💬 isn't part of the solutions, but any other words in the solutions *are* part of them, and similar explanations should be included in your own solutions.

Enjoy learning the new skills!

2 Expressions

In this section you'll learn some terminology used in algebra, and a useful technique – collecting like terms.

2.1 What is an expression?

In the module you've worked with various formulas, such as

$$P = 0.55n \quad \text{and} \quad T = \frac{D}{5} + \frac{H}{600}.$$

These formulas involve the elements

$$P, \quad 0.55n, \quad T \quad \text{and} \quad \frac{D}{5} + \frac{H}{600},$$

which are all examples of *algebraic expressions*. An **algebraic expression**, or just **expression** for short, is a collection of letters, numbers and/or mathematical symbols (such as $+$, $-$, $\times$, $\div$, brackets, and so on), arranged in such a way that if numbers are substituted for the letters, then you can work out the value of the expression.

So, for example, $5n + 20$ is an expression, but $5n + \div 20$ is not an expression, because '$+ \div$' doesn't make sense.

To make expressions easier to work with, we write them concisely in the ways you saw earlier in the module. In particular, we usually omit multiplication signs; things that are multiplied are just written next to each other instead. For example, $0.55 \times n$ is written as $0.55n$. But it's sometimes helpful to include some multiplication signs in an expression – and a multiplication sign between two numbers can't be omitted.

When you're working with expressions, the following is the key thing to remember.

> Letters represent numbers, so the normal rules of arithmetic apply to them in exactly the same way as they apply to numbers.

In particular, the BIDMAS rules apply to the letters in expressions.

When you substitute numbers for the letters in an expression and work out its value, you're **evaluating** the expression.

> The first formula here is the 'baker's profit' formula from Subsection 1.2, and the second is Naismith's Rule from Unit 2.

> You saw how to write formulas concisely in Unit 2, Subsection 3.2.

> The BIDMAS rules were covered in Unit 1, Subsection 2.1 and are summarised in the Handbook.

Example 1 *Evaluating an expression*

Evaluate the expression

$$4x^2 - 5y$$

when $x = 2$ and $y = -3$.

Solution

If $x = 2$ and $y = -3$, then

$$\begin{aligned} 4x^2 - 5y &= 4 \times 2^2 - 5 \times (-3) \\ &= 4 \times 4 - (-15) \\ &= 16 + 15 \\ &= 31. \end{aligned}$$

Activity 6 *Evaluating expressions*

Evaluate the following expressions when $a = -2$ and $b = 5$.

(a) $\frac{5}{2} + a$ (b) $-a + ab$ (c) ab^2 (d) $b + 3(b - a)$

> Remember to apply the BIDMAS rules. Be particularly careful in part (d).

Expressions don't have to contain letters – for example, $(2+3) \times 4$ is an expression.

Every expression can be written in many different ways. For example, multiplication signs can be included or omitted. As another example, the expression $x + x$ can also be written as $2x$. That's because adding a number to itself is the same as multiplying it by 2.

For instance, $3 + 3$ means the same as 2×3.

If two expressions are really just the same, but written differently, then we say that they're different *forms* of the same expression, or that they're **equivalent** to each other. We indicate this by writing an equals sign between them. For example, because $x + x$ is equivalent to $2x$, we write

$$x + x = 2x.$$

If two expressions are equivalent, then, whatever values you choose for their letters, the two expressions have the same value as each other.

Activity 7   *Checking whether expressions are equivalent*

Which of the following statements are correct?

(a) $u + u + u = 3u$ (b) $a^2 \times a = a^3$ (c) $2a \div 2 = a$

(d) $p^2 \times p^3 = p^6$ (e) $z + 2z = 3z$ (f) $6c \div 2 = 3c$

(g) $a - b - 2c = a + (-b) + (-2c)$ (h) $3n \div n = n$

You saw another example of equivalent expressions in Subsection 1.2, when two different formulas, $P = 1.24n - 0.69n$ and $P = 0.55n$, were found for the baker's profit. Since the formulas must give the same values,

$$1.24n - 0.69n = 0.55n.$$

When we write an expression in a different way, we say that we're **rearranging**, *manipulating* or *rewriting* the expression. Often the aim of doing this is to make the expression simpler, as with the formula for the baker's profit. In this case we say that we're **simplifying** the expression.

The first known use of an equals sign was by the Welsh mathematician Robert Recorde, in his algebra textbook *The whetstone of witte*, published in 1557. He justified the use of two parallel line segments to indicate equality as follows: *bicause noe 2 thynges can be moare equalle.*

We use equals signs when we're working with expressions, but expressions don't *contain* equals signs. For example, the statements

$$x + x = 2x \quad \text{and} \quad 1.24n - 0.69n = 0.55n$$

aren't expressions – they're equations. An **equation** is made up of *two* expressions, with an equals sign between them.

There's a difference between the two equations above and the ones that arose from the questions about school places and toddlers in Subsection 1.3. In that subsection, the number of children who applied to a school was found using the equation

$$\tfrac{3}{10}N = 150.$$

This equation is correct for *only one* value of N (it turned out to be 500). In contrast, the equations

$$x + x = 2x \quad \text{and} \quad 1.24n - 0.69n = 0.55n$$

are correct for *every* value of x and n, respectively. Equations like these, which are true for all values of the variables, are called **identities**. The different types of equation don't usually cause confusion in practice, as you know from the context which type you're dealing with.

There are similar differences in the use of letters to represent numbers. When the equation $\frac{3}{10}N = 150$ was used in Subsection 1.3, the letter N represented a *particular* number – it was just that we didn't know what that number was. This type of letter is called an **unknown**. In contrast, in the equation $x + x = 2x$ above, the letter x represents *any* number. A letter that represents any number (or any number of a particular type, such as any integer) is called a **variable**, as you saw in Unit 2. Usually you don't need to think about whether a letter is an unknown or a variable. Both types represent numbers, so the same rules of arithmetic apply in each case.

The first person to systematically use letters to represent numbers was the French mathematician François Viète. His treatise *In artem analyticem isagoge* (Introduction to the analytic art) of 1591 gives methods for solving equations, including ones more complicated than those in this module. Viète represented unknowns by vowels and known numbers by consonants (he represented known numbers by letters to help him describe the methods). However, he used words for connectives such as plus, equals and so on, and also to indicate powers. For example, he wrote '=' as 'aequatur', a^2 as '*a* quadratus' and a^3 as '*a* cubus'. So his algebra was still far from symbolic.

Viète also wrote books on astronomy, geometry and trigonometry, but he was never employed as a professional mathematician. He was trained in law, and followed a legal career for a few years before leaving the profession to oversee the education of the daughter of a local aristocratic family. His later career was spent in high public office, apart from a period of five years when he was banished from the court in Paris for political and religious reasons. Throughout his life, the only time he could devote to mathematics was when he was free from official duties.

Figure 1 François Viète (1540–1603)

2.2 What is a term?

Some expressions are lists of things that are all added or subtracted. Here's an example:

$$-2xy + 3z - y^2.$$

The things that are added or subtracted in an expression of this sort are called the **terms**. The terms of the expression above are

$$-2xy, \quad +3z \quad \text{and} \quad -y^2.$$

The plus or minus sign at the start of each term is *part of the term*. While you're getting used to working with terms, it can be helpful to mark them like this:

$$\underline{-2xy} \; \underline{+3z} \; \underline{-y^2}.$$

You need to make sure that the sign *at the start* of each term is included along with the rest of the term.

A sign *after* a term is part of the next term.

If the first term of an expression has no sign, then the term is added to the other terms, so really it has a plus sign – it's just that we normally don't write a plus sign in front of the first term of an expression. For example, if you have the expression

$$4a + c - 7\sqrt{b} - 5,$$

then you could write a plus sign at the start and mark the terms like this:

$$\underline{+4a} \; \underline{+c} \; \underline{-7\sqrt{b}} \; \underline{-5} \; .$$

Its terms are

$$+4a, \quad +c, \quad -7\sqrt{b} \quad \text{and} \quad -5.$$

Activity 8 *Identifying terms of expressions*

For each expression below, copy the expression, mark the terms and write down a list of the terms.

(a) $x^3 - x^2 + x + 1$ (b) $2mn - 3r$ (c) $-20p^2q^2 + \frac{1}{4}p - 18 - \frac{1}{3}q$

Remember that when you handwrite a lower-case x in mathematics, you should make it look different from a multiplication sign. One way to do this is to write it as a 'backwards c' followed by a 'normal c', like this:

When we discuss the terms of an expression, we often omit the plus signs. This is convenient in the same way that it's convenient to write the number $+3$ as 3. So, for example, we might say that the expression

$$-2xy + 3z - y^2 \tag{2}$$

has terms

$$-2xy, \quad 3z \quad \text{and} \quad -y^2.$$

We *never* omit the minus signs! And, of course, we *never* omit the plus sign of a term when writing the term as part of an expression, unless it's the first term.

There's a useful way to think of the relationship between an expression and its terms.

An expression is equivalent to the sum of its terms.

Remember that a *sum* of numbers is what you get by adding them. For example, the sum of 1, 4 and 7 is $1 + 4 + 7 = 12$.

For example, here is expression (2) written as the sum of its terms:

$$-2xy + 3z - y^2 = -2xy + 3z + (-y^2).$$

The expression on the right is obtained by adding the terms of expression (2) on the left. The two expressions are equivalent because subtracting y^2 is the same as adding the negative of y^2.

You saw in Unit 1 that subtracting a number is the same as adding its negative. For example, $1 - 3$ is the same as $1 + (-3)$.

You saw another example of an expression written as the sum of its terms in Activity 7(g):

$$a - b - 2c = a + (-b) + (-2c).$$

Because the order in which numbers are added doesn't matter, you can change the order of the terms in an expression however you like, and you will obtain an equivalent expression, as long as you keep each term together with its sign. For example, you can swap the order of the first two terms in the expression

$$-2xy + 3z - y^2$$

to give

$$3z - 2xy - y^2.$$

Or you can reverse the original order of the terms to give

$$-y^2 + 3z - 2xy.$$

All three of these expressions are equivalent to each other.

When you do the next activity, you'll probably find it helpful to begin by marking the terms in the way shown on page 14, including their signs, of course. Then think of moving the marked terms around.

Remember that you may need to write a plus sign in front of the first term.

Activity 9   *Changing the order of terms*

Write each of the following expressions with its terms in reverse order.

(a) $-X + 20Y - 5Z$ (b) $2u - 3uv$ (c) $4i - j + 5$

(d) $a - b + c + d$

Changing the order of the terms doesn't simplify an expression, but some methods for simplifying expressions are easier to apply if you rearrange the terms first.

A term in an expression may be just a number, like 4, $\frac{1}{2}$ or -5. If so, we say that it's a **constant term**, or just a *constant* for short. For example, the expression

$$3pq - 2 + 5p^2$$

has one constant term, -2.

It's called a constant term because, unlike other terms, its value doesn't change when the values of the letters in the expression are changed.

On the other hand, if a term is of the form

  a number $\times$ a combination of letters,

then the number is called the **coefficient** of the term, and we say that the term is a term *in* whatever the combination of letters is. For example,

The word 'coefficient' was introduced by François Viète (see page 13).

  $2xy$ has coefficient 2 and is a term in xy;

  $-3z$ has coefficient -3 and is a term in z;

  $\frac{2}{3}c^2$ has coefficient $\frac{2}{3}$ and is a term in c^2.

You may be tempted to think that terms like a and $-a$ don't have coefficients. However, because they are equivalent to $1a$ and $-1a$, respectively, they have coefficients 1 and -1, respectively. (We normally write a rather than $1a$, and $-a$ rather than $-1a$, for conciseness.)

Here are some more examples:

  y^3 has coefficient 1 and is a term in y^3;

  $-ab^2c$ has coefficient -1 and is a term in ab^2c.

Activity 10   *Identifying coefficients*

Write down the coefficient of:

(a) the third term in $2x^2 + 3xy + 4y^2$

(b) the second term in $2\sqrt{p} - 9\sqrt{q} - 7$

(c) the third term in $2x + 5\sqrt{2} + x^2$

(d) the first term in $-a^2b + 2c$

(e) the term in m^2 in $1 + 2m - 3m^2$

(f) the term in b in $ab + 2b + b^2$.

For each of parts (a)–(f) in Activity 10 above, write down any constant terms in the expression.

2.3 Collecting like terms

In this subsection you'll learn the first of several useful techniques for simplifying expressions: *collecting like terms*.

Let's look first at how it works with numbers. If you have 2 batches of 4 dots, and another 3 batches of 4 dots, then altogether you have

$2 + 3$ batches of 4 dots, that is, 5 batches of 4 dots.

This is shown in Figure 2, and you can express it by writing

$2 \times 4 + 3 \times 4 = 5 \times 4.$

Of course, this doesn't work just with batches of four dots. For example, Figure 3 illustrates that

$2 \times 7 + 3 \times 7 = 5 \times 7.$

In fact, no matter what number a is,

$2a + 3a = 5a.$

This gives you a way to simplify expressions that contain a number of batches of something, added to another number of batches *of the same thing*. For example, consider the expresssion

$5bc + 4bc.$

Adding 4 batches of bc to 5 batches of bc gives 9 batches of bc:

$5bc + 4bc = (5 + 4)bc = 9bc.$

Terms that are 'batches of the same thing' are called **like terms**. For terms to be like terms, the letters and the powers of the letters in each term must be the same.   So, for example,

$7\sqrt{A}$ and $3\sqrt{A}$ are like terms because they are both terms in $\sqrt{A}$;
$2x^2$ and $-0.5x^2$ are like terms because they are both terms in x^2.

However,

$5c$ and $4c^2$ are not like terms because $5c$ is a term in c and $4c^2$ is a term in c^2.

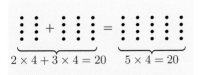

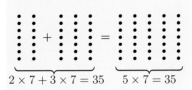

Figure 2

Figure 3

Which of the following are pairs of like terms?

(a) $3b$ and $6b^2$ (b) $5D$ and $5D$ (c) z and $-z$ (d) 3 and $2m$

Like terms can always be collected in a similar way to the examples above: you just add the coefficients (including negative ones). You can add any number of like terms.

Example 2   *Collecting like terms*

Simplify the following expressions.

(a) $12m + 15m - 26m$ (b) $0.5XY^2 + 0.1XY^2$ (c) $5p - p$

(d) $\frac{1}{3}d - 2d$

Solution

(a) $12m + 15m - 26m = (12 + 15 - 26)m = 1m = m$

(b) $0.5XY^2 + 0.1XY^2 = (0.5 + 0.1)XY^2 = 0.6XY^2$

(c) $5p - p = 5p - 1p = (5 - 1)p = 4p$

(d) $\frac{1}{3}d - 2d = \left(\frac{1}{3} - 2\right)d = \left(\frac{1}{3} - \frac{6}{3}\right)d = -\frac{5}{3}d$

So I've worked out that we need $\frac{68}{7}$ litres of magnolia paint, $3\sqrt{5}$ metres of skirting board and $47 + \frac{9\pi}{4}$ metres of that wallpaper we liked!

Notice that in the solution to Example 2(d), the fractional coefficients were not converted to approximate decimal values. In algebra you should work with *exact* numbers, such as $\frac{1}{3}$ and $\sqrt{5}$, rather than decimal approximations, wherever possible. However, if you're using algebra to solve a practical problem, then you may have to use decimal approximations.

Activity 13   *Collecting like terms*

Simplify the following expressions.

(a) $8A + 7A$ (b) $-5d + 8d - 2d$ (c) $-7z + z$

(d) $1.4pq + 0.7pq - pq$ (e) $\frac{1}{2}n^2 - \frac{1}{3}n^2$

It's easier to spot like terms if you make sure that all the letters in each term are written in alphabetical order. For example, $5st$ and $2ts$ are like terms – this is easier to see if you write the second one as $2st$.

You can always change the order in which things are multiplied, as this doesn't affect the overall result. For example, $3 \times 4 = 4 \times 3$, and $ts = st$.

Example 3   *Recognising like terms*

Simplify the following expressions.

(a) $5st + 2ts$ (b) $-6q^2rp + 4prq^2$

Solution

(a) $5st + 2ts = 5st + 2st = 7st$

(b) $-6q^2rp + 4prq^2 = -6pq^2r + 4pq^2r = -2pq^2r$

The lower- and upper-case versions of the same letter are *different* symbols in mathematics. So, for example, $4y$ and $9Y$ are not like terms.

Any two constant terms are like terms. They can be collected using the normal rules of arithmetic.

Activity 14   Recognising like terms

Which of the following are pairs of like terms?

(a) $2ab$ and $5ab$ (b) $-2rst$ and $20rst$ (c) $2xy$ and $-3yx$

(d) $4c^2a$ and $9ac^2$ (e) abc and cba (f) $8c^2d$ and $9d^2c$

(g) $2A^2$ and $10a^2$ (h) $3fh$ and $3gh$ (i) 22 and -81

Often an expression contains some like terms and some unlike terms. You can simplify the expression by first changing the order of its terms so that the like terms are grouped together, and then collecting the like terms. This leaves an expression in which all the terms are unlike, which can't be simplified any further. Here's an example.

Example 4   Collecting more like terms

Simplify the following expressions.

(a) $2a + 5b - 7a + 3b$ (b) $12 - 4pq - 2q + 1 - qp - 2$

Solution

(a) ☁ Group the like terms, then collect them. ☁

$$2a + 5b - 7a + 3b = 2a - 7a + 5b + 3b$$
$$= -5a + 8b$$

(b) ☁ Write qp as pq, group the like terms, then collect them. ☁

$$12 - 4pq - 2q + 1 - qp - 2 = 12 - 4pq - 2q + 1 - pq - 2$$
$$= 12 + 1 - 2 - 4pq - pq - 2q$$
$$= 11 - 5pq - 2q$$

☁ The terms in the final expression can be written in any order. For example, an alternative answer is $11 - 2q - 5pq$. ☁

Activity 15   Collecting more like terms

You may find it helpful to mark the terms before rearranging them.

Simplify the following expressions.

(a) $4A - 3B + 3C + 5A + 2B - A$ (b) $-8v + 7 - 5w - 2v - 8$

(c) $20y^2 + 10xy - 10y^2 - 5y - 5xy$ (d) $-4ef + 8e^2f + 10fe - 3f^2e$

(e) $\frac{1}{2}a + \frac{1}{3}b + 2a + \frac{1}{4}b$

As you become more used to working with expressions, you'll probably find that you can collect like terms without grouping them together first. The worked examples in the module will usually do this, and you should do so too, as soon as you feel comfortable with it.

Sometimes when you collect two or more like terms, you find that the result is zero – that is, the terms **cancel** each other out. Here's an example.

Example 5 *Terms that cancel out*

Simplify the expression

$M + 2N + 3M - 2N.$

Solution

$M + 2N + 3M - 2N = 4M + 0 = 4M$

In the example above, $2N$ is added and then subtracted, and the addition and subtraction cancel each other out.

Activity 16 *Terms that cancel out*

Simplify the following expressions.

(a) $2a^3 - 3a - 2a^3 - 3a$ (b) $2m + n - 5m + 2n + 3m$

(c) $b + 2b + 3b - 6b$

Earlier in the unit, the formula

$P = 1.24n - 0.69n$

was found for a baker's profit, where P is the profit in £, and n is the number of loaves. Then the simpler formula

$P = 0.55n$

was found for the profit, by thinking about the situation in a different way. Notice that the simpler formula could have been obtained directly from the first formula, by collecting the like terms on the right-hand side:

$P = 1.24n - 0.69n = 0.55n.$

In the next activity there is another formula that can be simplified in this way.

Activity 17 *Collecting like terms in a formula*

A primary school parents' group is organising an outing to a children's activity centre, for c children and a adults, travelling by train.

(a) The cost of a ticket for the activity centre is £10 for a child and £2 for an adult. Find a formula for A, where £A is the total cost of admission to the activity centre for the group.

(b) The cost of a return train ticket to get to the activity centre is £7 for a child and £14 for an adult. Find a formula for T, where £T is the total cost of travel for the group.

(c) By adding your answers to parts (a) and (b), find a formula for C, where £C is the total cost of the trip for the group.

(d) Simplify the formula found in part (c) by collecting like terms, if you haven't already done so in part (c).

(e) Use the formula found in part (d) to find the cost of the trip for 22 children and 10 adults.

Remember that you should not include units, such as £, in a formula. However, if a quantity found using a formula has units, then these should be included in the answer. For example, the answer to part (e) of this activity should include £.

In this section you have been introduced to some terminology used in algebra, and you have learned the algebraic technique of collecting like terms. In the next two sections you'll learn some more algebraic techniques that you will often need to use.

3 Simplifying terms

E = c²m?
I've never heard of that one!

E = c²m

Sometimes the terms in an expression need to be simplified, to make the expression easier to work with, and to make it easy to recognise any like terms. You'll learn how to do that in this section. We begin by looking at terms individually, and later in the section we consider expressions with more than one term.

3.1 Simplifying single terms

As you've seen, if a term consists of numbers and letters all multiplied together, then it should be written with the coefficient first, followed by the letters. It's often useful to write the letters in alphabetical order – for example, $3B^2DA$ as $3AB^2D$ – as this can help you to identify like terms in a complicated expression. This is usually done in this module. (However, there are some contexts where tradition requires a non-alphabetical order.)

Remember that the 2 in p^2 and the 3 in p^3 are called *powers*, *indices* (the singular is *index*) or *exponents*. As you saw in Unit 3, we also call p^2 and p^3 *powers* of p, so the word 'power' has two different, but related, meanings in mathematics.

If a term includes a letter multiplied by itself, then index notation should be used. For example,

$p \times p$ should be simplified to p^2,

and

$p \times p \times p$ should be simplified to p^3.

Example 6   *Simplifying terms*

Write the following terms in their shortest forms.

(a) $3 \times c \times g \times 4 \times b$ (b) $b \times a \times 5 \times b \times b$

Solution

(a) $3 \times c \times g \times 4 \times b = 12bcg$

(b) $b \times a \times 5 \times b \times b = 5ab^3$

When you simplify a term you should normally use index notation only for letters and not for numbers. For example,

$3 \times 3 \times a$ should be simplified to $9a$,   not 3^2a.

Activity 18   *Using index notation*

Write the following terms in their shortest forms.

(a) $y \times z \times 6 \times x \times 4$ (b) $7p \times 2qr$ (c) $QR \times G \times 5F$

(d) $2 \times a \times a \times 3 \times a$ (e) $m \times n \times m \times 4$

(f) $5y \times 2yx$ (g) $4AB \times 4AB$

If a term contains more than one power of the same letter, multiplied together, then the indices need to be *added*. For example,

$$x^3 \times x^2 = x^5.$$

Remember that x is the same as x^1; for example,

$$x \times x^7 = x^8.$$

In Unit 3 you met the index law $a^m \times a^n = a^{m+n}$.

Example 7 *Multiplying powers*

Write the following term in its shortest form:

$$2A^5B \times 3A^4B^7.$$

Solution

$$2A^5B \times 3A^4B^7 = 2 \times 3 \times A^{5+4}B^{1+7} = 6A^9B^8$$

Activity 19 *Multiplying powers*

Write the following terms in their shortest forms.

(a) $8P^8 \times 5P$ (b) $2c^{10}d^3 \times 2c^2d^3$

If a term consists of numbers and letters multiplied together, and some of these have minus signs, then the overall sign of the term can be worked out using the rules below. The rest of the term can be simplified in the usual way.

Similar rules were given for numbers in Unit 1, Subsection 3.1. The following table might help you to remember them.

	+	−
+	+	−
−	−	+

> When multiplying or dividing:
>
> two signs the same give a plus sign;
>
> two different signs give a minus sign.

It indicates that a positive times a positive is a positive, a positive times a negative is a negative, and so on.

Here are some examples to illustrate these rules.

$$2 \times (-3) = -6, \qquad (-2) \times (-3) = 6,$$
$$a \times (-b) = -ab, \qquad (-a) \times (-b) = ab.$$

Example 8 *Simplifying terms involving minus signs*

Write the following terms in their shortest forms.

(a) $4q \times (-2p)$ (b) $-B^3 \times (-5B)$ (c) $-a \times (-b) \times (-a)$

Solution

(a) ✑ A positive times a negative gives a negative. ✑

$$4q \times (-2p) = -4q \times 2p$$
$$= -8pq$$

Instead of 'a positive times a negative gives a negative', we sometimes say, informally, 'a plus times a minus gives a minus'.

(b) ✑ A negative times a negative gives a positive. ✑

$$-B^3 \times (-5B) = +B^3 \times 5B$$
$$= +5B^4$$
$$= 5B^4$$

The overall sign is found in the same way as when you multiply several negative numbers together. See Unit 1, Subsection 3.1.

(c) 🔍 The first negative times the second negative gives a positive, then that positive times the third negative gives a negative. 💬

$$-a \times (-b) \times (-a) = -a \times b \times a$$
$$= -a^2 b$$

The box below summarises how to simplify a term.

> **Strategy** *To simplify a term*
>
> 1. Find the overall sign and write it at the front.
> 2. Simplify the rest of the coefficient and write it next.
> 3. Write the letters in alphabetical order (usually), using index notation as appropriate.

If the coefficient of a term is 1 or -1, then the 1 should be omitted. For example,

   $1xy$ should be simplified to xy,

and

   $-1c^2$ should be simplified to $-c^2$.

In the next activity, try to simplify the terms in a single step, using the strategy above. This skill will be helpful later, when you learn to simplify more complicated expressions.

Activity 20 *Simplifying terms involving minus signs*

Write the following terms in their shortest forms.

(a) $9X \times (-XY)$ (b) $3s \times \frac{1}{3}r$ (c) $-3a^3 \times (-4a^4)$

(d) $-2pq \times (-3qp^2)$ (e) $-0.5g \times 2f^5$ (f) $-a \times b \times (-c) \times (-d)$

(g) $(-x) \times (-y) \times (-x^2) \times (-4y)$ (h) $(-3cd)^2$ (i) $-(3cd)^2$

Hint for parts (h) and (i): something^2 = the something $\times$ the something.

Expressions can contain terms of the form

   $+(-\text{something})$ or $-(-\text{something})$.

These should be simplified by using the following facts.

You saw these rules for numbers in Unit 1, Subsection 3.1.

> *   Adding the negative of something is the same as subtracting the something.
> *   Subtracting the negative of something is the same as adding the something.

Here are some examples:

$$+(-8) = -8, \qquad -(-5) = +5 = 5,$$
$$+(-2M^2) = -2M^2, \qquad -(-x) = +x = x.$$

Also, any unnecessary brackets in a term should usually be removed. For example:

$$+(pq) = +pq = pq,$$
$$-(7z) = -7z.$$

The brackets in these terms aren't needed, because by the BIDMAS rules multiplication is done before addition and subtraction.

Before removing unnecessary brackets, check carefully that they really are unnecessary! If you're not sure, leave the brackets in.

Activity 21   *Simplifying the signs of terms*

Write the following terms in their shortest forms.

(a) $+(-ab)$ (b) $-(-6x^2)$ (c) $-(2M^4)$ (d) $+(-7y)$

(e) $+(5p)$ (f) $-\left(-\frac{3}{4}n\right)$

3.2 Simplifying two or more terms

So far in this section you've been simplifying single terms. To simplify an expression with two or more terms, you need to simplify each term individually, in the way that you've seen. Before you can do that, you need to identify which bits of the expression belong to which term. The easiest way to do that is to use the following fact.

> Each term after the first starts with a plus or minus sign that isn't inside brackets.

Example 9   *Identifying terms*

 Tutorial clip

Mark the terms in the following expressions.

(a) $-2a - (-5a^2) + (-4a)$ (b) $2x \times 4xy - 2y \times (-5x)$

Solution

(a) 💭 Begin by marking the start of the first term. 💭

$$\underline{-}2a - (-5a^2) + (-4a)$$

💭 Extend the line under the first term until you reach a plus or minus sign that isn't inside brackets. That's the start of the next term. 💭

$$\underline{-2a} - (-5a^2) + (-4a)$$

💭 Extend the line under the second term until you reach a plus or minus sign that isn't inside brackets. That's the start of the next term. 💭

$$\underline{-2a} \,\underline{- (-5a^2)} + (-4a)$$

💭 Extend the line under the third term until you reach a plus or minus sign that isn't inside brackets. This time you don't reach one –

you just reach the end of the expression. So this expression has three terms, as marked. 💭

$$\underset{\underline{}}{-2a} \;\underset{\underline{}}{-\,(-5a^2)} \;\underset{\underline{}}{+\,(-4a)}$$

(b) 💭 Mark the start of the first term. 💭

$$\underset{\underline{}}{2}x \times 4xy - 2y \times (-5x)$$

💭 When you reach a plus or minus sign that isn't inside brackets, that's the start of the next term. 💭

$$\underset{\underline{}}{2x \times 4xy} \;\underset{\underline{}}{-}\; 2y \times (-5x)$$

💭 You don't reach another plus or minus sign that isn't inside brackets, so this expression has two terms. 💭

$$\underset{\underline{}}{2x \times 4xy} \;\underset{\underline{}}{-\,2y \times (-5x)}$$

Example 9 showed you how to carry out the first step in the following strategy. The other two steps use techniques that you've seen already.

Strategy   *To simplify an expression with more than one term*

1. Identify the terms. Each term after the first starts with a plus or minus sign that isn't inside brackets.

2. Simplify each term, using the strategy on page 22. Include the sign (plus or minus) at the start of each term.

3. Collect any like terms.

As usual, a plus sign in front of a first term can be omitted.

In the next example, this strategy is used to simplify the expressions in Example 9.

Tutorial clip

Example 10   *Simplifying expressions with more than one term*

Simplify the following expressions.

(a) $-2a - (-5a^2) + (-4a)$ (b) $2x \times 4xy - 2y \times (-5x)$

Solution

(a) 💭 First identify the terms. Then simplify each term individually. Finally, collect like terms. 💭

$$\underset{\underline{}}{-2a} \;\underset{\underline{}}{-\,(-5a^2)} \;\underset{\underline{}}{+\,(-4a)} = -2a + 5a^2 - 4a$$
$$= 5a^2 - 6a$$

💭 This could also be written as $-6a + 5a^2$. 💭

(b) 💭 Identify the terms, then simplify each term individually. Finally, check for like terms – there are none here. 💭

$$\underset{\underline{}}{2x \times 4xy} \;\underset{\underline{}}{-\,2y \times (-5x)} = 8x^2y + 10xy$$

In the next activity, begin each part by marking the terms, as shown in Example 9. As you become more used to manipulating expressions, you'll probably find that you can identify and simplify the terms without needing to mark them.

Activity 22 *Simplifying expressions*

Simplify the following expressions.

(a) $5m \times 2m - 2n \times n^2$ (b) $3p \times 2q + 2r \times (-7p)$

(c) $2P - (-3Q) + (-P) + (2Q)$ (d) $3 \times (-2a) - 1c^2 + 9ac$

(e) $4s \times \frac{1}{2}rst - 2(-\frac{1}{2}s)$ (f) $-5xy + (-3y \times x^2) - (-y^2)$

(g) $-3r \times (-2r) - (-2r \times r) + (r^2 \times 9)$

Don't be concerned if you find this activity difficult – it's one of the harder ones in the unit. Take your time, and follow the strategy carefully. Remember that some terms may not need to be simplified, as they may already be in their simplest forms.

---

4 Brackets

In this section you'll learn how to rewrite expressions that contain brackets as expressions without brackets, and you'll also see some applications of algebra, including how to prove that the number trick in Subsection 1.1 always works.

4.1 Multiplying out brackets

Any expression that contains brackets, such as

$$8a + 3b(b - 2a)$$

or

$$(2m + 3n) - (m + n - 3r),$$

can be rewritten without brackets. To see how to do this, let's start by looking at an expression that involves only numbers:

$$(2 + 3) \times 4.$$

When you learned to collect like terms, you saw that $2 + 3$ batches of 4 dots is the same as 2 batches of 4 dots plus 3 batches of 4 dots, as illustrated in Figure 4. So $(2 + 3) \times 4$ is equivalent to

$$2 \times 4 + 3 \times 4.$$

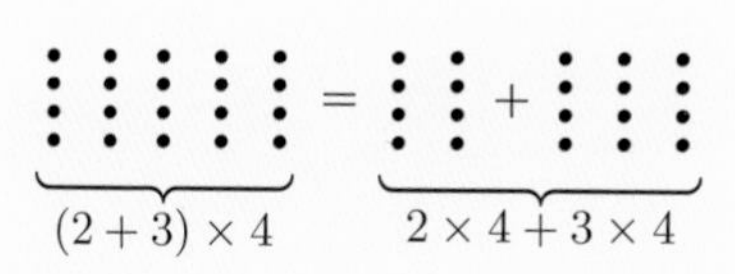

Here an expression containing brackets has been rewritten as an expression without brackets:

$$(2 + 3) \times 4 = 2 \times 4 + 3 \times 4.$$

It's usual to write numbers in front of brackets, so let's write the 4 first in each multiplication:

$$4(2 + 3) = 4 \times 2 + 4 \times 3.$$

Here you can see how to rewrite an expression with brackets as one without brackets: you multiply each of the numbers inside the brackets individually by the number outside the brackets. This is called **multiplying out the brackets**, *expanding the brackets*, or simply *removing the brackets*. The number outside the brackets is called the **multiplier**. Here's another example, with multiplier 7.

$$7(1 + 5) = 7 \times 1 + 7 \times 5$$

Figure 4

Multiplying out the brackets can be particularly helpful for expressions that contain letters. The rule above applies in just the same way.

> **Strategy** *To multiply out brackets*
>
> Multiply each term inside the brackets by the multiplier.

Remember that you must multiply *every* term inside the brackets, not just the first term.

Here are two examples, with multipliers a and 3, respectively.

$$a(b + c) = ab + ac$$

$$3(p + q^2 + r) = 3p + 3q^2 + 3r$$

It doesn't matter whether the multiplier is before or after the brackets. Here's an example of multiplying out where the multiplier is after the brackets:

$$(x + y)z = xz + yz.$$

If you prefer the multiplier to be before the brackets, then you can change the order before multiplying out. For example,

$$(x + y)z = z(x + y) = zx + zy = xz + yz.$$

When you multiply out brackets, you often need to simplify the resulting terms, as illustrated in the next example.

Tutorial clip

Example 11 *Multiplying out brackets*

Multiply out the brackets in the following expression:

$$2a(3a + 2b).$$

Solution

$$2a(3a + 2b) = 2a \times 3a + 2a \times 2b$$
$$= 6a^2 + 4ab$$

Activity 23 *Multiplying out brackets*

Multiply out the brackets in the following expressions.

(a) $3p(pq + 4)$ (b) $x^2(x + 2y)$

Once you're familiar with how to multiply out brackets, it's usually best to simplify the terms as you multiply out, instead of first writing down an expression containing multiplication signs. This leads to tidier expressions and fewer errors.

For example, if you look at the expression in Example 11,

$$2a(3a + 2b),$$

you can see that when you multiply out the brackets, the first term will be $2a$ times $3a$. You simplify this to $6a^2$, using the strategy of first finding the sign, then the rest of the coefficient and then the letters, and write it down. Then you see that the second term is $2a$ times $+2b$, simplify this to $+4ab$, and write it down after the first term. This gives

$$2a(3a + 2b) = 6a^2 + 4ab.$$

Try this shorter form of working in the following activity.

Activity 24 *Multiplying out brackets efficiently*

Multiply out the brackets in each of the following expressions.

(a) $f(e + 5g)$ (b) $5(2A + B)$ (c) $3c(4c + 2d)$

(d) $(a - b)c^2$ (e) $2y(x + 2y + 4z)$ (f) $2\left(\frac{1}{2}A^2 + \frac{3}{2}\right)$

(g) $a(x + y)z$ (h) $2b(b^2 + 2b^4)$

Simplifying the terms at the same time as multiplying out is particularly helpful when some of the terms inside the brackets, or the multiplier, have minus signs. For example, let's multiply out the brackets in the expression

$$3m(-2m + 3n - 6).$$

The first term is $3m$ times $-2m$, which simplifies to $-6m^2$. Working out the other terms in a similar way, we obtain

$$3m(-2m + 3n - 6) = -6m^2 + 9mn - 18m.$$

Here's another example. In this one the multiplier has a minus sign.

Example 12 *Multiplying out brackets involving minus signs*

 Tutorial clip

Multiply out the brackets in the following expression:

$$-a(b - a + 7).$$

Solution

$$-a(b - a + 7) = -ab + a^2 - 7a$$

The terms are
$$-a \times b = -ab,$$
$$-a \times (-a) = +a^2,$$
$$-a \times 7 = -7a.$$

Activity 25 *Multiplying out brackets involving minus signs*

Multiply out the brackets in the following expressions, simplifying where possible.

(a) $p(q - r)$ (b) $7a(-4a + 3b)$ (c) $6(0.2a - 0.3b + 1.4)$

(d) $10(\frac{1}{2}n + \frac{1}{5})$ (e) $-3(x - 2y)$ (f) $-b^2(-a + b)$

An expression containing brackets may have more than one term. For example, the expression

$$x(y + 1) + 2y(y + 3)$$

has two terms, each containing brackets, as follows:

$$\underbrace{x(y + 1)}\ \underbrace{+ 2y(y + 3)}.$$

The strategy for simplifying expressions is on page 24.

An expression like this can be dealt with term by term, using a similar strategy to the one for simplifying expressions.

> **Strategy** *To multiply out brackets in an expression with more than one term*
>
> 1. Identify the terms. Each term after the first starts with a plus or minus sign that isn't inside brackets.
> 2. Multiply out the brackets in each term. Include the sign (plus or minus) at the start of each resulting term.
> 3. Collect any like terms.

Stage 2 usually increases the number of terms.

While you're learning to multiply out brackets in expressions with more than one term, you'll probably find it helpful to mark the terms as you identify them. This should help you to avoid errors.

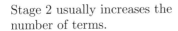 Tutorial clip

---
Example 13 *Expanding the brackets when there's more than one term*

Multiply out the brackets in the following expressions, simplifying where possible.

(a) $x(y + 1) + 2y(y + 3)$ (b) $2r^2 - r(r - s)$

Solution

(a) Identify the terms. Multiply out the brackets. Then check for like terms – there are none here.

$$\underbrace{x(y + 1)}\ \underbrace{+ 2y(y + 3)} = xy + x + 2y^2 + 6y$$

(b) Identify the terms. Multiply out the brackets. Collect like terms.

$$\underbrace{2r^2}\ \underbrace{- r(r - s)} = 2r^2 - r^2 + rs$$
$$= r^2 + rs$$

Activity 26 *Expanding the brackets when there's more than one term*

Multiply out the brackets in the following expressions, simplifying where possible.

(a) $f + g(f + h)$ (b) $x - y(x + 2y)$ (c) $2p - 3q(-3p + q)$

(d) $-2(a + b) + 4(a - b)$ (e) $2aE - 3E(-E - 5a)$ (f) $(d - c)c - c^2$

Some expressions, such as

$$-(a + 2b - c),$$

contain brackets with just a minus sign in front.

You can remove these brackets by using the fact that a minus sign in front is just the same as multiplying by -1:

$$-(a + 2b - c) = -1(a + 2b - c)$$
$$= -a - 2b + c.$$

You can see that the overall effect is that the sign of each term in the brackets has been changed.

An expression may also contain brackets with just a plus sign in front. These brackets can be removed by using the fact that a plus sign in front is just the same as multiplying by 1. For example, the expression

$$2x + (y - 3z)$$

can be simplified as follows:

$$2x + (y - 3z) = 2x + 1(y - 3z)$$
$$= 2x + y - 3z.$$

This time you can see that the effect is that all the signs in the brackets remain as they are.

Rather than introducing 1 or -1 into working, as was done above, it's better to remember the following strategy.

> **Strategy**   *To remove brackets with a plus or minus sign in front*
>
> - If the sign is plus, keep the sign of each term inside the brackets the same.
> - If the sign is minus, change the sign of each term inside the brackets.

This strategy applies even if there's just one term in the brackets. For example,
$$+(-2M^2) = -2M^2,$$
and
$$-(-x) = +x = x,$$
as you know already from the rules for adding and subtracting negatives, which were given on page 22.

   Tutorial clip

Example 14   *Plus and minus signs in front of brackets*

Remove the brackets in the following expressions.

(a) $-(-P^2 + 2Q - 3R)$ (b) $a + (2bc - d)$

Solution

(a) $-(-P^2 + 2Q - 3R) = +P^2 - 2Q + 3R$
$$= P^2 - 2Q + 3R$$

(b) $a + (2bc - d) = a + 2bc - d$

Activity 27   *Plus and minus signs in front of brackets*

Remove the brackets in each of the following expressions, and simplify them where possible.

(a) $-(4f - g^3)$ (b) $-(-x + 7y - 8z + 6)$ (c) $2(a - b) + (c - 2d)$

(d) $r + (-2s - r)$ (e) $-A + B - (-3A + 4B)$

(f) $-(-t - w) + (-t + w)$ (g) $-(L + 2M) - (-M)$

Some expressions, such as

$$(x + 2)(x - 5),$$

contain two, or even more, pairs of brackets multiplied together. You'll learn how to multiply out brackets like these in Unit 9.

You've seen that you should usually write expressions in the simplest way you can. For example, you should write

$$x + 2x + 3x \quad \text{as} \quad 6x.$$

The second form of this expression is clearly simpler than the first:

- it's shorter and easier to understand, and
- it's easier to evaluate for any particular value of x.

These are the attributes to aim for when you try to write an expression in a simpler way.

However, sometimes it's not so clear that one way of writing an expression is better than another. For example,

$$x(x + 1) \quad \text{is equivalent to} \quad x^2 + x.$$

Both these forms are reasonably short, and both are reasonably easy to evaluate. So this expression doesn't have a simplest form.

The same is true of many other expressions. You should try to write each expression that you work with in a reasonably simple way, but often there's no 'right answer' for the simplest form. One form might be better for some purposes, and a different form might be better for other purposes.

In Unit 7 you'll see that there's a reverse process to multiplying out the brackets: sometimes an expression can be made simpler or more useful by *introducing* brackets.

In particular, multiplying out the brackets in an expression doesn't always simplify it.

4.2 Algebraic fractions

It's usually best to use fraction notation, rather than a division sign, to indicate division in algebraic expressions. For example, the expression

$$a + b \div c \tag{3}$$

can be written as

$$a + \frac{b}{c}. \tag{4}$$

This makes it easy to see which parts of the expression are divided by which. In expression (3), it's just b, not $a + b$, that's divided by c, by the BIDMAS rules. This is clearer in expression (4).

Similarly, the expression

$$(8a + 3) \div (2a)$$

can be written in fraction notation as

$$\frac{8a + 3}{2a}. \tag{5}$$

The brackets can be omitted because the fraction notation makes it clear that the whole of $8a + 3$ is divided by $2a$.

Algebraic expressions written using fraction notation are called **algebraic fractions**. The expressions above and below the line in an algebraic fraction are called the *numerator* and *denominator*, respectively, just as they are for ordinary fractions.

When you write an algebraic fraction, you must make sure that the horizontal line extends to the full width of the numerator or denominator, whichever is the wider. For example,

$$(8a + 3) \div (2a) \text{ should be written as } \frac{8a + 3}{2a}, \text{ not } \frac{8a + 3}{2a}.$$

I told you that removing the brackets isn't always a good idea!

This is because the line acts as brackets for the numerator and denominator, as well as indicating division.

Try not to use division signs in expressions, or whenever you carry out algebraic manipulation, from now on; use fraction notation instead. However, occasionally it's useful to use division signs in algebraic expressions, just as occasionally it's useful to use multiplication signs.

If you need to type an algebraic fraction in a line of text, for example when sending an email, then use brackets and a slash. For example,

$$\frac{8a + 3}{2a}$$

can be typed as $(8a + 3)/(2a)$.

Activity 28   *Using fraction notation*

Rewrite the following expressions using fraction notation.

(a) $(a + b) \div 3$ (b) $a + b \div 3$ (c) $(x + 2) \div (y + 3)$

(d) $(x + 2) \div y + 3$ (e) $x + 2 \div (y + 3)$ (f) $x + 2 \div y + 3$

Activity 29   *Working with fraction notation*

Multiply out the brackets in the following expressions.

(a) $6\left(1 + \dfrac{h}{2}\right)$ (b) $6\left(\dfrac{1 + h}{2}\right)$

Hint for part (b): First write the expression in the form 'number $\times (1 + h)$'.

There's a technique, based on multiplying out brackets, that can be useful when you're working with algebraic fractions. As with multiplying out brackets, this technique doesn't necessarily simplify an expression; it just gives a different way of writing it. It applies to algebraic fractions where there's more than one term in the *numerator*, such as

$$\frac{2a - 5b + c}{3d}. \tag{6}$$

Since dividing by something is the same as multiplying by its reciprocal, you can write this expression as

$$\frac{1}{3d}(2a - 5b + c).$$

You can then multiply out the brackets to give

$$\frac{2a}{3d} - \frac{5b}{3d} + \frac{c}{3d}. \tag{7}$$

If you compare expressions (6) and (7), you can see that the overall effect is that each term on the numerator has been individually divided by the denominator. This is called **expanding** the algebraic fraction.

Once an algebraic fraction has been expanded, it may be possible to simplify some of the resulting terms, as illustrated in the next example.

Example 15   *Expanding an algebraic fraction*

Expand the algebraic fraction $\dfrac{10x + x^2 - 8}{x}$.

Solution

$$\frac{10x + x^2 - 8}{x} = \frac{10x}{x} + \frac{x^2}{x} - \frac{8}{x}$$

$$= 10 + x - \frac{8}{x}$$

Remember: $\dfrac{x^2}{x} = \dfrac{\cancel{x} \times x}{\cancel{x}} = x$.

Remember that an algebraic fraction can be expanded only if it has more than one term in the *numerator*. The following fraction, which has more than one term in the denominator, can't be expanded:

$$\frac{a}{2a + 5b - c}.$$

Activity 30 *Expanding algebraic fractions*

Expand the following algebraic fractions, and simplify the resulting expressions where possible.

(a) $\dfrac{A - 6B}{3}$ (b) $\dfrac{10z^2 + 5z - 20}{5}$ (c) $\dfrac{3A^2 + A}{A}$

You'll learn more about working with algebraic fractions in Unit 9.

4.3 Using algebra

You've now covered all the algebra needed to prove that the number trick in Subsection 1.1 works for every possible starting number.

To do this, you carry out the trick starting with a letter (n, say), which represents any number at all. After each step you simplify the resulting expression.

Think of a number:	n
Double it:	$2n$
Add 7:	$2n + 7$
Double the result:	$2(2n + 7) = 4n + 14$
Add 6:	$4n + 14 + 6 = 4n + 20$
Divide by 4:	$\dfrac{4n + 20}{4} = \dfrac{4n}{4} + \dfrac{20}{4} = n + 5$
Take away the number you first thought of:	$n + 5 - n = 5$

So, because n represents any number at all, you can see that you'll always end up with the answer 5.

Notice that it was important to include the brackets when the expression $2n + 7$ was doubled in the above calculation. Doubling $2n + 7$ does *not* give $2 \times 2n + 7 = 4n + 7$; the correct calculation is

$$2(2n + 7) = 4n + 14.$$

Activity 31 *Checking a number trick*

Here's another number trick.

Think of a number.
Multiply it by 3.
Add 2.
Double the result.
Add 2.
Divide by 6.
Take away the number you first thought of.

(a) Test the trick with whatever starting number you wish. What's the final answer?

(b) By starting with n, prove that the trick always gives the same answer.

In the next example you'll see how multiplying out brackets can be useful when you're finding a formula.

Example 16   *Finding and simplifying a formula*

Each week Arthur works for at least 37 hours. He's paid £15 per hour for the first 37 hours, and £25 per hour for each additional hour. Find a formula for P, where £P is Arthur's pay for the week if he works for n hours.

Solution

Arthur's pay in £ for the first 37 hours is

$37 \times 15 = 555$.

The number of additional hours that Arthur works is $n - 37$, so his pay in £ for these additional hours is

$(n - 37) \times 25 = 25(n - 37)$.

The question states that Arthur works for at least 37 hours, so there's no need to worry about $n - 37$ going negative.

So a formula for Arthur's pay is

$P = 555 + 25(n - 37)$.

The formula can be simplified by multiplying out the brackets:

$P = 555 + 25n - 925$

$\quad = 25n - 370$.

So the simplified formula is

$P = 25n - 370$.

Activity 32   *Finding and simplifying a formula*

A print company charges £175 to print 200 leaflets of a particular size, plus an extra £0.25 per leaflet for any further leaflets.

(a) Find a formula for C, where £C is the cost of printing n leaflets, assuming that n is at least 200.

(b) Write the formula as simply as you can.

(c) Use the formula to find the cost of printing 450 leaflets.

Remember that the units for C are pounds. Don't convert any of the costs to pence.

Finally in this section, you'll see some more examples of how algebra can be used to prove mathematical facts. First try the following activity.

Activity 33 *Adding three consecutive integers*

Choose any three consecutive integers and add them together. Is the total divisible by 3? Now try another three consecutive integers.

As with the number tricks you saw earlier, the property in Activity 33 seems to hold for any integers you choose. But how can you be sure that it always holds? You can't check *all* choices of three consecutive integers individually, as there are infinitely many choices. The way to prove that the property always holds is to use algebra.

 Tutorial clip

Example 17 *Proving a property of numbers*

Prove that the sum of any three consecutive integers is divisible by 3.

Solution

Represent the first of the three integers by n. Then the other two integers are $n+1$ and $n+2$. So their sum is

$$n + (n+1) + (n+2) = n + n + 1 + n + 2$$
$$= 3n + 3.$$

To confirm that $3n + 3$ is a multiple of 3, you can either divide by 3 and check that you get an integer, as is done in the example, or you can argue as follows. The number $3n$ is a multiple of 3, since n is an integer, so $3n + 3$ must also be a multiple of 3, since adding 3 to a multiple of 3 gives another multiple of 3.

Dividing by 3 gives

$$\frac{3n+3}{3} = \frac{3n}{3} + \frac{3}{3}$$
$$= n + 1.$$

Now $n + 1$ is an integer, because n is an integer. So dividing the sum of the three numbers by 3 gives an integer. That is, the sum is divisible by 3.

Activity 34 *Proving a property of numbers*

(a) Choose any three integers such that the second and third are each 2 more than the one before (such as 5, 7 and 9, or 20, 22 and 24). Is their sum divisible by 3?

(b) Choose another three integers of the same type, and check whether their sum is divisible by 3.

(c) Prove that the same thing always happens. Write out your proof in a similar way to the proof in Example 17.

You can use similar methods to prove many more properties of numbers. Here are another two proofs for you to try.

Activity 35 *Proving another property of numbers*

Prove that if you add up any four consecutive integers, then the answer is *not* divisible by 4.

The facts that you saw in Example 17 and Activity 34 are particular cases of the more general fact explored in the next activity.

Activity 36   *Proving a more general property of numbers*

In this activity you are asked to prove the following fact.

> If you add up any three integers such that the second and third integers are each the same amount more than the one before, then the answer is divisible by 3.

Do this by following the steps below.

(a) Try a numerical example first – you could use one of the two examples in the margin, or choose your own example. Write down the first integer, the amount by which the second and third integers are more than the one before, and the sum of the three integers. Check that the sum of the three integers is divisible by 3.

(b) Use the letter n to represent the first integer and the letter d to represent the amount by which the second and third integers are more than the one before. Write down expressions for the second and third integers in terms of n and d.

(c) Use your answers to part (b) to find an expression for the sum of the three integers, and hence prove the fact above.

For example, the integers 15, 19 and 23 have this property, since they have the following pattern:

$$15 \xrightarrow{\ +\,4\ } 19 \xrightarrow{\ +\,4\ } 23.$$

Similarly, the integers 107, 117 and 127 have the property, since they have the following pattern:

$$107 \xrightarrow{\ +\,10\ } 117 \xrightarrow{\ +\,10\ } 127.$$

5 Linear equations

In Section 1 you met the idea that some mathematical questions can be answered by solving equations. In this section you'll learn how to solve equations of a particular type – *linear equations in one unknown* – and see how to use them to answer some simple mathematical questions.

You'll soon see that linear equations are common in mathematics and can be extremely useful. Later in the module, you'll see how they can be used to model and solve some more complex real-world problems.

5.1 Solutions of equations

As you saw earlier, an equation consists of two expressions, with an equals sign between them. Here's an example:

$$2(r + 3) = 5r - 6. \tag{8}$$

The expressions to the left and right of the equals sign in an equation are referred to as the *left-hand side* (LHS) and *right-hand side* (RHS), respectively. For equation (8) above,

$$\text{LHS} = 2(r + 3) \quad \text{and} \quad \text{RHS} = 5r - 6.$$

This section is about equations that contain an *unknown* – a letter representing a number that you don't know. For example, earlier you saw the equation

$$\tfrac{3}{10}N = 150, \tag{9}$$

where N is an unknown representing the number of children who applied

This equation was in Subsection 1.3 (see page 9).

to a school. It turned out that $N = 500$, because equation (9) is correct when you substitute 500 for N:

$$\tfrac{3}{10} \times 500 = 150.$$

The process of finding the value of the unknown in an equation is called **solving the equation**, and the value found is called a *solution* of the equation. We also say that this value **satisfies** the equation.

Example 18   *Checking a solution of an equation*

Show that $r = 4$ is a solution of the equation

$$2(r + 3) = 5r - 6.$$

Solution

If $r = 4$, then

$$\text{LHS} = 2(4 + 3) = 2 \times 7 = 14$$

and

$$\text{RHS} = 5 \times 4 - 6 = 20 - 6 = 14.$$

Since LHS = RHS, $r = 4$ is a solution.

When you check whether a number is a solution of an equation, you should set out your working in a similar way to Example 18. Evaluate the left- and right-hand sides *separately*, and check whether each side gives the same answer.

If one side of the equation is a constant term, then you just need to evaluate the other side, and check whether you get the right number. You can set out your working in the way shown in Example 19 below.

Example 19   *Checking a solution of another equation*

Show that $x = -2$ is a solution of the equation

$$\tfrac{1}{2}(x + 8) = 3.$$

Solution

If $x = -2$, then

$$\text{LHS} = \tfrac{1}{2}(-2 + 8) = \tfrac{1}{2} \times 6 = 3 = \text{RHS}.$$

Hence $x = -2$ is a solution.

Activity 37   *Checking solutions of equations*

Determine whether each of the following statements is true.

(a) The equation $4p = 12$ has solution $p = 3$.

(b) The equation $10 - 2A = 1 + A$ has solution $A = 2$.

(c) The equation $4z + 2 = 3(z - 1)$ has solution $z = -5$.

It's possible for an equation to have more than one solution. For example, the equation $a^2 = 4$ has two solutions, $a = 2$ and $a = -2$, because $2^2 = 4$ and $(-2)^2 = 4$. It's also possible for an equation to have no solution at all. For example, the equation $a^2 = -1$ has no solution, because squaring a real number always gives a non-negative answer.

All the equations that you'll be asked to solve in this unit have exactly one solution. They're all of a particular type – **linear equations in one unknown** – and each equation of this type has exactly one solution. The phrase 'in one unknown' means that there's only one unknown in the equation (though it can appear more than once). The word 'linear' means that if the unknown is x, say, then after expanding any brackets or fractions in the equation, each term is either a constant term or a number times x. In particular, the equation doesn't involve powers like x^2, x^3 or x^{-1}, but only x itself. Linear equations are related to straight lines, as you'll see in the next unit.

You'll learn more about different types of equations, and how many solutions they have, as part of your work in the next few units of the module.

It's traditional to use the letter x for a single unknown. You can use any letter, but x is often used in general discussions about equations.

> Traditionally, unknowns have been represented by letters from near the end of the alphabet. This convention was introduced by the French philosopher and mathematician René Descartes.

Figure 5 René Descartes (1596–1650)

5.2 How to solve linear equations

The method for solving linear equations that you'll learn in this section is based on a simple idea. Consider the following equation:

$$6 = 6. \tag{10}$$

This equation may seem rather boring, but every equation is much like it! In every equation, the expressions on each side of the equals sign represent *equal numbers*.

If you've got two equal numbers, then you can do the same thing to each of them and you'll still have two equal numbers. For example, you can add 4 to each side of equation (10) to obtain

$$6 + 4 = 6 + 4; \quad \text{that is,} \quad 10 = 10.$$

But if you do something to *just one side* of an equation, then things go wrong. For example, if you add 4 to just the left-hand side of equation (10), then you obtain $10 = 6$, which is wrong.

> If you do any of the following things to *both sides* of a correct equation, then you obtain another correct equation.
>
> - Add a number.
> - Subtract a number.
> - Multiply by a number.
> - Divide by a non-zero number.

You might find it helpful to think of the two sides of an equation as the two pans of a set of weighing scales. To keep the scales balanced, the same thing must be done to the weights on each side.

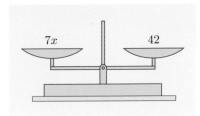

Multiplying by 7 and dividing by 7 are **inverse** operations – each undoes the effect of the other.

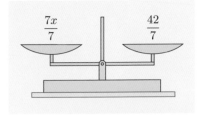

This fact can be used to solve equations. Let's use it now to solve the equation

$$7x = 42. \tag{11}$$

The idea is to do the same thing to both sides and end up with an equation of the form

$$x = \text{(a number)},$$

since that will give the solution. So what should we do to both sides? Well, since x is *multiplied* by 7 in the equation, we need to *divide* by 7, to give x by itself. Dividing both sides by 7 gives

$$\frac{7x}{7} = \frac{42}{7}.$$

Simplifying gives

$$x = 6,$$

which is the solution.

Once you've found the solution to an equation, it's a good idea to check it, to make sure that you haven't made a mistake. For equation (11), if $x = 6$, then

$$\text{LHS} = 7 \times 6 = 42 = \text{RHS}.$$

So the solution found above is correct.

Here's another example, which illustrates how you should set out your working when you solve an equation.

Example 20 *Solving an equation*

Solve the equation $P - 33 = 48$.

Solution

The equation is: $P - 33 = 48$

$\vars,$ P has 33 subtracted, so add 33. Add it to both sides. ς

Add 33: $P - 33 + 33 = 48 + 33$

Simplify: $P = 81$

The solution is $P = 81$.

(Check: if $P = 81$, then

$$\text{LHS} = 81 - 33 = 48 = \text{RHS},$$

so the solution is correct.)

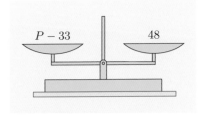

Adding 33 is the inverse operation to subtracting 33.

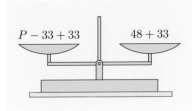

Activity 38 *Solving equations*

Solve the following equations by doing the same thing to both sides.

(a) $5x = 20$ (b) $t - 6 = 7$ (c) $x + 4 = 1$

(d) $\dfrac{z}{2} = 8$ (e) $x - 1.7 = 3$ (f) $3X = 4$

In part (f), remember that it's usually best to give *exact* answers, so use fractions.

(g) $-2y = 10$ (h) $\dfrac{c}{-5} = -6$ (i) $-m = 12$

You can use the idea of doing the same thing to both sides to solve more complicated equations. Given a complicated equation, you first do the same thing to both sides to obtain a simpler equation. Then you do the same thing to both sides of the simpler equation to obtain an even simpler equation, and so on, until eventually you end up with an equation of the form

$$x = \boxed{\text{a number}},$$

which gives the solution.

The tricky bit is deciding what to do in each step! The best approach is to first aim to obtain an equation of the form

$$\boxed{\text{a number}} \times x = \boxed{\text{a number}},$$

that is, something like $5x = 20$, $3x = -4$ or $-2x = 10$. You can often obtain an equation of this form by adding or subtracting terms on both sides of the original equation. Once you've obtained an equation of this form, you need to carry out just one further step – dividing both sides by the coefficient of x – to obtain the solution. Here's an example.

Example 21 *Solving a more complicated equation*

Tutorial clip

Solve the equation

$$5x = 3x + 10.$$

Solution

The equation is: $5x = 3x + 10$

💬 First aim to get an equation of the form 'a number × x = a number'. The equation is nearly in this form: the only problem is the $3x$ on the right-hand side. To cancel out the $3x$, subtract $3x$ from both sides. 💬

Subtract $3x$: $5x - 3x = 3x + 10 - 3x$

Simplify: $2x = 10$

Since $3x$ represents a number, it's fine to subtract it from both sides.

💬 This is in the form wanted. To find the solution, divide both sides by 2. 💬

Divide by 2: $\dfrac{2x}{2} = \dfrac{10}{2}$

Simplify: $x = 5$

The solution is $x = 5$.

(Check: if $x = 5$, then

$$\text{LHS} = 5 \times 5 = 25$$

and

$$\text{RHS} = 3 \times 5 + 10 = 15 + 10 = 25.$$

Since LHS = RHS, the solution is correct.)

Activity 39 *Solving more complicated equations*

Solve each of the following equations by first adding or subtracting a term on both sides to obtain an equation of the form 'a number $\times x =$ a number', and then dividing both sides by the coefficient of x. Set out your working in the way shown in Examples 20 and 21.

(a) $9x = 12 + 5x$ (b) $6x + 8 = 2$ (c) $9x = 6 - 3x$

When you're solving an equation, you may need to first add or subtract one term on both sides, and then add or subtract another term on both sides, to obtain an equation of the form 'a number $\times x =$ a number'. This is illustrated in the next example.

Tutorial clip

Example 22 *Solving an even more complicated equation*

Solve the equation

$$7x - 4 = 2x - 14.$$

Solution

The equation is: $7x - 4 = 2x - 14$

💭 For the form 'a number $\times x =$ a number', there must be one term in x, on the left-hand side. To cancel out the $2x$ on the right-hand side, subtract $2x$ from both sides. 💭

Subtract $2x$: $7x - 4 - 2x = 2x - 14 - 2x$

Simplify: $5x - 4 = -14$

💭 For the form 'a number $\times x =$ a number', there must be one constant term, on the right-hand side. To cancel out the -4 on the left-hand side, add 4 to both sides. 💭

Add 4: $5x - 4 + 4 = -14 + 4$

Simplify: $5x = -10$

💭 This is in the form wanted. To find the solution, divide both sides by 5. 💭

Divide by 5: $\dfrac{5x}{5} = \dfrac{-10}{5}$

Simplify: $x = -2$

The solution is $x = -2$.

(Check: if $x = -2$, then

$$\text{LHS} = 7(-2) - 4 = -14 - 4 = -18$$

and

$$\text{RHS} = 2(-2) - 14 = -4 - 14 = -18.$$

Since LHS = RHS, the solution is correct.)

Activity 40 *Solving even more complicated equations*

Solve each of the following equations using the method illustrated in Example 22. That is, first add or subtract a term on both sides, and then add or subtract another term on both sides, to obtain an equation of the form 'a number $\times x$ = a number'. Then divide both sides by the coefficient of x. Set out your working in the way shown in Example 22.

(a) $3x + 2 = x + 10$ (b) $5x + 9 = -x - 3$

Sometimes when you're solving an equation, you can make the working easier by swapping the sides. For example, suppose that you want to solve the equation

$$x + 16 = 5x.$$

You could begin by swapping the sides, because that gives an equation that's closer to the form 'a number $\times x$ = a number':

$$5x = x + 16.$$

(Then you just need to subtract x from both sides to obtain the form you want.)

You can swap the sides of an equation at any stage of your working.

An alternative to swapping the sides is to aim to get a term in x on the *right*-hand side only, and a constant term on the *left*-hand side only, instead of the other way round. Then you end up with a final equation of the form

$$\text{(a number)} = x$$

instead of the usual

$$x = \text{(a number)}.$$

Here's a summary of the method that you've seen for solving equations. It can be used for any linear equation that doesn't contain fractions or brackets.

Strategy *To solve a linear equation in one unknown with no fractions or brackets*

Carry out a sequence of steps. In each step, do one of the following:

- do the same thing to both sides
- simplify one side or both sides
- swap the sides.

Aim to do the following, in order.

1. Add or subtract terms on both sides to obtain an equation of the form

   $$\text{(a number)} \times \text{(the unknown)} = \text{(a number)}.$$

2. Divide both sides by the coefficient of the unknown.

As you get more used to solving equations, you'll probably find that you can do the same thing to both sides and simplify the resulting equation all in one step. The worked examples in this unit will usually do this from now on, and you should too, as soon as you feel comfortable with it. Don't try to do too much in one step, however – that can lead to mistakes, and it can also make it hard for other people to follow your working.

Here's an example illustrating this slightly shorter form of working.

Example 23   *Solving an equation efficiently*

Solve the equation

$$3x - 4 = 2 - x.$$

Solution

The equation is:	$3x - 4 = 2 - x$
Add x:	$4x - 4 = 2$
Add 4:	$4x = 6$
Divide by 4:	$x = \dfrac{6}{4} = \dfrac{3}{2}$

The solution is $x = \frac{3}{2}$.

(Check: if $x = \frac{3}{2}$, then

$$\text{LHS} = 3 \times \tfrac{3}{2} - 4 = \tfrac{9}{2} - 4 = \tfrac{9}{2} - \tfrac{8}{2} = \tfrac{1}{2}$$

and

$$\text{RHS} = 2 - \tfrac{3}{2} = \tfrac{4}{2} - \tfrac{3}{2} = \tfrac{1}{2}.$$

Since LHS = RHS, the solution is correct.)

Try this shorter form of working in the following activity.

Activity 41   *Solving equations efficiently*

Solve the following equations.

(a) $4z + 7 = -2z + 6$ (b) $18 = 60 - 7t$

You've seen that, given any correct equation, you can do the same thing to both sides, manipulate the expressions in the equation, or swap the sides of the equation, and you'll obtain another correct equation. If we do any of these things, then we say that we're **rearranging** or *manipulating* the equation. If an equation can be obtained from another equation in this way, then we say that the two equations are **equivalent** or different forms of the same equation.

The ancient Egyptians of around 1800 BC were able to solve linear equations in one unknown. The Rhind papyrus, which dates from about 1650 BC but is a copy of a text from about two centuries earlier, contains a succession of mathematical problems and their solutions, some of which are of this type. However, no general methods of solving linear equations are given, and no letters or other symbols are used to represent unknowns. The Rhind papyrus, which is in the British Museum, is named after the antiquarian Alexander Henry Rhind, who acquired it in Egypt in 1858. It is over five metres long and was first translated in the late nineteenth century.

Figure 6 Part of the Rhind papyrus

The ancient Babylonians of around the same time also developed methods for solving linear equations, and for solving problems involving more than one equation. (You'll learn about problems of this type in Unit 7.) Like the ancient Eygptians, the ancient Babylonians didn't use letters or symbols to represent unknowns. The Babylonians lived in Mesopotamia, a region that is now largely Iraq. Our knowledge of Babylonian mathematics is derived from a large number of clay tablets unearthed since the 1850s.

Figure 7 A Babylonian clay tablet

5.3 Linear equations with fractions and brackets

Some linear equations contain fractions or brackets. You can solve an equation like this by using the usual method of a sequence of steps, in each of which you do the same thing to both sides, simplify one side or both sides or swap the sides. In the first few steps you remove the fractions and brackets, and then you continue as before.

Removing a fraction from an equation is often called **clearing** the fraction, and it can be done by multiplying both sides by a suitable number. But you must multiply the *whole* of each side. To see why, consider the following equation, which involves only numbers:

$$\tfrac{1}{2} + 3 = \tfrac{7}{2}. \tag{12}$$

This equation is correct, as each side has value $\tfrac{7}{2}$.

If you multiply the whole of each side of the equation by 2, say, then you obtain another correct equation:

$$2\left(\tfrac{1}{2} + 3\right) = 2 \times \tfrac{7}{2}.$$

Each side of this new equation has value 7.

But if you multiply just part of one side by 2, then things go wrong. For example, if you start with equation (12) and multiply the right-hand side by 2, but multiply only the fraction on the left-hand side by 2, then you obtain

$$2 \times \tfrac{1}{2} + 3 = 2 \times \tfrac{7}{2}.$$

This equation is incorrect, because the left- and right-hand sides have values 4 and 7, respectively.

So remember that when you do the same thing to both sides of an equation, you must do it to the whole of each side.

Removing fractions isn't essential (if they're numerical rather than algebraic fractions), but it makes equations easier to manipulate.

The next example illustrates how to solve an equation that contains fractions and brackets. It's usually best to consider the fractions first, because when you clear a fraction you often need to introduce extra brackets as part of the working. But there are are no hard-and-fast rules. As you become more familiar with solving equations, you'll begin to see the best way to proceed for any particular equation.

Tutorial clip

Example 24   *Solving an equation with fractions and brackets*

Solve the equation

$$4(x - 5) = \frac{x}{2} + 8.$$

Solution

The equation is: $\qquad\qquad\qquad 4(x - 5) = \frac{x}{2} + 8$

There's a fraction with denominator 2, so multiply both sides by 2 to clear it. The *whole* of each side must be multiplied by 2, so introduce brackets on the right-hand side.

Multiply by 2: $\qquad\qquad\qquad 2 \times 4(x - 5) = 2\left(\frac{x}{2} + 8\right)$

Simplify: $\qquad\qquad\qquad\qquad 8(x - 5) = 2\left(\frac{x}{2} + 8\right)$

Next multiply out the brackets. Multiply *every term* in brackets by the appropriate multiplier.

Multiply out the brackets: $\qquad 8x - 40 = x + 16$

Now there are no fractions or brackets, so continue in the usual way.

Subtract x: $\qquad\qquad\qquad\qquad 7x - 40 = 16$

Add 40: $\qquad\qquad\qquad\qquad\qquad 7x = 56$

Divide by 7: $\qquad\qquad\qquad\qquad\quad x = 8$

The solution is $x = 8$.

(Check: if $x = 8$, then

$$\text{LHS} = 4(8 - 5) = 4 \times 3 = 12$$

and

$$\text{RHS} = \frac{8}{2} + 8 = 4 + 8 = 12.$$

Since LHS = RHS, the solution is correct.)

The strategy used in Example 24 is summarised in the box on the next page. It's just the strategy from the previous subsection, with the extra stage of removing fractions and brackets.

Strategy   *To solve a linear equation in one unknown*

Carry out a sequence of steps. In each step, do one of the following:

- do the same thing to both sides
- simplify one side or both sides
- swap the sides.

Aim to do the following, in order.

1. Clear any fractions and multiply out any brackets. To clear fractions, multiply both sides by a suitable number.

2. Add or subtract terms on both sides to obtain an equation of the form

$$\text{(a number)} \times \text{(the unknown)} = \text{(a number)}.$$

3. Divide both sides by the coefficient of the unknown.

When you multiply both sides by a number, you must multiply the *whole* of each side.

Activity 42   *Solving equations with fractions and brackets*

Solve the following equations.

(a) $x + 8 = 3(x - 2)$ (b) $\dfrac{2 - x}{7} = 3$ (c) $3(b - 5) = \dfrac{b}{3} + 17$

(d) $3\left(1 + \dfrac{y}{2}\right) = 2(y - 1)$ (e) $\dfrac{1 + a}{2} = 1 + \dfrac{3a}{5}$

Hint for part (e): In this part there are *two* fractions to be cleared. First multiply both sides by a number that will clear one of the fractions, then multiply out any brackets that you have introduced. Then do the same for the other fraction. (A shortcut is to multiply both sides by a number that will clear both fractions at once – the number has to be a common multiple of the two denominators.)

5.4   Using linear equations

Earlier in the unit, you met the idea that some mathematical questions can be answered by using equations. Here's the strategy that can be used.

Strategy   *To find an unknown number*

- Represent the number that you want to find by a letter.
- Express the information that you know about the number as an equation.
- Solve the equation.

In this subsection you'll see many different mathematical questions that can be answered by using this strategy. Here's the first example.

Example 25   *Finding an unknown number*

The price of a packet of cereal on special offer has been reduced by 20% and is now £1.80. What's the normal price?

Solution

💭 Represent the number that you want to find by a letter. 💭

Let the normal price, in £, be c.

💭 Express what you know about the number as an equation. 💭

The price has been reduced by 20%, so the reduced price is 80% of the normal price. That is, the reduced price, in £, is

$$\frac{80}{100} \times c, \quad \text{which simplifies to } 0.8c.$$

We know that the reduced price is £1.80, so we obtain the equation

$$0.8c = 1.8.$$

💭 Solve the equation. 💭

We now solve this equation.

Divide by 0.8: $c = \dfrac{1.8}{0.8} = 2.25$

💭 State a conclusion in the context of the question. 💭

So the normal price is £2.25.

(Check: 80% of £2.25 = $0.8 \times$ £2.25 = £1.80.)

When you use the strategy given at the beginning of this subsection, it can be helpful to choose a letter that reminds you of what the letter represents. For example, in Example 25 the letter c stands for cost. But avoid letters that resemble numbers, such as o and l, which look like 0 and 1, respectively. And if the question involves money, then it's best to avoid the letter p, as it can be confused with 'pence'.

Activity 43   *Finding unknown numbers*

Use equations to answer the following questions.

(a) Laura's age, multiplied by four, is 92. How old is Laura?

(b) In a village raffle, 8% of the people who bought a ticket won a prize. There were 16 prizes. How many people bought a ticket?

(c) Rahul celebrated his thirty-fourth birthday in 2008. In what year was he born?

   Hint: The equation needed here involves addition rather than multiplication.

(d) Jakub's house is valued at £175 000. House prices in his area have increased by 25% over the last five years. If Jakub's house is typical, what was it worth five years ago?

In the next example there's more than one unknown number. Since the unknown numbers are related, the question can still be answered by using an equation.

Example 26 *Finding related unknown numbers*

Callum, Ewan and Finlay have helped out in their grandfather John's garden, and John has given them £90 to share between them. The money is to be shared according to how much work each grandson has done: Callum and Ewan are to receive three times as much and twice as much, respectively, as Finlay. How much money should each grandson receive?

Solution

⊜ There are three numbers (Callum's, Ewan's and Finlay's money) to be found, but once one number has been found, it'll be straightforward to find the other two. So represent just one of the three numbers by a letter. ⊜

Let the amount of money that Finlay receives, in £, be m.

⊜ Express what you know about the number as an equation. ⊜

Then the amounts that Callum and Ewan receive, in £, are $3m$ and $2m$, respectively. The total amount, in £, is

$$m + 2m + 3m.$$

We know that the total amount of money is £90, so we obtain the equation

$$m + 2m + 3m = 90.$$

⊜ Solve the equation. ⊜

We now solve this equation.

Simplify: $6m = 90$

Divide by 6: $m = 15$

⊜ State a conclusion in the context of the question. ⊜

So Finlay receives £15. Hence Callum receives

$$3 \times £15 = £45,$$

and Ewan receives

$$2 \times £15 = £30.$$

(Check: £15 + £30 + £45 = £90.)

Activity 44 *Finding related unknown numbers*

Use an equation to answer the following question.

Lydia and Meena share a flat. Meena has a larger bedroom than Lydia, so they have agreed that the rent that Meena pays should be 1.25 times the rent that Lydia pays. The monthly rent for the flat is £945. How much should each flatmate pay?

Usually the most difficult part of the strategy on page 45 is finding the equation that you need. It's often helpful to write down a rough 'word equation', and then find algebraic expressions to replace the words. This is illustrated in the next example, which is about a 'find-the-age' number puzzle. Puzzles like this aren't so puzzling if you know how to solve equations!

Example 27 *Solving a find-the-age puzzle*

In ten years' time, Matthew will be four times the age he was eight years ago. How old is Matthew?

Solution

Represent the number that you want to find by a letter.

Let Matthew's age be a.

Write down a word equation. To do this, use the information given in the puzzle to find two things that are equal to each other. It's sometimes helpful to look out for the word 'is' (or 'was' or 'will be') in a question or puzzle: this can be the verbal equivalent of an equals sign.

We're told that

   Matthew's age 10 years from now $= 4 \times$ Matthew's age 8 years ago.

Now replace the words in the word equation by expressions involving the unknown a. A table can help you to find the right expressions.

Time	Matthew's age
Now	a
10 years from now	$a + 10$
8 years ago	$a - 8$

Replacing the words in the word equation by the expressions from the table gives the equation

   $a + 10 = 4(a - 8)$.

The brackets are essential: Matthew's age eight years ago is $a - 8$, so four times his age eight years ago is $4(a - 8)$, not $4a - 8$.

Solve the equation.

We now solve this equation.

Multiply out the brackets:	$a + 10 = 4a - 32$
Subtract a:	$10 = 3a - 32$
Add 32:	$42 = 3a$
Divide by 3:	$14 = a$

The solution is $a = 14$.

State a conclusion in the context of the question.

That is, Matthew's age is 14.

(Check: In ten years' time Matthew will be 24, and eight years ago he was 6. So his age in ten years' time will be four times the age he was eight years ago.)

Here are some find-the-age puzzles for you to solve. In each part of Activity 45 you might find it easier to compile the age table before writing down the word equation. Do whichever is easier for you.

Activity 45   *Solving find-the-age puzzles*

Solve the following puzzles.

(a) Mariko is four times the age she was 63 years ago. How old is Mariko?

(b) In four years' time, Gregor will be three times the age he was six years ago. How old is Gregor?

(c) Five years ago, Aisha was three times as old as her son Jamil was then. Aisha is 47. How old is Jamil?

Hint: For part (c) you'll need a table with two 'age' columns, one for Aisha's age and one for Jamil's age.

Finally in this unit, we'll use an equation to answer the seemingly complicated question about a charitable donation that you saw in Subsection 1.3. Here's the question.

> Catherine wants to contribute to a charitable cause, using her credit card and a donations website. The donations company states that from each donation, first it will deduct a 2% charge for credit card use, then it will deduct a charge of £3 for use of its website, and then the remaining money will be increased by 22% due to tax payback. How much money (to the nearest penny) must Catherine pay if she wants the cause to receive £40?

To answer this question, let's begin by denoting the amount in £ that Catherine must pay by m. Then we have the following word equation:

amount in £ paid to cause if £m is paid to company = 40.

The next step is to find an expression involving m to replace the left-hand side of this word equation. This can be done by starting with m and using successive steps – it's just like following through a think-of-a-number trick. In the next activity you are asked to do this, and then to solve the resulting equation to find the answer to the question.

Activity 46   *Finding another unknown number*

(a) Follow the steps below to find an expression for the amount in £ paid to the charitable cause if £m is paid to the donations company.

> Money paid to company (in £): m
>
> Multiply by 0.98 (because of the 2% reduction):
>
> Subtract 3 (the charge for use of the website):
>
> Multiply by 1.22 (because of tax payback):

(b) Hence write down an equation whose solution gives the answer to the question above.

(c) Solve the equation found in part (b) and hence state the answer to the question.

Remember that:

- if you deduct 2% of a quantity, then you end up with 0.98 times what you started with

- if you increase a quantity by 22%, then you end up with 1.22 times what you started with.

Percentage increases and decreases were covered in Unit 1.

Now that you've reached the end of this unit, you should have acquired fundamental algebraic skills that will be needed later in this module, and in any further mathematics modules that you study.

Learning checklist

After studying this unit, you should be able to:

- appreciate some of the uses of algebra
- recognise some technical terms used in algebra
- collect like terms
- simplify expressions term by term
- multiply out brackets
- use algebraic fraction notation
- prove some simple facts about numbers
- simplify some formulas
- solve linear equations
- use equations to answer some mathematical questions.

Solutions and comments on Activities

Activity 1

Was your answer *elephant*?

Activity 2

Was your answer *elephant* again? Or perhaps *elk*, or *eel*? See the discussion in the text after the activity.

Activity 3

Substituting $n = 48$ into the formula

$P = 1.24n - 0.69n$

gives

$$P = 1.24 \times 48 - 0.69 \times 48$$
$$= 59.52 - 33.12$$
$$= 26.4.$$

So the profit is £26.40.

Activity 4

Substituting $n = 48$ into the formula

$P = 0.55n$

gives

$P = 0.55 \times 48 = 26.4.$

So the profit is £26.40.

Activity 5

(a) $\frac{2}{5}T = 24$

(b) Two-fifths of T is 24,

so one-fifth of T is $24 \div 2 = 12$,

so T is $5 \times 12 = 60$.

So there are 60 toddlers in the village.

(You can confirm that this is the right answer by checking that the equation in part (a) is correct when $T = 60$ is substituted in.)

Activity 6

Substitute $a = -2$ and $b = 5$ in each case.

(a) $\frac{5}{2} + a = \frac{5}{2} + (-2)$

$$= \frac{5}{2} - 2$$
$$= \frac{5}{2} - \frac{4}{2}$$
$$= \frac{1}{2}$$

(b) $-a + ab = -(-2) + (-2) \times 5$

$$= 2 + (-10)$$
$$= 2 - 10$$
$$= -8$$

(c) $ab^2 = (-2) \times 5^2$

$$= -2 \times 25$$
$$= -50$$

(d) $b + 3(b - a) = 5 + 3(5 - (-2))$

$$= 5 + 3 \times 7$$
$$= 5 + 21$$
$$= 26$$

Activity 7

(a) This is correct. Adding three copies of a number together is the same as multiplying it by 3.

(b) This is correct, by an index law. (The index laws were covered in Unit 3.)

(c) This is correct. Multiplying a number by 2 and then dividing by 2 results in the number you started with.

(d) This is incorrect. By an index law, $p^2 \times p^3 = p^5$.

(The statement is correct for $p = 0$ and $p = 1$, but these are the *only* values for which it is correct, so the expressions aren't equivalent.)

(e) This is correct. $2z$ is the same as $z + z$, so $z + 2z$ is the same as $z + z + z$, which is the same as $3z$.

(f) This is correct. Since $6 = 3 \times 2$, multiplying a number by 6 and then dividing by 2 results in 3 times the number you started with.

(g) This is correct. Adding the negative of a number is the same as subtracting the number. (For example, $6 + (-3)$ is the same is $6 - 3$. You met this property of numbers in Unit 1.)

(h) This is incorrect. Multiplying the number 3 by n and then dividing by n gives the result 3.

(The statement is correct for $n = 3$, but this is the *only* value for which it's correct, so the expressions aren't equivalent.)

Activity 8

(a) The expression is

$\underline{+x^3}\ \underline{-x^2}\ \underline{+x}\ \underline{+1}$.

Its terms are $+x^3$, $-x^2$, $+x$ and $+1$.

(b) The expression is

$\underline{+2mn}\ \underline{-3r}$.

Its terms are $+2mn$ and $-3r$.

(c) The expression is

$\underline{-20p^2q^2}\ \underline{+\frac{1}{4}p}\ \underline{-18}\ \underline{-\frac{1}{3}q}$.

Its terms are $-20p^2q^2$, $+\frac{1}{4}p$, -18 and $-\frac{1}{3}q$.

Activity 9

(a) The expression is

$$\underbrace{-X}\ \underbrace{+\,20Y}\ \underbrace{-\,5Z}\ .$$

Reversing the order of the terms gives

$-5Z + 20Y - X$.

(b) The expression is

$$\underbrace{+2u}\ \underbrace{-\,3uv}\ .$$

Reversing the order of the terms gives

$-3uv + 2u$.

(c) The expression is

$$\underbrace{+4i}\ \underbrace{-\,j}\ \underbrace{+\,5}\ .$$

Reversing the order of the terms gives

$5 - j + 4i$.

(d) The expression is

$$\underbrace{+a}\ \underbrace{-\,b}\ \underbrace{+\,c}\ \underbrace{+\,d}\ .$$

Reversing the order of the terms gives

$d + c - b + a$.

Activity 10

(a) The third term is $4y^2$, with coefficient 4.

(b) The second term is $-9\sqrt{q}$, with coefficient -9.

(c) The third term is x^2, with coefficient 1.

(d) The first term is $-a^2b$, with coefficient -1.

(e) The term in m^2 is $-3m^2$, with coefficient -3.

(f) The term in b is $2b$, with coefficient 2. (The term b^2 is a term in b^2, not b.)

Activity 11

(a) There is no constant term.

(b) There is a constant term, -7.

(c) There is a constant term, $5\sqrt{2}$.

(d) There is no constant term.

(e) There is a constant term, 1.

(f) There is no constant term.

Activity 12

(a) These are unlike terms: the first is a term in b, and the second is a term in b^2.

(b) These are like terms: both are terms in D.

(c) These are like terms: both are terms in z. (The first term has coefficient 1, and the second has coefficient -1.)

(d) These are unlike terms: the first is a constant term, and the second is a term in m.

Activity 13

(a) $8A + 7A = (8 + 7)A = 15A$

(b) $-5d + 8d - 2d = (-5 + 8 - 2)d = 1d = d$

($1d$ is usually written as d.)

(c) $-7z + z = -7z + 1z = (-7 + 1)z = -6z$

(d) $1.4pq + 0.7pq - pq = 1.4pq + 0.7pq - 1pq$
$$= (1.4 + 0.7 - 1)pq$$
$$= 1.1pq$$

(e) $\frac{1}{2}n^2 - \frac{1}{3}n^2 = \frac{3}{6}n^2 - \frac{2}{6}n^2 = \left(\frac{3}{6} - \frac{2}{6}\right)n^2 = \frac{1}{6}n^2$

(You should give the exact answer, $\frac{1}{6}n^2$, not an approximation such as $0.167n^2$.)

Activity 14

(a) These are like terms: both are terms in ab.

(b) These are like terms: both are terms in rst.

(c) These are like terms: both are terms in xy. (The second term can be written as $-3xy$.)

(d) These are like terms: both are terms in ac^2. (The first term can be written as $4ac^2$.)

(e) These are like terms: both are terms in abc. (The second term can be written as abc.)

(f) These are unlike terms. If we write the second term with the letters in alphabetical order, then it's $9cd^2$. So the first term is a term in c^2d (that is, $c \times c \times d$), and the second is a term in cd^2 (that is, $c \times d \times d$).

(g) These are unlike terms: the first is a term in A^2, and the second is a term in a^2.

(h) These are unlike terms: the first is a term in fh, and the second is a term in gh.

(i) These are like terms, as they're both constant terms.

Activity 15

(a) $4A - 3B + 3C + 5A + 2B - A$
$$= 4A + 5A - A - 3B + 2B + 3C$$
$$= 8A - B + 3C$$

(b) $-8v + 7 - 5w - 2v - 8$
$$= -8v - 2v - 5w + 7 - 8$$
$$= -10v - 5w - 1$$

(c) $20y^2 + 10xy - 10y^2 - 5y - 5xy$
$$= 20y^2 - 10y^2 + 10xy - 5xy - 5y$$
$$= 10y^2 + 5xy - 5y$$

(d) $-4ef + 8e^2f + 10fe - 3f^2e$
$$= -4ef + 8e^2f + 10ef - 3ef^2$$
$$= -4ef + 10ef + 8e^2f - 3ef^2$$
$$= 6ef + 8e^2f - 3ef^2$$

(e) $\frac{1}{2}a + \frac{1}{3}b + 2a + \frac{1}{4}b$

$= \frac{1}{2}a + 2a + \frac{1}{3}b + \frac{1}{4}b$

$= \frac{1}{2}a + \frac{4}{2}a + \frac{4}{12}b + \frac{3}{12}b$

$= \frac{5}{2}a + \frac{7}{12}b$

Activity 16

(a) $2a^3 - 3a - 2a^3 - 3a = -6a$

(b) $2m + n - 5m + 2n + 3m = 3n$

(c) $b + 2b + 3b - 6b = 0$

Activity 17

(a) The formula is
$A = 10c + 2a$.

(b) The formula is
$T = 7c + 14a$.

(c) The formula is
$C = 10c + 2a + 7c + 14a$.

(d) Collecting like terms gives
$C = 17c + 16a$.

(e) Substituting $c = 22$ and $a = 10$ in the formula found in part (d) gives
$C = 17 \times 22 + 16 \times 10 = 374 + 160 = 534$.
The cost of the trip is £534.

Activity 18

(a) $y \times z \times 6 \times x \times 4 = 24xyz$

(b) $7p \times 2qr = 14pqr$

(c) $QR \times G \times 5F = 5FGQR$

(d) $2 \times a \times a \times 3 \times a = 6a^3$

(e) $m \times n \times m \times 4 = 4m^2n$

(f) $5y \times 2yx = 10xy^2$

(g) $4AB \times 4AB = 16A^2B^2$

Activity 19

(a) $8P^8 \times 5P = 40P^9$

(b) $2c^{10}d^3 \times 2c^2d^3 = 4c^{12}d^6$

Activity 20

(a) $9X \times (-XY) = -9X^2Y$

(b) $3s \times \frac{1}{3}r = 1rs = rs$

(c) $-3a^3 \times (-4a^4) = +12a^7 = 12a^7$

(d) $-2pq \times (-3qp^2) = +6p^3q^2 = 6p^3q^2$

(e) $-0.5g \times 2f^5 = -1f^5g = -f^5g$

(f) $-a \times b \times (-c) \times (-d) = -abcd$

(g) $(-x) \times (-y) \times (-x^2) \times (-4y)$
$= +4x^3y^2 = 4x^3y^2$

(h) $(-3cd)^2 = (-3cd) \times (-3cd) = +9c^2d^2 = 9c^2d^2$

(i) $-(3cd)^2 = -(3cd \times 3cd) = -9c^2d^2$

You could do parts (c), (d), (g) and (h) in one step if you prefer.

Activity 21

(a) $+(-ab) = -ab$

(b) $-(-6x^2) = +6x^2 = 6x^2$

(c) $-(2M^4) = -2M^4$

(d) $+(-7y) = -7y$

(e) $+(5p) = +5p = 5p$

(f) $-\left(-\frac{3}{4}n\right) = \frac{3}{4}n$

Activity 22

(a) $\underline{5m \times 2m} \ \underline{-2n \times n^2} = 10m^2 - 2n^3$

(b) $\underline{3p \times 2q} \ \underline{+2r \times (-7p)} = 6pq - 14pr$

(c) $\underline{2P} \ \underline{-(-3Q)} \ \underline{+(-P)} \ \underline{+(2Q)}$
$= 2P + 3Q - P + 2Q$
$= P + 5Q$

(d) $\underline{3 \times (-2a)} \ \underline{-1c^2} \ \underline{+9ac} = -6a - c^2 + 9ac$

(Only the first and second terms were simplified. The third term was already in its simplest form.)

(e) $\underline{4s \times \frac{1}{2}rst} \ \underline{-2(-\frac{1}{2}s)} = 2rs^2t + s$

(f) $\underline{-5xy} \ \underline{+(-3y \times x^2)} \ \underline{-(-y^2)}$
$= -5xy - 3x^2y + y^2$

(Only the second and third terms were simplified. The first term was already in its simplest form.)

(g) $\underline{-3r \times (-2r)} \ \underline{-(-2r \times r)} \ \underline{+(r^2 \times 9)}$
$= 6r^2 + 2r^2 + 9r^2$
$= 17r^2$

Activity 23

(a) $3p(pq + 4) = 3p \times pq + 3p \times 4 = 3p^2q + 12p$

(b) $x^2(x + 2y) = x^2 \times x + x^2 \times 2y = x^3 + 2x^2y$

Activity 24

(a) $f(e + 5g) = ef + 5fg$

(b) $5(2A + B) = 10A + 5B$

(c) $3c(4c + 2d) = 12c^2 + 6cd$

(d) $(a - b)c^2 = ac^2 - bc^2$

(e) $2y(x + 2y + 4z) = 2xy + 4y^2 + 8yz$

(f) $2\left(\frac{1}{2}A^2 + \frac{3}{2}\right) = A^2 + 3$

(g) $a(x + y)z = axz + ayz$

(h) $2b(b^2 + 2b^4) = 2b^3 + 4b^5$

Activity 25

(a) $p(q - r) = pq - pr$

(b) $7a(-4a + 3b) = -28a^2 + 21ab$

(c) $6(0.2a - 0.3b + 1.4) = 1.2a - 1.8b + 8.4$

(d) $10(\frac{1}{2}n + \frac{1}{5}) = 5n + 2$

(e) $-3(x - 2y) = -3x + 6y$

(f) $-b^2(-a + b) = ab^2 - b^3$

Activity 26

(a) $\underline{f} + \underline{g(f + h)} = f + fg + gh$

(b) $\underline{x} - \underline{y(x + 2y)} = x - xy - 2y^2$

(c) $\underline{2p} - \underline{3q(-3p + q)} = 2p + 9pq - 3q^2$

(d) $\underline{-2(a + b)} + \underline{4(a - b)} = -2a - 2b + 4a - 4b$

$\qquad = 2a - 6b$

(e) $\underline{2aE} - \underline{3E(-E - 5a)} = 2aE + 3E^2 + 15aE$

$\qquad = 17aE + 3E^2$

(f) $\underline{(d - c)c} - \underline{c^2} = dc - c^2 - c^2$

$\qquad = cd - 2c^2$

Activity 27

(a) $-(4f - g^3) = -4f + g^3$

(b) $-(-x + 7y - 8z + 6) = x - 7y + 8z - 6$

(c) $\underline{2(a - b)} + \underline{(c - 2d)} = 2a - 2b + c - 2d$

(d) $\underline{r} + \underline{(-2s - r)} = r - 2s - r = -2s$

(e) $\underline{-A} + \underline{B} - \underline{(-3A + 4B)}$

$\qquad = -A + B + 3A - 4B = 2A - 3B$

(f) $\underline{-(-t - w)} + \underline{(-t + w)} = t + w - t + w$

$\qquad = 2w$

(g) $\underline{-(L + 2M)} - \underline{(-M)} = -L - 2M + M$

$\qquad = -L - M$

Activity 28

(a) $(a + b) \div 3 = \dfrac{a + b}{3}$

(b) $a + b \div 3 = a + \dfrac{b}{3}$

(c) $(x + 2) \div (y + 3) = \dfrac{x + 2}{y + 3}$

(d) $(x + 2) \div y + 3 = \dfrac{x + 2}{y} + 3$

(e) $x + 2 \div (y + 3) = x + \dfrac{2}{y + 3}$

(f) $x + 2 \div y + 3 = x + \dfrac{2}{y} + 3$

Activity 29

(a) $6\left(1 + \dfrac{h}{2}\right) = 6 + \dfrac{6h}{2} = 6 + 3h$

(b) $6\left(\dfrac{1 + h}{2}\right) = \dfrac{6}{2}(1 + h) = 3(1 + h) = 3 + 3h$

Activity 30

(a) $\dfrac{A - 6B}{3} = \dfrac{A}{3} - \dfrac{6B}{3} = \dfrac{A}{3} - 2B$

(b) $\dfrac{10z^2 + 5z - 20}{5} = \dfrac{10z^2}{5} + \dfrac{5z}{5} - \dfrac{20}{5}$

$\qquad = 2z^2 + z - 4$

(c) $\dfrac{3A^2 + A}{A} = \dfrac{3A^2}{A} + \dfrac{A}{A} = 3A + 1$

Activity 31

(a) For example, here's the trick with starting number 7.

Think of a number:	7
Multiply it by 3:	21
Add 2:	23
Double the result:	46
Add 2:	48
Divide by 6:	8
Take away the number you first thought of:	1

The answer is 1.

(b) Here's the trick starting with n.

Think of a number:	n
Multiply it by 3:	$3n$
Add 2:	$3n + 2$
Double the result:	$2(3n + 2) = 6n + 4$
Add 2:	$6n + 4 + 2 = 6n + 6$
Divide by 6:	$\dfrac{6n + 6}{6} = \dfrac{6n}{6} + \dfrac{6}{6} = n + 1$

Take away the number
you first thought of: $\quad n + 1 - n = 1$

So the trick always gives the answer 1.

Activity 32

(a) The cost for the first 200 leaflets is £175. The remaining number of leaflets is $n - 200$, and the cost in £ for these leaflets is

$(n - 200) \times 0.25 = 0.25(n - 200).$

The total cost in £ is

$175 + 0.25(n - 200).$

So the formula is

$C = 175 + 0.25(n - 200).$

(b) The formula can be simplified as follows:
$$C = 175 + 0.25(n - 200)$$
$$= 175 + 0.25n - 50$$
$$= 125 + 0.25n.$$

The formula is

$C = 125 + 0.25n.$

(c) If $n = 450$, then
$$C = 125 + 0.25 \times 450$$
$$= 125 + 112.5$$
$$= 237.5.$$

So the cost of printing 450 leaflets is £237.50.

Activity 33

For example, the consecutive integers 1, 2 and 3 add up to 6, which is divisible by 3. Then, for example, the consecutive integers 7, 8 and 9 add up to 24, which is also divisible by 3.

Activity 34

(a) For example, $5 + 7 + 9 = 21$, which is divisible by 3.

(b) For example, $20 + 22 + 24 = 66$, which is divisible by 3.

(c) Represent the first of the three integers by n. Then the other two integers are $n + 2$ and $n + 4$. So their sum is
$$n + (n + 2) + (n + 4) = n + n + 2 + n + 4$$
$$= 3n + 6.$$

Dividing by 3 gives
$$\frac{3n + 6}{3} = \frac{3n}{3} + \frac{6}{3} = n + 2.$$

Now $n + 2$ is an integer, because n is an integer. So dividing the sum of the three numbers by 3 gives an integer. That is, the sum is divisible by 3.

Activity 35

Represent the first of the four integers by n. Then

the other three integers are $n + 1$, $n + 2$ and $n + 3$. So their sum is
$$n + (n + 1) + (n + 2) + (n + 3)$$
$$= n + n + 1 + n + 2 + n + 3$$
$$= 4n + 6.$$

Dividing by 4 gives
$$\frac{4n + 6}{4} = \frac{4n}{4} + \frac{6}{4} = n + \frac{3}{2}.$$

Since n is an integer, $n + \frac{3}{2}$ is *not* an integer. So the sum is not divisible by 4.

Activity 36

(a) For example, if you choose the first example in the margin, then the first integer is 15 and the amount by which the second and third integers are more than the one before is 4. The three integers are 15, 19 and 23, and their sum is $15 + 19 + 23 = 57$, which is divisible by 3, since $57 \div 3 = 19$.

(b) An expression for the second integer is $n + d$, and an expression for the third integer is $n + d + d$, which simplifies to $n + 2d$.

(c) An expression for the sum of the three integers is
$$n + (n + d) + (n + 2d) = n + n + d + n + 2d$$
$$= 3n + 3d.$$

Dividing the expression in part (c) by by 3 gives
$$\frac{3n + 3d}{3} = \frac{3n}{3} + \frac{3d}{3} = n + d.$$

Since n and d are both integers, so is $n + d$. So dividing the sum of the three integers by 3 gives an integer. That is, the sum is divisible by 3.

Activity 37

(a) If $p = 3$, then

$\text{LHS} = 4 \times 3 = 12 = \text{RHS},$

so $p = 3$ is a solution. Hence the statement is true.

(b) If $A = 2$, then

$\text{LHS} = 10 - 2 \times 2 = 10 - 4 = 6$

and

$\text{RHS} = 1 + 2 = 3.$

Thus the LHS and the RHS are not equal, so $A = 2$ is not a solution. Hence the statement is false.

(c) If $z = -5$, then

$\text{LHS} = 4 \times (-5) + 2 = -20 + 2 = -18$

and

$\text{RHS} = 3(-5 - 1) = 3 \times (-6) = -18.$

Thus LHS = RHS, so $z = -5$ is a solution. Hence the statement is true.

Activity 38

(a) The equation is: $5x = 20$

Divide by 5: $\dfrac{5x}{5} = \dfrac{20}{5}$

Simplify: $x = 4$

The solution is $x = 4$.

(Check: if $x = 4$, then

LHS $= 5 \times 4 = 20 =$ RHS,

so the solution is correct.)

(b) The equation is: $t - 6 = 7$

Add 6: $t - 6 + 6 = 7 + 6$

Simplify: $t = 13$

The solution is $t = 13$.

(Check: if $t = 13$, then

LHS $= 13 - 6 = 7 =$ RHS,

so the solution is correct.)

(c) The equation is: $x + 4 = 1$

Subtract 4: $x + 4 - 4 = 1 - 4$

Simplify: $x = -3$

The solution is $x = -3$.

(Check: if $x = -3$, then

LHS $= -3 + 4 = 1 =$ RHS,

so the solution is correct.)

(d) The equation is: $\dfrac{z}{2} = 8$

Multiply by 2: $\dfrac{z}{2} \times 2 = 8 \times 2$

Simplify: $z = 16$

The solution is $z = 16$.

(Check: if $z = 16$, then

LHS $= \dfrac{16}{2} = 8 =$ RHS,

so the solution is correct.)

(e) The equation is: $x - 1.7 = 3$

Add 1.7: $x - 1.7 + 1.7 = 3 + 1.7$

Simplify: $x = 4.7$

The solution is $x = 4.7$.

(Check: if $x = 4.7$, then

LHS $= 4.7 - 1.7 = 3 =$ RHS,

so the solution is correct.)

(f) The equation is: $3X = 4$

Divide by 3: $\dfrac{3X}{3} = \dfrac{4}{3}$

Simplify: $X = \tfrac{4}{3}$

The solution is $X = \tfrac{4}{3}$.

(Give the exact answer, $\tfrac{4}{3}$, not an approximation such as 1.33. You could convert the top-heavy fraction $\tfrac{4}{3}$ to the mixed number $1\tfrac{1}{3}$, but you don't have to do that.)

(Check: if $X = \tfrac{4}{3}$, then

LHS $= 3 \times \tfrac{4}{3} = 4 =$ RHS,

so the solution is correct.)

(g) The equation is: $-2y = 10$

Divide by -2: $\dfrac{-2y}{-2} = \dfrac{10}{-2}$

Simplify: $y = -5$

The solution is $y = -5$.

(Check: if $y = -5$, then

LHS $= -2 \times (-5) = 10 =$ RHS,

so the solution is correct.)

(h) The equation is: $\dfrac{c}{-5} = -6$

Multiply by -5: $\dfrac{c}{-5} \times (-5) = (-6) \times (-5)$

Simplify: $c = 30$

The solution is $c = 30$.

(Check: if $c = 30$, then

LHS $= \dfrac{30}{-5} = -6 =$ RHS,

so the solution is correct.)

(i) The equation is: $-m = 12$

Multiply by -1: $-m \times (-1) = 12 \times (-1)$

Simplify: $m = -12$

The solution is $m = -12$.

(Check: if $m = -12$, then

LHS $= -(-12) = 12 =$ RHS,

so the solution is correct.)

Activity 39

(a) The equation is: $9x = 12 + 5x$

Subtract $5x$: $9x - 5x = 12 + 5x - 5x$

Simplify: $4x = 12$

Divide by 4: $\dfrac{4x}{4} = \dfrac{12}{4}$

Simplify: $x = 3$

The solution is $x = 3$.

(Check: if $x = 3$, then

LHS $= 9 \times 3 = 27$

and

RHS $= 12 + 5 \times 3 = 12 + 15 = 27$.

Since LHS $=$ RHS, the solution is correct.)

(b) The equation is: $6x + 8 = 2$

Subtract 8: $\quad 6x + 8 - 8 = 2 - 8$

Simplify: $\quad 6x = -6$

Divide by 6: $\quad \dfrac{6x}{6} = \dfrac{-6}{6}$

Simplify: $\quad x = -1$

The solution is $x = -1$.

(Check: if $x = -1$, then

$\quad$ LHS $= 6 \times (-1) + 8 = -6 + 8 = 2 =$ RHS,

so the solution is correct.)

(c) The equation is: $9x = 6 - 3x$

Add $3x$: $\quad 9x + 3x = 6 - 3x + 3x$

Simplify: $\quad 12x = 6$

Divide by 12: $\quad \dfrac{12x}{12} = \dfrac{6}{12}$

Simplify: $\quad x = \frac{1}{2}$

The solution is $x = \frac{1}{2}$.

(Check: if $x = \frac{1}{2}$, then

$\quad$ LHS $= 9 \times \frac{1}{2} = \frac{9}{2}$

and

$\quad$ RHS $= 6 - 3 \times \frac{1}{2} = \frac{12}{2} - \frac{3}{2} = \frac{9}{2}$.

Since LHS = RHS, the solution is correct.)

Activity 40

(a) The equation is: $3x + 2 = x + 10$

Subtract x: $\quad 3x + 2 - x = x + 10 - x$

Simplify: $\quad 2x + 2 = 10$

Subtract 2: $\quad 2x + 2 - 2 = 10 - 2$

Simplify: $\quad 2x = 8$

Divide by 2: $\quad \dfrac{2x}{2} = \dfrac{8}{2}$

Simplify: $\quad x = 4$

The solution is $x = 4$.

(Check: if $x = 4$, then

$\quad$ LHS $= 3 \times 4 + 2 = 12 + 2 = 14$

and

$\quad$ RHS $= 4 + 10 = 14$.

Since LHS = RHS, the solution is correct.)

(b) The equation is: $5x + 9 = -x - 3$

Add x: $\quad 5x + 9 + x = -x - 3 + x$

Simplify: $\quad 6x + 9 = -3$

Subtract 9: $\quad 6x + 9 - 9 = -3 - 9$

Simplify: $\quad 6x = -12$

Divide by 6: $\quad \dfrac{6x}{6} = \dfrac{-12}{6}$

Simplify: $\quad x = -2$

The solution is $x = -2$.

(Check: if $x = -2$, then

$\quad$ LHS $= 5 \times (-2) + 9 = -10 + 9 = -1$

and

$\quad$ RHS $= -(-2) - 3 = 2 - 3 = -1$.

Since LHS = RHS, the solution is correct.)

Activity 41

(a) The equation is: $4z + 7 = -2z + 6$

Add $2z$: $\quad 6z + 7 = 6$

Subtract 7: $\quad 6z = -1$

Divide by 6: $\quad z = \dfrac{-1}{6} = -\frac{1}{6}$

The solution is $z = -\frac{1}{6}$.

(Check: if $z = -\frac{1}{6}$, then

$\quad$ LHS $= 4(-\frac{1}{6}) + 7$

$\quad\quad = -\frac{2}{3} + 7 = -\frac{2}{3} + \frac{21}{3} = \frac{19}{3}$

and

$\quad$ RHS $= -2(-\frac{1}{6}) + 6$

$\quad\quad = \frac{1}{3} + 6 = \frac{1}{3} + \frac{18}{3} = \frac{19}{3}$.

Since LHS = RHS, the solution is correct.)

(b) The equation is: $18 = 60 - 7t$

Swap the sides: $\quad 60 - 7t = 18$

Subtract 60: $\quad -7t = -42$

Divide by -7: $\quad t = 6$

The solution is $t = 6$.

(An alternative way to solve the equation is as follows.

The equation is: $18 = 60 - 7t$

Add $7t$: $\quad 18 + 7t = 60$

Subtract 18: $\quad 7t = 42$

Divide by 7: $\quad t = 6$)

(Check: if $t = 6$, then

$\quad$ RHS $= 60 - 7 \times 6 = 60 - 42 = 18 =$ LHS,

so the solution is correct.)

Activity 42

(a) The equation is: $\quad\quad\quad\quad x + 8 = 3(x - 2)$

Multiply out the brackets: $\quad x + 8 = 3x - 6$

Subtract x: $\quad\quad\quad\quad\quad 8 = 2x - 6$

Add 6: $\quad\quad\quad\quad\quad\quad 14 = 2x$

Divide by 2: $\quad\quad\quad\quad 7 = x$

The solution is $x = 7$.

(Check: if $x = 7$, then LHS $= 7 + 8 = 15$ and RHS $= 3(7 - 2) = 3 \times 5 = 15$, so the solution is correct.)

(b) The equation is: $\dfrac{2-x}{7} = 3$

Multiply by 7: $\quad 2 - x = 21$

Subtract 2: $\quad -x = 19$

Multiply by -1: $\quad x = -19$

The solution is $x = -19$.

(Check: if $x = -19$, then

LHS $= \dfrac{2-(-19)}{7} = \dfrac{21}{7} = 3 = $ RHS,

so the solution is correct.)

(c) The equation is: $\quad 3(b-5) = \dfrac{b}{3} + 17$

Multiply by 3: $\quad 3 \times 3(b-5) = 3\left(\dfrac{b}{3} + 17\right)$

Simplify: $\quad 9(b-5) = 3\left(\dfrac{b}{3} + 17\right)$

Multiply out the brackets: $\quad 9b - 45 = b + 51$

Subtract b: $\quad 8b - 45 = 51$

Add 45: $\quad 8b = 96$

Divide by 8: $\quad b = 12$

The solution is $b = 12$.

(Check: if $b = 12$, then

LHS $= 3(12 - 5) = 3 \times 7 = 21$

and

RHS $= \dfrac{12}{3} + 17 = 4 + 17 = 21$.

Since LHS $=$ RHS, the solution is correct.)

(d) The equation is: $\quad 3\left(1 + \dfrac{y}{2}\right) = 2(y-1)$

Multiply by 2: $\quad 2 \times 3\left(1 + \dfrac{y}{2}\right)$
$$= 2 \times 2(y-1)$$

Simplify: $\quad 6\left(1 + \dfrac{y}{2}\right) = 4(y-1)$

Multiply out the brackets: $\quad 6 + 3y = 4y - 4$

Subtract $3y$: $\quad 6 = y - 4$

Add 4: $\quad 10 = y$

The solution is $y = 10$.

(Check: if $y = 10$, then

LHS $= 3\left(1 + \dfrac{10}{2}\right) = 3(1 + 5) = 3 \times 6 = 18$

and

RHS $= 2(10 - 1) = 2 \times 9 = 18$.

Since LHS $=$ RHS, the solution is correct.)

(e) The equation is: $\quad \dfrac{1+a}{2} = 1 + \dfrac{3a}{5}$

Multiply by 2: $\quad 1 + a = 2\left(1 + \dfrac{3a}{5}\right)$

Multiply out the brackets: $\quad 1 + a = 2 + \dfrac{6a}{5}$

Multiply by 5: $\quad 5(1 + a) = 5\left(2 + \dfrac{6a}{5}\right)$

Multiply out the brackets: $\quad 5 + 5a = 10 + 6a$

Subtract $5a$: $\quad 5 = 10 + a$

Subtract 10: $\quad -5 = a$

The solution is $a = -5$.

(Check: if $a = -5$, then

LHS $= \dfrac{1 + (-5)}{2} = \dfrac{1 - 5}{2} = \dfrac{-4}{2} = -2$

and

RHS $= 1 + \dfrac{3 \times (-5)}{5} = 1 + \dfrac{-15}{5} = 1 + (-3) = -2$.

Since LHS $=$ RHS, the solution is correct.)

(If instead you begin by multiplying by a number that will remove both fractions, the working begins as follows.

The equation is: $\quad \dfrac{1+a}{2} = 1 + \dfrac{3a}{5}$

Multiply by 10: $\quad 10\left(\dfrac{1+a}{2}\right) = 10\left(1 + \dfrac{3a}{5}\right)$

Simplify the LHS: $\quad 5(1 + a) = 10\left(1 + \dfrac{3a}{5}\right)$

Multiply out the brackets: $\quad 5 + 5a = 10 + 6a$

The working continues as above.)

Activity 43

(a) Let Laura's age be a. Then four times her age is $4a$. We're told that this is equal to 92, so we obtain the equation
$$4a = 92.$$

We now solve this equation.

Divide by 4: $\quad a = \dfrac{92}{4} = 23$

So Laura is 23.

(Check: $4 \times 23 = 92$.)

(b) Let the number of people who bought a ticket be n. We're told that 8% of this number is 16, so we obtain the equation
$$\dfrac{8}{100} \times n = 16.$$

We now solve this equation.

Multiply by 100: $8n = 1600$

Divide by 8: $n = 200$

So 200 people bought a ticket.

(Check: $\dfrac{8}{100} \times 200 = 16$.)

(The initial equation could have been simplified to $0.08n = 16$. Then it could have been solved by dividing both sides by 0.08.)

(c) Let the year of Rahul's birth be y. Then the year in which he had his thirty-fourth birthday is $y + 34$. We're told that this is 2008, so we obtain the equation

$y + 34 = 2008.$

We now solve this equation.

Subtract 34: $y = 1974$

So Rahul was born in 1974.

(Check: $1974 + 34 = 2008$.)

(d) Let the value, in £, of Jakub's house five years ago be v.

Then its value now, in £, is

$$\frac{125}{100} \times v = 1.25v.$$

We know that this value is £175 000, so we obtain the equation

$1.25v = 175\,000.$

We now solve this equation.

Divide by 1.25: $v = \dfrac{175\,000}{1.25} = 140\,000$

So the value five years ago was £140 000.

(Check: $1.25 \times £140\,000 = £175\,000$.)

Activity 44

Let Lydia's share of the rent, in £, be r. Then Meena's share, in £, is $1.25r$. The total rent, in £, is

$r + 1.25r.$

The total rent is £945, so we obtain the equation

$r + 1.25r = 945.$

We now solve this equation.

Simplify: $2.25r = 945$

Divide by 2.25: $r = \dfrac{945}{2.25} = 420$

So Lydia's share is £420. Hence Meena's share is

$1.25 \times £420 = £525.$

(Check: $£420 + £525 = £945$.)

Activity 45

(a) Let Mariko's age be a.

We're told that

Mariko's age now = $4 \times$ her age 63 years ago.

Time	Mariko's age
Now	a
63 years ago	$a - 63$

Replacing the words in the word equation by the expressions from the table gives the equation

$a = 4(a - 63).$

We now solve this equation.

Multiply out the brackets: $a = 4a - 252$

Subtract a: $0 = 3a - 252$

Add 252: $252 = 3a$

Divide by 3: $84 = a$

So Mariko is 84.

(Check: 63 years ago, Mariko's age was $84 - 63 = 21$. Since $4 \times 21 = 84$, Mariko is four times the age she was 63 years ago.)

(b) Let Gregor's age be a.

We're told that

Gregor's age in 4 years' time $= 3 \times$ his age 6 years ago.

Time	Gregor's age
Now	a
4 years from now	$a + 4$
6 years ago	$a - 6$

Replacing the words in the word equation by the expressions from the table gives the equation

$a + 4 = 3(a - 6).$

We now solve this equation.

Multiply out the brackets: $a + 4 = 3a - 18$

Subtract a: $4 = 2a - 18$

Add 18: $22 = 2a$

Divide by 2: $11 = a$

So Gregor is 11.

(Check: In four years' time, Gregor will be 15, and six years ago he was 5. So his age in four years' time will be three times the age he was six years ago.)

(c) Let Jamil's age be a.

We're told that

    Aisha's age 5 years ago
    $= 3 \times$ Jamil's age 5 years ago.

Time	Aisha's age	Jamil's age
Now	47	a
5 years ago	42	$a - 5$

Replacing the words in the word equation by the expressions from the table gives the equation

    $42 = 3(a - 5)$.

We now solve this equation.

Multiply out the brackets: $42 = 3a - 15$

Add 15: $57 = 3a$

Divide by 3: $19 = a$

So Jamil is 19.

(Check: Five years ago Aisha was 42, and Jamil was 14. Since $3 \times 14 = 42$, at that time Aisha was three times as old as Jamil.)

Activity 46

(a) Money paid to company (in £): m

Multiply by 0.98 (because of the 2% reduction): $0.98m$

Subtract 3 (the charge for use of the website): $0.98m - 3$

Multiply by 1.22 (because of tax payback): $1.22(0.98m - 3)$
    $= 1.1956m - 3.66$

(b) The equation is

    $1.1956m - 3.66 = 40$.

(c) Start with the equation in part (b).

Add 3.66: $1.1956m = 43.66$

Divide by 1.1956: $m = \dfrac{43.66}{1.1956} = 36.52$ (to 2 d.p.)

So Catherine must donate £36.52.

(Check: $0.98 \times £36.52 = £35.7896$.
$£35.7896 - £3 = £32.7896$.
$1.22 \times £32.7896 \approx £40$.)

Graphs

Introduction

This unit extends your work on graphs, which you began in Unit 2, by looking at some connections between algebra and graphs. You have seen that relationships between quantities can often be expressed using algebraic formulas. For example, in Unit 2 you saw a formula expressing the relationship between the distance, speed and time for a journey, and a formula expressing the relationship between the number of days for which you hire a car and the cost of hiring it. This unit is about relationships between *two* quantities, such as the car hire relationship, or the relationship between distance and time if you travel at a constant speed. Relationships between two quantities can be visualised by using graphs, and this unit concentrates on relationships that correspond to *straight lines* on graphs. You will see other types of relationships between two quantities later in the module.

Section 1 shows you how to use a formula expressing the relationship between two quantities to draw a graph of the relationship. It also shows you how sets of paired data can sometimes be modelled by straight lines on graphs.

Section 2 concentrates on two key characteristics of a straight-line graph: its slope (how steep it is) and its position. You will learn how to measure the slope of a line, and how to interpret it. The slope of a straight-line graph indicates how one quantity changes in comparison with the other, and it can give you valuable information about the relationship between the two quantities that would be difficult to spot from a table of numbers.

In Section 3 you will see that every straight-line graph can be described by an algebraic equation and learn how this algebraic equation is linked to the characteristics of the graph. In mathematics it is often useful to be able to look at a problem both algebraically and graphically, so the ideas in this section are important and you will need them in future units. In this section you will also meet a particular type of algebraic relationship between quantities, *direct proportion*, which occurs in many practical situations. The graphs that illustrate relationships of this type are all straight lines that pass through the origin.

In Section 4 you will apply what you have learned in earlier sections to some real-world problems in which data are modelled by straight lines on graphs. In particular, you will see models for the growth of the world's tallest-ever man and investigate some possible relationships in the backache data that you met in Unit 4.

1   Plotting graphs

The idea of a *subject* of a formula was introduced in Unit 2, Subsection 3.1.

This section shows you how to plot a graph to illustrate an equation or formula involving two variables. (Remember that a formula is just an equation that has a *subject* – a variable that appears by itself on one side of the equals sign and not at all on the other side.) The first subsection provides some brief revision of graphs and coordinates, and in the second subsection you will see an example of an equation plotted as a graph, and have the opportunity to plot some graphs yourself. In the third subsection you will see how to plot a *scatterplot* to illustrate paired data, and why this can be useful.

1.1 Graph axes and coordinates

The graph axes form an important part of every graph. In general discussions about graphs, it is standard to label the horizontal and vertical axes with the letters x and y, respectively, and the axes are then referred to as the x-axis and the y-axis. Each axis should have scale markings and arrows, as shown in Figure 1, and the distance between two consecutive integers on an axis is referred to as 1 unit. The graph axes are often extended to include negative numbers, as illustrated.

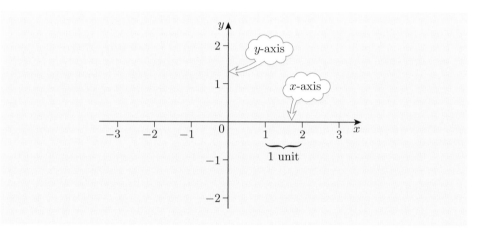

Figure 1   Standard graph axes

As you saw in Unit 2, each point that can be plotted on a graph is represented by a pair of numbers called the **coordinates** of the point. The first number specifies the position of the point along the x-axis from 0, and the second number specifies its position along the y-axis from 0. These two numbers are called the x- and y-coordinates of the point, respectively. Figure 2 shows the positions of some points, and their coordinates.

The French mathematician René Descartes (see page 37) developed this way of specifying the position of a point in 1637. It is known as the **Cartesian coordinate system**, after him.

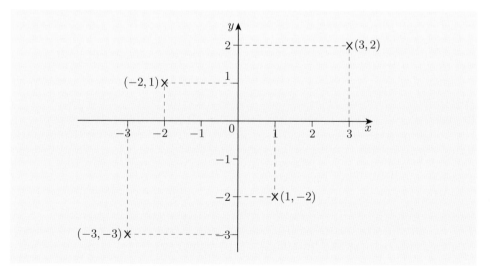

Figure 2   The coordinates of some points

Recall from Unit 2 that you can use either a small cross or a dot to mark a point on a graph.

Each point that is plotted on a graph can be labelled with its coordinates, as in Figure 2, or with a letter, or with both. For example, the point labelled $(3, 2)$ in Figure 2 could alternatively be labelled P or $P(3, 2)$.

If you are drawing a graph by hand, it can be useful to use graph paper so that you can plot points and read off their values accurately. However, for many purposes it is sufficient to use a blank sheet of paper, and measure the positions of the points using a ruler or set square with millimetre markings. You can also use square-ruled paper. There are examples of graphs with all three types of background throughout this unit.

You can print out graph paper and square-ruled paper from the module website.

Activity 1   *Writing down coordinates and plotting points*

For help with coordinates, see Maths Help Module 5, Section 3.

(a) Write down the coordinates of the points A, B, C and D shown below.

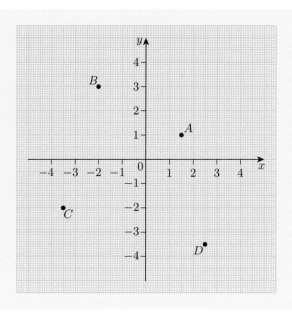

(b) Mark the following points on a graph. You can either mark them on the graph in part (a), or draw your own axes and mark the scales.

(i) $E(-1, -3)$ (ii) $F(0.5, 2.75)$

(iii) $G(-3.5, 3.5)$ (iv) $H(4, -1)$

Although x and y are the standard labels for graph axes, other labels can be used. For example, if you are drawing a graph to illustrate the relationship between the variables c and f, then you should use these letters to label the axes. Alternatively, you can use the names (and units, if appropriate) of the quantities that these variables represent.

The words used for a graph are adjusted according to the axis labels. If the axes are labelled c and f, then they are called the c-axis and the f-axis, and a point on the graph has a c-coordinate and an f-coordinate. You can also refer to the horizontal and vertical axes, and horizontal and vertical coordinates.

No matter how the axes are labelled, the first number in a pair of coordinates always gives the position along the *horizontal* axis, and the second number always gives the position along the *vertical* axis.

1.2   Graphs of equations

You can plot a graph to illustrate an equation that relates the variables x and y by first choosing some values of x and working out the corresponding values of y. This will give you the coordinates of some points to plot on the graph. It is convenient to record the values of x and y in a table of values, as illustrated in the example below.

Example 1   *Plotting a graph to illustrate an equation*

Plot a graph to illustrate the equation

$$y = \tfrac{1}{2}x + 3.$$

Solution

Construct a table of values. Choose some equally-spaced numbers for x, and work out the corresponding values of y by substituting into the equation. For example, substituting $x = -2$ into the equation gives $y = \tfrac{1}{2} \times (-2) + 3 = -1 + 3 = 2.$

A table of values for the equation $y = \tfrac{1}{2}x + 3$ is as follows.

x	-2	-1	0	1	2
y	2	2.5	3	3.5	4

Draw the axes and plot the points. They seem to lie in a straight line, so draw the straight line through them.

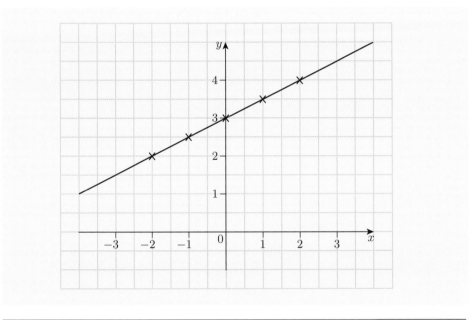

In Example 1 a straight line was drawn through the five points plotted. This is because if you were to choose some more values of x, find the corresponding values of y and plot these new points on the graph, then you would find that they all lie on the same straight line. Although this has not been checked for the example above, later in the unit you will see how you can be sure of this just by looking at the form of the equation relating x and y.

So the points that lie on the line in Example 1 are the points that have coordinates (x, y) such that

$$y = \tfrac{1}{2}x + 3.$$

Because of this, we say that $y = \tfrac{1}{2}x + 3$ is the **equation** of the line, and we often refer to the line as 'the line $y = \tfrac{1}{2}x + 3$'. Only part of the line is shown on the graph – it actually extends infinitely far in each direction.

You can check whether any particular point lies on the line $y = \frac{1}{2}x + 3$ by checking whether the coordinates of the point **satisfy** the equation of the line. In other words, you have to check whether the equation is correct when the coordinates are substituted in. A convenient method of doing this for an equation like $y = \frac{1}{2}x + 3$ is illustrated in the next example.

Example 2   *Checking whether coordinates satisfy an equation*

Determine whether each of the following points lies on the line $y = \frac{1}{2}x + 3$.

(a) $(8, 7)$ (b) $(-8, -3)$

Solution

For each pair of coordinates, substitute the x-coordinate into the equation and check whether you obtain the y-coordinate.

(a) Substituting $x = 8$ into the equation gives

$$y = \frac{1}{2} \times 8 + 3 = 4 + 3 = 7.$$

So the point $(8, 7)$ lies on the line.

(b) Substituting $x = -8$ into the equation gives

$$y = \frac{1}{2} \times (-8) + 3 = -4 + 3 = -1.$$

So the point $(-8, -3)$ does not lie on the line.

Activity 2   *Checking whether coordinates satisfy an equation*

Determine whether each of the following points lies on the line $y = \frac{1}{2}x + 3$.

(a) $(6, 5)$ (b) $(-5, 0.5)$

When you plot a graph to illustrate an equation, the word 'graph' can be used to refer either to the whole picture, including the axes and all the other elements, or just to the line or curve on the picture that illustrates the equation. So the line plotted in Example 1 is the **graph** of the equation $y = \frac{1}{2}x + 3$.

In the next activity you are asked to plot the graph of another equation.

Activity 3   *Plotting a graph to illustrate an equation*

Complete the table of values below for the equation

$$y = -3x - 1,$$

and hence plot a graph to illustrate the equation.

x	-2	-1	0	1	2
y					

In the next activity, you are asked to plot a graph to illustrate a practical formula in which the variables are letters other than x and y. In a formula like this, the subject is known as the **dependent variable**, since its value depends on the value of the other variable, and the other variable is known as the **independent variable**.

When you plot a graph of a formula like this, you should put the independent variable on the horizontal axis, and the dependent variable on the vertical axis. In other words, you should plot the dependent variable **against** the independent variable.

In the table of values, the independent and dependent variables should be in the first and second lines, respectively, so that the coordinates will be in the correct order when you read down the columns.

Activity 4 *Plotting the graph of a practical formula*

You saw in Unit 2 that the formula for converting a temperature from Celsius to Fahrenheit is

$$f = 1.8c + 32,$$

where f is the temperature in degrees Fahrenheit and c is the temperature in degrees Celsius.

(a) Which variable is the independent variable?

(b) Construct a table of values for the formula, using the values -20, 0, 20 and 40 for the independent variable.

(c) Plot a graph to illustrate the formula, drawing a straight line through the points plotted. (Use graph paper if you have some available.)

(d) Use your graph to make the following conversions.

    (i) Convert $10°C$ to $°F$.   (ii) Convert $-10°C$ to $°F$.

    (iii) Convert $-10°F$ to $°C$.   (iv) Convert $0°F$ to $°C$.

All the relationships that you have seen in this subsection have graphs that are straight lines. Relationships of this type are called **linear relationships**. You will meet other types of relationship later in the module.

The method that you have seen for plotting the graph of a relationship – constructing a table of values and plotting points – can be used to plot many types of relationship.

1.3 Scatterplots

In the previous subsection you saw how to plot the graph of an equation that expresses the relationship between two quantities. Sometimes when you are dealing with two quantities, you don't know an equation relating them – you just have some paired data that give you information about how the quantities are related. As you saw in Unit 2, in this situation you can plot the paired data on a graph to give you a visual idea of the relationship between the quantities. When you do this you might find that the points plotted lie at least approximately in a straight line.

For example, Table 1 presents some data collected by a greengrocer. She recorded the price that she charged for tomatoes, and the quantity of tomatoes that she sold, for a number of weeks. The greengrocer was

interested in the relationship between these two quantities because every week she decides what price she will charge for tomatoes (this depends on the price that she has to pay for them at the market) and then she needs to obtain the quantity of tomatoes that she is likely to sell at that price.

In the table the price in £ is denoted by P and the quantity sold in kg is denoted by Q.

Table 1 P, price in £ charged for tomatoes, and Q, quantity in kg sold

P	3.00	3.25	3.25	3.75	3.75	4.25	4.50	5.00	5.20	5.75
Q	841	787	852	728	769	618	568	587	574	479

To produce a graph of the data pairs in Table 1, you can put price on the horizontal axis and quantity sold on the vertical axis, and plot the points $(3, 841)$, $(3.25, 787)$, $(3.25, 852)$, and so on. The graph is shown in Figure 3(a).

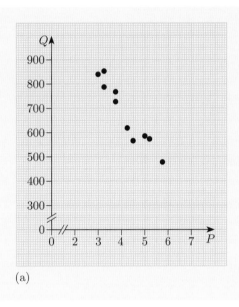

(a)

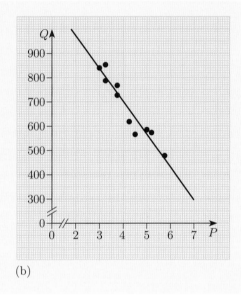

(b)

Figure 3   (a) Q, quantity in kg of tomatoes sold, plotted against P, price in £. (b) The same graph with a straight line superimposed.

Remember that the pairs of angled parallel lines in the axes in Figure 3 indicate breaks in the scales.

A graph on which data pairs are plotted is called a **scatterplot**, and the points plotted are referred to as **data points**. The data points on the scatterplot in Figure 3(a) do not lie exactly in a straight line, so the relationship between the selling price of the tomatoes and the quantity sold does not correspond exactly to a straight line. However, the data points lie approximately in a straight line, so the relationship can be *modelled* by a straight line. A suitable line has been added to the scatterplot in Figure 3(b). Lines like this can used to obtain useful approximate answers.

Activity 5   *Using the greengrocer's graph to make predictions*

For each of the following selling prices, use the graph in Figure 3(b) to predict the approximate quantity of tomatoes that the greengrocer will sell at that price.

(a) £3.50 per kg   (b) £4.75 per kg

From your work in the previous subsection, you might expect that there is an equation in the variables P and Q whose graph is the line in

Figure 3(b). There is indeed such an equation, and it would be helpful for the greengrocer to know what it is, because then she could use it to work out the quantity of tomatoes that she is likely to sell, rather than having to read it off the graph. In Section 2 of this unit you will learn about some characteristics of straight lines on graphs, and in Section 3 you will see how to use these characteristics to find the equation corresponding to any straight line on a graph.

The straight line in Figure 3(b) seems to model the data points reasonably well, but it is not clear whether it is the *best* straight line to model them. In the final section of the unit, you will see a method for finding the best straight line in this sort of situation, and a measure of how well such a line fits the data points.

2 Characteristics of straight-line graphs

In Section 1, and also in Unit 2, you have seen that a graph that illustrates the relationship between two quantities can be a straight line. This section is about the main features of graphs of this type.

2.1 Gradient

One of the main characteristics of a straight line is how steep it is. The steepness of a line is measured by its *gradient*. This subsection explains how to calculate the gradient of a line, and later in the section you will see how gradients are interpreted in practical situations.

To understand what is meant by the gradient of a line, imagine tracing the tip of your pencil along the line. The **gradient** (or *slope*) of the line is the number of units that your pencil tip moves up as it moves 1 unit horizontally to the right. For example, Figure 4 shows the line that passes through the points $(1, 2)$ and $(3, 8)$. You can see from the grid on the graph that for each 1 unit your pencil tip moves to the right, it moves up by 3 units. So the gradient of this line is 3.

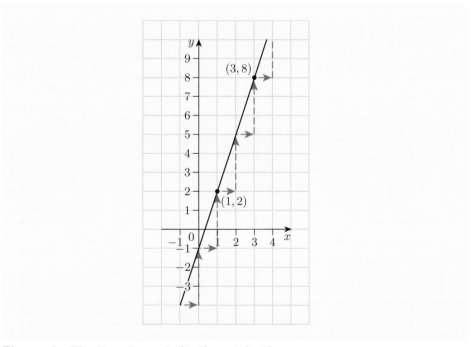

Figure 4   The line through $(1, 2)$ and $(3, 8)$

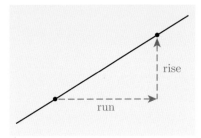

Figure 5   The run and rise

Often the gradient of a line is not as obvious as in Figure 4, and it may not be a whole number: for example, your pencil tip might move up 2.37 units as it moves one unit to the right. One way to work out the gradient of a line is to choose any two points on the line and consider what happens as your pencil tip moves from the left-hand point to the right-hand point. The increase in the x-coordinate is known as the **run**, and the increase in the y-coordinate is known as the **rise**, as illustrated in Figure 5. The gradient of the line can be calculated by dividing the rise by the run.

To illustrate this method, consider again the line in Figure 4, which passes through the points $(1, 2)$ and $(3, 8)$. As your pencil tip moves from the left-hand point $(1, 2)$ to the right-hand point $(3, 8)$, the x-coordinate increases from 1 to 3, which is an increase of 2, and the y-coordinate increases from 2 to 8, which is an increase of 6. So the run is 2 and the rise is 6, as shown in Figure 6. Therefore the gradient is $6/2 = 3$, as expected.

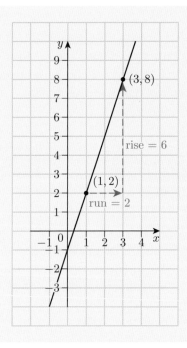

Figure 6   The run and rise between the points $(1, 2)$ and $(3, 8)$

To see why this method works, notice that saying that your pencil tip moves six units up for every two units right is the same as saying that it moves three units up for every one unit right.

The method is summarised below.

Try to remember that the gradient is the increase in the y-coordinate divided by the increase in the x-coordinate, not the other way round. You might like to remember this by the fact that you can pronounce yox (y over x) but not xoy (x over y)!

Strategy   *To calculate the gradient (slope) of a straight line*

Choose two points on the line. Then

$$\text{gradient} = \frac{\text{increase in } y\text{-coordinate}}{\text{increase in } x\text{-coordinate}} = \frac{\text{rise}}{\text{run}}.$$

(The run and rise are calculated from the *scales on the axes*, not from the physical distances on the paper or screen.)

Some lines, like the one in Figure 7, slope down rather than up from left to right. As you move your pencil tip from a left-hand point to a right-hand point along a line like this, the y-coordinate decreases rather than increases. A decrease can be thought of as a 'negative increase', so this means that the rise is negative.

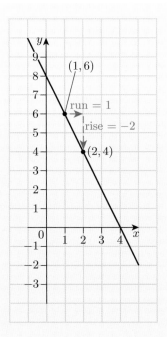

Figure 7   A negative rise

For example, consider the two points plotted in Figure 7. As your pencil tip moves from the left-hand point $(1,6)$ to the right-hand point $(2,4)$, the x-coordinate increases from 1 to 2, which is an increase of 1, and the y-coordinate decreases from 6 to 4, which is a decrease of 2, or an increase of -2. So the run is 1 and the rise is -2. The gradient is therefore

$$\frac{\text{rise}}{\text{run}} = \frac{-2}{1} = -2.$$

Any line that slopes down from left to right has a negative gradient, since the y-coordinate decreases as the x-coordinate increases.

> ### The sign of the gradient
>
> Lines that slope up from left to right have a *positive* gradient.
>
> Lines that slope down from left to right have a *negative* gradient.

When you calculate the gradient of a line, you should always check that the sign of the gradient agrees with the direction in which the line slopes.

There is a systematic way to work out the run and rise between two points on a line. Since the run is the increase in the x-coordinate, you can calculate it by subtracting the x-coordinate of the left-hand point from the x-coordinate of the right-hand point. Similarly, since the rise is the increase in the y-coordinate, you can calculate it by subtracting the y-coordinate of the left-hand point from the y-coordinate of the right-hand point, and this works even if the rise is negative. For example, for the points $(1,6)$ and $(2,4)$ in Figure 7, the run is

$$2 - 1 = 1$$

and the rise is

$$4 - 6 = -2,$$

as found above. This way of working out the run and rise is used in the next example.

Tutorial clip

Example 3   *Calculating gradients of lines*

Calculate the gradients of the lines shown below.

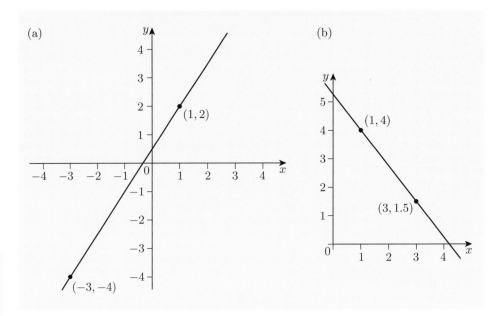

(a)

(b)

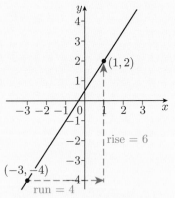

Solution

(a)   The run is the increase in the x-coordinate, which is $1 - (-3) = 4$.

The rise is the increase in the y-coordinate, which is $2 - (-4) = 6$.

So the gradient is $\dfrac{\text{rise}}{\text{run}} = \dfrac{6}{4} = 1.5$.

(Check: The line slopes up, so the gradient should be positive, which it is.)

(b)   The run is the increase in the x-coordinate, which is $3 - 1 = 2$.

The rise is the increase in the y-coordinate, which is $1.5 - 4 = -2.5$.

So the gradient is $\dfrac{\text{rise}}{\text{run}} = \dfrac{-2.5}{2} = -1.25$.

(Check: The line slopes down, so the gradient should be negative, which it is.)

The gradients calculated in Example 3 are expressed as decimals, but you can also express gradients as fractions. If the decimal form of a gradient does not terminate, then it is usually best to express it as a fraction, if possible, so that it is an exact value. For example, if the rise is 2 and the run is 3, then the gradient should be written as $\frac{2}{3}$, rather than a rounded decimal such as 0.67.

Recall that a *terminating* decimal is one that has a finite number of digits after the decimal point.

The next activity asks you to calculate the gradients of some lines. Although you can use any two points on a line to find the gradient, if a question gives you the coordinates of two points on a line, then you should use these points rather than reading off new coordinates from a graph, as your readings may not be accurate.

Activity 6 *Calculating gradients of lines*

(a) Calculate the gradients of the lines shown below.

(i)

(ii)

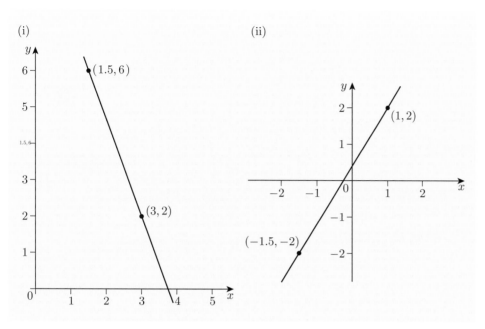

(b) For each of the following pairs of points, calculate the gradient of the line that passes through them.

(i) $A(2, 2)$ and $B(-2, 2)$

(ii) $A(2, 2)$ and $C(-1.5, -2.5)$

(iii) $A(2, 2)$ and $D(3, -1)$

(You might find it helpful to first sketch these points on a graph.)

(c) What is the rise between any two points on a *horizontal* line? What is the gradient of a horizontal line?

When a line is drawn on a graph, how steep it looks on the page or screen depends not only on its gradient but also on the scales used on the axes. For example, the three graphs in Figure 8 all show the line passing through the points $(1, 2)$ and $(5, 7)$, so the gradient is the same in all three cases (namely $\frac{5}{4}$), but the steepnesses of the lines look different.

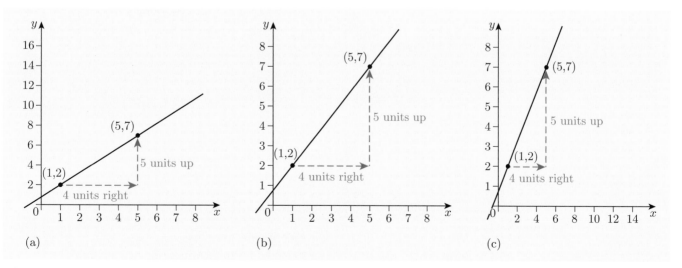

Figure 8 The effect of changing the axis scales

Because of this, when you draw a graph using the standard x- and y-axes, it is usually a good idea to use the same scale on each axis. Figure 9 shows lines with gradients 1 and -1 drawn on graphs with the same scale on each axis. As you can see, these lines make angles of 45° with the x-axis.

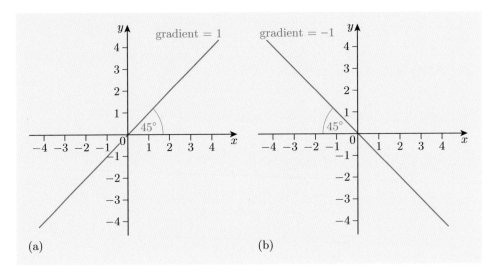

(a)   (b)

Figure 9   Lines with gradients 1 and -1 drawn on axes with equal scales

The gradients of other lines drawn on graphs with the same scale on each axis can be compared to these gradients, as follows.

By the **size** of a number we mean its value without its negative sign, if it has one. For example, the size of 3 is 3 and the size of -3 is also 3. The size of a number is often referred to as its *modulus*, *magnitude* or *absolute value*.

- A line whose gradient is greater than 1 makes an angle greater than 45° with the x-axis. So does a line whose gradient is greater than 1 in size, but negative. For example, the blue lines in Figure 10 have gradients 3 and -3 and make angles greater than 45° with the x-axis.

- A line whose gradient is smaller than 1, but positive, makes an angle less than 45° with the x-axis. So does a line whose gradient is smaller than 1 in size, but negative. For example, the green lines in Figure 10 have gradients $\frac{1}{3}$ and $-\frac{1}{3}$ and make angles less than 45° with the x-axis.

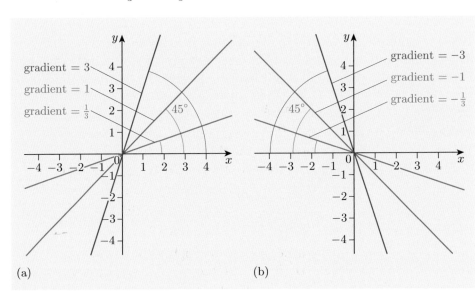

(a)   (b)

Figure 10   (a) Positive gradients of lines and angles made with the x-axis. (b) Negative gradients of lines and angles made with the x-axis.

When you calculate the gradient of a line that has been drawn using axes with equal scales, it is a good idea to make sure that the size of the gradient seems to agree with the angle that the line makes with the x-axis.

Activity 7 *Estimating the gradients of graphs*

For each of the graphs below, decide how the angle that the line makes with the x-axis compares with 45°, and hence state which of the following apply to the gradient of the line:

> about 1,   about −1,   greater than 1,   less than −1,
> between 0 and 1,   between −1 and 0.

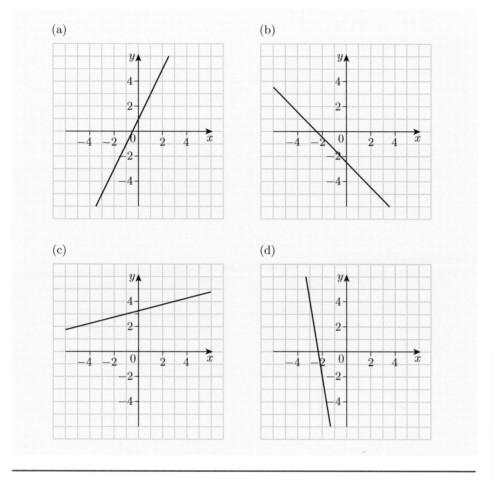

Horizontal and vertical lines

You saw in Activity 6(e) that the gradient of every horizontal line is zero. This is because the gradient of a line is the rise divided by the run, and the rise between any two points on a horizontal line is zero, as shown in Figure 11.

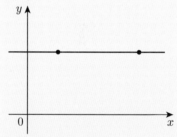

Figure 11 The rise between two points on a horizontal line is zero

What about vertical lines? For example, consider the line passing through the points $(1, 1)$ and $(1, 4)$, which is shown in Figure 12.

Here we do not have a left-hand point and a right-hand point, and whichever way round we take the points, the run is zero. Since the gradient of a line is the rise divided by the run, and it is not possible to divide a number by zero, it is not possible to calculate the gradient of this line. The same is true for every vertical line. So the gradient of a vertical line is undefined.

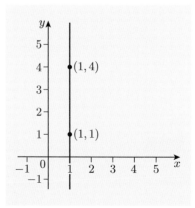

Figure 12 A vertical line

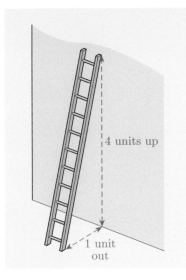

There are many situations where it is important to know how steep something is. For example, you may need to decide whether a ladder has been put up safely (Figure 13), determine how steep a hill is on a proposed walk, or even decide whether an avalanche is likely given the slope of a snowfield.

Figure 13   The recommended slope for a ladder is 1 unit out and 4 units up, which is a gradient of $\frac{4}{1} = 4$

2.2   A formula for gradient

In the previous subsection you saw a method for calculating the gradient of a line, using the coordinates of two points on the line. If letters are used to represent the coordinates of the points, then this method can be summarised as a formula.

Since coordinates are written in the form (x, y), and there are two points, it is convenient to represent the coordinates of the left-hand point by (x_1, y_1) and those of the right-hand point by (x_2, y_2), as shown in Figure 14. The small numbers after the x and y are known as **subscripts**. They are labels that distinguish one point from another.

x_1 is read as 'x-one'.

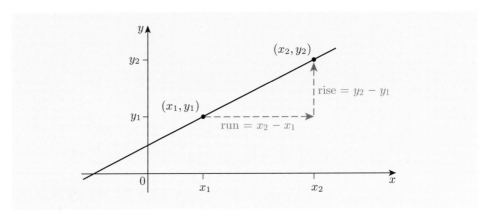

Figure 14   The run and rise between the points (x_1, y_1) and (x_2, y_2)

The run is calculated by subtracting the x-coordinate of the left-hand point from the x-coordinate of the right-hand point, so

$$\text{run} = x_2 - x_1.$$

Similarly, the rise is calculated by subtracting the y-coordinate of the left-hand point from the y-coordinate of the right-hand point, so

$$\text{rise} = y_2 - y_1.$$

Hence

$$\text{gradient} = \frac{\text{rise}}{\text{run}} = \frac{y_2 - y_1}{x_2 - x_1}.$$

This formula is used to calculate the gradient of a line in the next example.

Tutorial clip

Example 4   *Using the formula for gradient*

Use the formula

$$\text{gradient} = \frac{y_2 - y_1}{x_2 - x_1},$$

to find the gradient of the line through the points $(1, 1)$ and $(3, -1)$.

Solution

A sketch of the line is shown in the margin.

The left-hand point is $(1,1)$, so $x_1 = 1$ and $y_1 = 1$.

The right-hand point is $(3,-1)$, so $x_2 = 3$ and $y_2 = -1$.

The formula gives

$$\text{gradient} = \frac{y_2 - y_1}{x_2 - x_1} = \frac{-1-1}{3-1} = \frac{-2}{2} = -1.$$

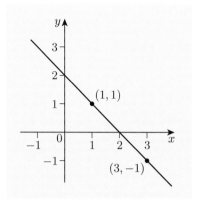

(Check: The line slopes down, so the gradient should be negative, which it is. Also, the same scale has been used on each axis in the diagram, and the line seems to make an angle of about $45°$ with the x-axis, so the size of the gradient should be about 1, which it is.)

In Example 4, the formula

$$\text{gradient} = \frac{y_2 - y_1}{x_2 - x_1} \tag{1}$$

was used to work out the gradient of a line, with $(x_1, y_1) = (1,1)$ and $(x_2, y_2) = (3,-1)$. What happens if you take the points the other way round? With $(x_1, y_1) = (3,-1)$ and $(x_2, y_2) = (1,1)$, the formula gives

$$\text{gradient} = \frac{y_2 - y_1}{x_2 - x_1} = \frac{1-(-1)}{1-3} = \frac{2}{-2} = -1.$$

This is the same value as found in Example 4, so here it does not matter whether (x_1, y_1) is taken to be the left-hand point and (x_2, y_2) the right-hand point, or the other way round. But is this true in general?

You know that formula (1) holds if (x_1, y_1) is the left-hand point and (x_2, y_2) the right-hand point, because that was worked out at the beginning of this subsection. To check whether it holds if (x_1, y_1) is the right-hand point and (x_2, y_2) the left-hand point, let's use the usual method to work out the gradient in this case. The run is calculated by subtracting the x-coordinate of the left-hand point from the x-coordinate of the right-hand point, so

$$\text{run} = x_1 - x_2.$$

Similarly, the rise is calculated by subtracting the y-coordinate of the left-hand point from the y-coordinate of the right-hand point, so

$$\text{rise} = y_1 - y_2.$$

Hence

$$\text{gradient} = \frac{\text{rise}}{\text{run}} = \frac{y_1 - y_2}{x_1 - x_2}. \tag{2}$$

This formula looks different from formula (1), but it is just the same formula in disguise. If you multiply top and bottom of the fraction in formula (2) by -1, then you obtain

$$\begin{aligned}
\text{gradient} &= \frac{(-1) \times (y_1 - y_2)}{(-1) \times (x_1 - x_2)} \\
&= \frac{-y_1 + y_2}{-x_1 + x_2} \\
&= \frac{y_2 - y_1}{x_2 - x_1},
\end{aligned}$$

Remember that multiplying both top and bottom of a fraction by a non-zero number does not change the value of the fraction.

which is the same as formula (1).

So the result that you have seen in this subsection can be summarised as follows.

> **A formula for gradient**
>
> The gradient of the line through the points (x_1, y_1) and (x_2, y_2) is given by
>
> $$\text{gradient} = \frac{y_2 - y_1}{x_2 - x_1}.$$
>
> (It does not matter which point you take to be (x_1, y_1) and which you take to be (x_2, y_2).)

In the next activity you are asked to use this formula to calculate some gradients. Notice that the graph in this activity has been drawn with different scales on the x- and y-axes. This is because it would be difficult to read off the coordinates of the points if the graph were drawn with equal scales.

Activity 8   Using the formula for gradient

Consider the following graph.

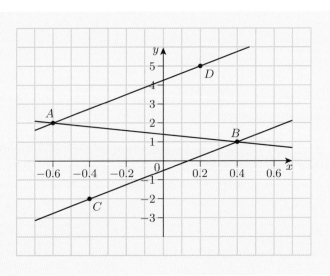

(a) Write down the coordinates of the points A, B, C and D.

(b) Use the formula for gradient to calculate the gradients of the lines that pass through the following pairs of points.

   (i) A and B (ii) A and D (iii) B and C

(c) What do you notice about the gradients of the lines in parts (b)(ii) and (b)(iii)?

Two lines are said to be **parallel** if they never cross, even when extended infinitely far in each direction. For example, in the graph in Activity 8, the line though the points A and D is parallel to the line through the points B and C. You saw in the solution to part (c) of the activity that these two lines have the same gradient. In general, saying that two lines are parallel means the same as saying that they have the same gradient (except for vertical lines, which are parallel but whose gradient is undefined).

2.3 Interpreting gradient

In this subsection you will see some real-life examples of graphs and learn how gradients can be interpreted practically.

A straight-line graph that illustrates a relationship between real-life quantities usually has axis scales that represent particular units. So the gradient of the line also has units, which should be quoted when the gradient is stated. The units of the gradient are the units on the vertical axis divided by the units on the horizontal axis, since this corresponds to the formula for gradient.

If the units on the two axes are the same, *then when you divide one by the other they cancel out and so the gradient has no units.*

For example, the graph in Figure 15 illustrates the growth of a bamboo plant.

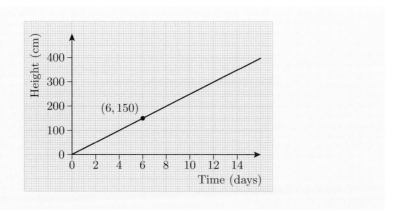

Figure 15 The growth of a bamboo plant

The vertical axis measures the height of the bamboo plant in centimetres, and the horizontal axis measures the time in days. So the units for the gradient are cm/day, or centimetres per day.

The line on the graph passes through the points $(0, 0)$ and $(6, 150)$, so the numerical value of the gradient is

$$\frac{150 - 0}{6 - 0} = \frac{150}{6} = 25,$$

and hence the gradient is 25 cm/day. This quantity measures the number of centimetres that the bamboo plant grows in 1 day.

In other words, the gradient gives the *rate* at which the bamboo grows. In general, the gradient of a graph tells you the amount that the variable on the vertical axis changes when the variable on the horizontal axis increases by one unit. So if the variables on the horizontal and vertical axes are x and y respectively then the gradient is the **rate of change** of y with respect to x.

To save time when doing calculations like the one above, you can do the calculation and quote the units at the same time, in the following way. The gradient is

$$\frac{150 - 0}{6 - 0} = \frac{150}{6} = 25 \, \text{cm/day}.$$

It is not strictly correct to write this, since whatever is on the left of an equals sign should be exactly equal to whatever is on the right – so if units are included on one side, then they should also be included on the other side. However, calculations can look unnecessarily complicated if units are included all the way through, so in practice it is sometimes convenient to omit them until the final answer is obtained.

Some types of bamboo grow at about a metre per day in favourable conditions.

Here are some more examples of interpreting gradients in practical situations.

Example 5   Interpreting gradients

Graph (a) below shows the wages earned by a factory worker for shifts of different lengths, and graph (b) shows the depth of a river over a 9-hour period after heavy rainfall. For each graph, find the gradient and explain what it measures.

(a)

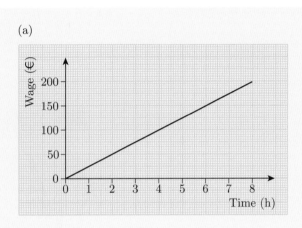

(b)

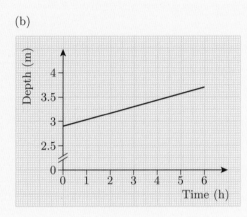

Figure 16 A gauge used to measure the depth of a river

Solution

(a) Choose two points on the line whose coordinates can be easily read off the graph.

The points $(0, 0)$ and $(4, 100)$ lie on the line, so its gradient is

$$\frac{100 - 0}{4 - 0} = \frac{100}{4} = 25 \text{ euro/hour}.$$

The gradient measures the number of € earned by the worker per hour.

(b) The points $(0, 2.9)$ and $(6, 3.7)$ lie on the line, so its gradient is

$$\frac{3.7 - 2.9}{6 - 0} = \frac{0.8}{6} = 0.13 \text{ m/h (to 2 d.p.)}.$$

The gradient measures the number of metres by which the river rises per hour.

Activity 9   Interpreting gradients

Graph (a) on the next page shows the distance travelled by a car plotted against the amount of fuel used, and graph (b) shows the distance travelled plotted against the time taken. For each graph, find the gradient and explain what it measures.

(a)

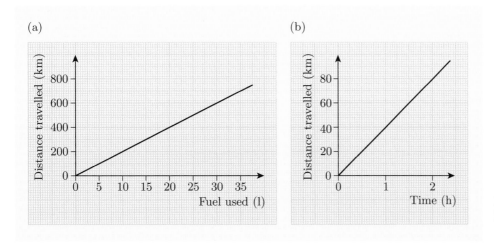

(b)

Remember that 'l' stands for litres.

Figure 17 is an example of a real-life graph with a negative gradient. It shows the depth of the river in Example 5(b) over an earlier 10-hour period.

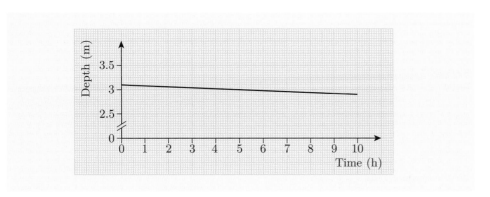

Figure 17   The depth of a river over a 10-hour period

The points $(0, 3.1)$ and $(10, 2.9)$ lie on the line, so its gradient is

$$\frac{2.9 - 3.1}{10 - 0} = \frac{-0.2}{10} = -0.02 \, \text{m/h}.$$

The fact that the gradient is negative tells you that the depth of the river *decreases* with time during this period. Its depth decreases by 0.02 metres per hour, or 2 centimetres per hour. The box below summarises what the sign of the gradient of a graph tells you.

Interpreting the sign of the gradient of a graph

- A *positive* gradient indicates that the quantity on the vertical axis *increases* as the quantity on the horizontal axis increases.

- A *negative* gradient indicates that the quantity on the vertical axis *decreases* as the quantity on the horizontal axis increases.

- A *zero* gradient indicates that the quantity on the vertical axis *remains constant* as the quantity on the horizontal axis increases.

So you can see from the gradient of the graph that our profits are looking healthy!

Sometimes when you want to model a situation, it is helpful to use a graph that consists of more than one straight line. For example, consider the graph in Figure 18. It shows the depth of the river in Example 5(b), over an extended period that includes the 6-hour period in the example, the 10-hour period in Figure 17, and another 4-hour period in between.

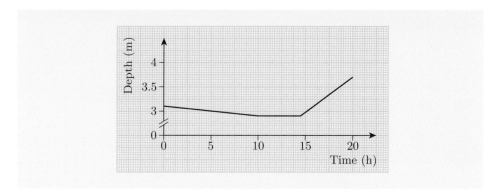

Figure 18   The depth of a river over a 20-hour period

The graph shows that in the first 10 hours the depth of the river fell from 3.1 m to 2.9 m, over the next four hours it remained constant at 2.9 m, and over the final six hours, after the heavy rain, its depth increased to 3.7 m. The gradients of the three line segments that make up the graph can be calculated in the usual way. Each of these gradients indicates the rate of change of the depth of the river with respect to time during one of the three time periods.

It is likely that the graph in Figure 18 is a simplified model, perhaps based on only four measurements, at 0 hours, 10 hours, 14 hours and 20 hours. If more measurements had been taken, then it might have been possible to use a curved graph to provide a more accurate model. However the graph in Figure 18 is sufficient for many purposes.

2.4   Intercepts

Note that the word 'intercept' is different from 'intersect'. Two lines *intersect* if they cross each other.

The value on the axis scale where a straight-line graph crosses one of the graph axes is another important characteristic of the graph, and is called an **intercept**. In particular, if the graph is drawn using the standard x- and y-axes, then the x-intercept is the value where the line crosses the x-axis, and the y-intercept is the value where the line crosses the y-axis. In other words, the x-intercept is the value of x when $y = 0$, and the y-intercept is the value of y when $x = 0$.

For example, the x- and y-intercepts of the line shown in Figure 19 are -3 and 2, respectively. Notice that an intercept is a value and not a point. The points corresponding to these intercepts are $(-3, 0)$ and $(0, 2)$.

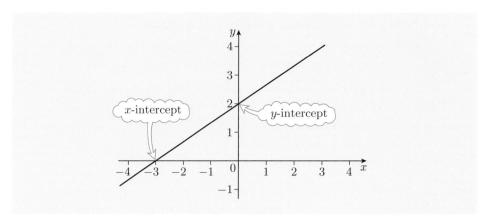

Figure 19   The x- and y-intercepts of a line

If the part of a line shown on a graph does not cross an axis, then it may be necessary to extend the line to find the intercept.

As with some other terms used for graphs, the terms used for intercepts are adjusted according to the axis labels. For example, if a graph has a c-axis and an f-axis, then it has a c-intercept and an f-intercept. You can also refer to horizontal and vertical intercepts.

If a line is drawn on a graph whose axis scales represent particular units, then the intercepts also have units, which should be quoted when the intercepts are stated.

The next example illustrates how some intercepts can be interpreted practically.

Example 6 *Interpreting vertical intercepts*

Graph (a) below is the Celsius–Fahrenheit conversion graph, and graph (b) shows the cost of printing pages on a home printer. For graph (a), write down the values of the intercepts, and state what they represent. Repeat this for graph (b), but only for the vertical intercept.

(a)

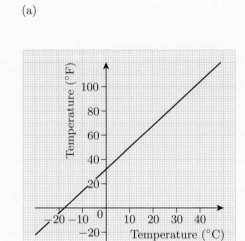

(b)

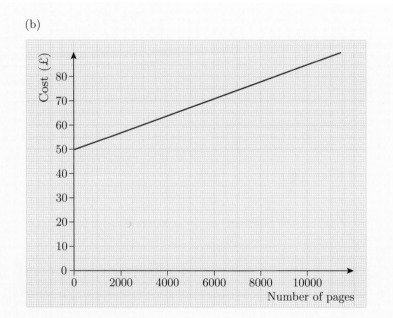

Solution

(a) The vertical intercept is 32°F. This is the temperature in °F when the temperature in °C is zero.

   The horizontal intercept is about −18°C. This is the temperature in °C when the temperature in °F is zero.

(b) The vertical intercept is £50. This is the cost when the number of pages printed is zero. That is, it is the initial cost of the printer.

You were asked to find this value earlier, in Activity 4(d)(iv).

The next activity asks you to find some intercepts.

Activity 10   *Interpreting intercepts*

Graph (a) below shows the distance of a participant in a sponsored walk from the finish line at different times after the start time, and graph (b) shows the cost of hiring a particular venue. For graph (a), write down the values of the intercepts, and state what they represent. Repeat this for graph (b), but only for the vertical intercept.

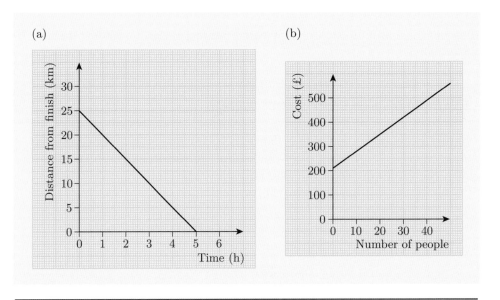

In this section, you have learned about the gradient and the intercepts of a straight line. The gradient measures the rate at which the vertical variable changes with respect to the horizontal variable, and you have learned how to calculate it from two points on the line. The intercepts are the scale values where the line crosses the axes. You have seen how to interpret both the gradient and the intercepts in practical situations.

3   Equations of straight lines

In Example 1 on page 65 you saw that the line shown in Figure 20 is described by the equation $y = \frac{1}{2}x + 3$. The points that lie on the line are the points whose coordinates (x, y) satisfy this equation.

In this section you will see that every straight line that can be drawn on a graph is described by an equation in a similar way. As usual, the ideas are explained using the standard variables x and y, but they apply to any pair of variables whose relationship is illustrated by a straight line on a graph.

The first subsection is about straight lines of a particular type – those that pass through the origin.

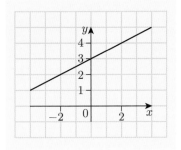

Figure 20   The line $y = \frac{1}{2}x + 3$

3.1   Lines that pass through the origin

Consider the line shown in Figure 21, which passes through the origin and has gradient 2.

Since the gradient is 2, if you position your pencil tip on the line and then move it a number of units right and twice that number of units up, then your pencil tip ends up at a point that is also on the line. So, since the origin is on the line, so are the points $(1, 2)$, $(3, 6)$ and $(4.5, 9)$, as shown in Figure 21, and so is any point with positive coordinates whose y-coordinate is twice its x-coordinate.

Similarly, if you position your pencil tip at a point on the line and move it a number of units to the left and twice that number of units down, then it ends up at another point on the line. So the points $(-1, -2)$ and $(-3, -6)$ also lie on the line, and so does any point with negative coordinates whose y-coordinate is twice its x-coordinate.

So every point whose y-coordinate is twice its x-coordinate lies on the line.

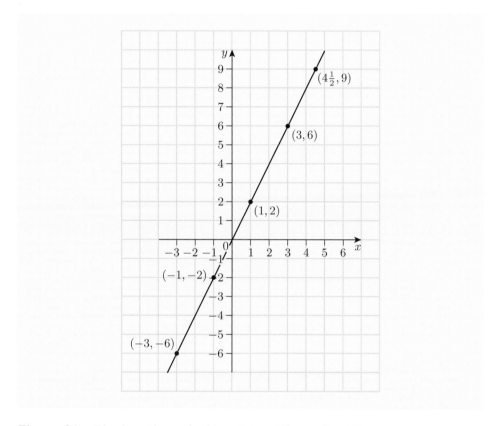

Figure 21   The line through the origin with gradient 2

You can also see that every point whose y-coordinate is *not* twice its x-coordinate does *not* lie on the line. For example, consider the point $(5, 3)$: the number 3 is not 2 times 5, and this point does not lie on the line.

Since the points that lie on the line are the points such that the y-coordinate is twice the x-coordinate, the equation of the line is $y = 2x$.

Other lines that pass through the origin have similar equations. For example, Figure 22(a) shows the line with gradient 3 that passes through the origin. The y-coordinate of every point on this line is three times its x-coordinate, so the equation of this line is $y = 3x$. Similarly, Figure 22(b) shows the line with gradient -1 that passes through the origin. The y-coordinate of every point on the line is -1 times its x-coordinate, so the equation of this line is $y = -1x$, or $y = -x$.

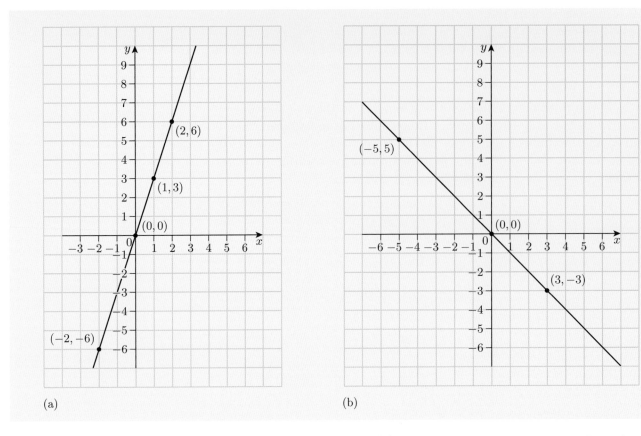

(a)   (b)

Figure 22   (a) The line through the origin with gradient 3. (b) The line through the origin with gradient -1.

In general, each line that passes through the origin has the equation

$$y = \text{gradient} \times x,$$

The equations of vertical lines are discussed later in the section.

with the exception of the vertical line through the origin (the y-axis) because it does not have a gradient. This fact can be stated as follows.

> **The equation of a line through the origin**
>
> It is traditional to use the letter m to represent gradient, though the reason is no longer known! The earliest known use of the letter m for gradient is by the Italian mathematician Vincenzo Riccati in 1757.
>
> The straight line that passes through the origin and has gradient m has equation $y = mx$.

It is traditional to use the letter m to represent gradient, though the reason is no longer known! The earliest known use of the letter m for gradient is by the Italian mathematician Vincenzo Riccati in 1757.

In the next activity you are asked to use Graphplotter, a computer tool that draws graphs, to view some more lines of the form $y = mx$, and to convince yourself that the gradient of each line is m, the coefficient of x. There are instructions for using Graphplotter in the MU123 Guide.

You will notice that Graphplotter uses the word 'function'. Whenever you have an equation that expresses one variable in terms of another variable, you can think of it as a rule that takes an input value and produces an output value. For example, if the equation is $y = 2x$, then inputting $x = 2$ gives the output $y = 4$, inputting $x = 3$ gives the output $y = 6$, and similarly for other values. A rule that takes input values and produces output values like this is often called a **function**.

So the graph of an equation of the form $y = mx$ is the graph of a function.

Graphplotter

Activity 11 *Investigating lines of the form $y = mx$*

(a) Open Graphplotter and choose the equation $y = mx + c$ from the drop-down list. Set $c = 0$, since this activity is about equations of the form $y = mx$.

(b) Use the slider to increase the value of m gradually up to 10, and then down again, to -10. Observe how the gradient of the line changes as you change the value of m.

(c) Use Graphplotter to plot the lines with equations $y = 3x$, $y = 0.5x$, $y = -2x$ and $y = -5x$, in turn, by typing the appropriate values of m into the box and pressing 'Enter'. (Do not change the axis scales – keep them the same for each graph.) Which of these lines makes the smallest angle with the x-axis?

Later in this section you will see how other types of lines – those that do not pass through the origin – are described by equations. First, however, in the next subsection you will learn about a commonly-occurring type of relationship between two quantities, and you will see that relationships of this type are illustrated by straight lines through the origin.

3.2 Direct proportion

Sometimes two quantities are related in such a way that if you multiply or divide one of the quantities by a number, then the other quantity is also multiplied or divided by the same number. For example, the relationship between distance in miles and the equivalent distance in kilometres is like this. If you double the number of miles, then the number of kilometres is also doubled. And if you halve the number of miles, then the number of kilometres is also halved, and so on.

If two quantities are related in this way, then they are said to be *directly proportional* to each other (or just proportional to each other, for short), and the relationship is known as **direct proportion**. So, for example, the number of miles is directly proportional to the equivalent number of kilometres.

Many everyday relationships between two quantities are direct proportion relationships. Here are two more examples.

- The number of people attending a concert is directly proportional to the money received from the ticket sales (if all the tickets have the same price).

- The volume of water that you need to boil to make tea is directly proportional to the number of cups of tea that you want to make (provided that each cup is to be filled with the same amount of tea).

On the other hand, there are many relationships between two quantities that are *not* direct proportion relationships. Here is an example.

- The speed at which you travel during a particular journey is *not* directly proportional to the time that the journey takes. For example, suppose that you have to make a 40-kilometre journey. If you travel at $40 \, \text{km/h}$, then the time taken is 1 hour; but if you travel at $80 \, \text{km/h}$, then the time taken is not 2 hours!

Sometimes a relationship that you might expect to be direct proportion is in fact not. For example, if you were buying some items, then you might expect to pay twice the price if you buy twice as many items. But in practice, twice the number of items may cost less than twice the price – there may be a discount, or a special offer such as 'buy one, get one free'.

Activity 12   *Identifying direct proportion relationships*

In each of parts (a) to (e), state whether the two quantities are directly proportional.

In each case, ask yourself: If I double the first quantity (or multiply or divide it by any number), is the second quantity also doubled (or multiplied or divided by the same number)?

(a) The time for which you travel and the distance that you travel, if you are travelling at a constant speed.

(b) The number of painters and the time it takes them to paint a bridge, if they all help and all work at the same rate.

(c) The number of pounds that you exchange for euros and the number of euros that you receive, if there is a transaction fee of €10.

(d) The number of songs that you download from a music website and the total cost, if each song costs the same amount.

Gross pay is pay before deductions such as taxes have been made.

(e) The number of hours that you work and the gross pay that you receive, if you are paid at a fixed hourly rate.

You saw earlier in this subsection that the relationship between distance in miles and the equivalent distance in kilometres is a direct proportion relationship. This relationship is described by the formula

$$K = 1.6M,$$

where K and M represent the number of kilometres and the number of miles, respectively. (This formula is only approximate.)

A more precise, but still not exact, formula is $K = 1.609M$.

Whenever two quantities are directly proportional, their relationship is described by a formula similar to this one.

Direct proportion relationships

If two quantities x and y are directly proportional to each other, then the relationship between them is described by an equation of the form

$$y = kx,$$

where k is a non-zero number, known as the **constant of proportionality**.

The statement 'y is directly proportional to x' is sometimes written as

$$y \propto x.$$

The symbol $\propto$ is read as 'is proportional to'.

A **constant** in an equation or expression is a quantity that does not change when the values of the variables change. Sometimes, as here, it is convenient to represent a constant by a letter.

If two variables are directly proportional and you know a value of one variable and the corresponding value of the other variable, then you can work out the constant of proportionality. The next example shows you how to do this.

Example 7   *Finding a constant of proportionality*

The two quantities x and y are directly proportional to each other, and $y = 24$ when $x = 16$.

(a) Find a formula for y in terms of x.

(b) Find the value of y when $x = 20$.

Solution

(a) Since x and y are directly proportional, their relationship is expressed by an equation of the form

$$y = kx,$$

where k is a constant.

💭 Use the given values of x and y to find the value of k. 💭

Also, $y = 24$ when $x = 16$. Substituting these values into the equation gives

$$24 = 16k.$$

We now solve this equation to find the value of k.

Divide by 16: $\qquad\qquad\qquad\qquad \frac{24}{16} = k$

Simplify the fraction and swap the sides: $\quad k = \frac{3}{2}$

Substituting $k = \frac{3}{2}$ into the equation $y = kx$ gives

$$y = \tfrac{3}{2}x.$$

This is the formula required.

(b) Substituting $x = 20$ into the formula found in part (a) gives

$$y = \tfrac{3}{2} \times 20 = 30.$$

Finding a constant of proportionality can be useful in many different practical situations – here is an example.

An art installation called 'Of all the people in all the world' has been exhibited at various venues throughout the world in recent years. It aims to help visitors to visualise the sizes of different groups of people by using one grain of rice per person. For example, one pile of rice might represent the number of millionaires in the world, while another might represent the number of refugees. The piles of rice representing different groups of people are juxtaposed in ways that are variously thought-provoking, shocking or amusing. Figure 23 overleaf shows part of one version of the installation.

All the rice used in each installation is later returned to be used for food.

For small groups of people, such as the number of people who have walked on the moon, the rice can be counted, but for large groups, such as the populations of countries, the rice has to be weighed. So the people setting out the piles of rice need a means of calculating the weight of rice required for a given number of people. One way to do this is to use a formula. Since the number of people represented and the weight of rice needed are directly proportional, the formula will be of the type that you have seen in this subsection. The next example shows how a suitable formula can be found.

Figure 23 Part of the art installation 'Of all the people in all the world' by the Birmingham-based theatre company *Stan's Cafe*

Example 8 *Finding a constant of proportionality for the rice*

The publicity information for 'Of all the people in all the world' states that 1 kg of rice is needed to represent 60 000 people.

(a) Find a formula for the weight of rice needed in terms of the number of people represented. Use the letters r and p to represent the weight of rice in kilograms and the number of thousands of people represented, respectively.

(b) Use the formula to find the weight of rice needed to represent the number of students of The Open University in 2006–07, which was about 224 000.

Solution

(a) Since r and p are directly proportional, the formula expressing their relationship is of the form

$$r = kp,$$

where k is a constant. Also, $r = 1$ when $p = 60$. Substituting these values into the formula gives

$$1 = k \times 60.$$

We now solve this equation to find the value of k.

Divide by 60: $\frac{1}{60} = k$

Substituting $k = \frac{1}{60}$ into the equation $r = kp$ gives

$$r = \frac{1}{60}p.$$

This is the required formula for r in terms of p.

(b) The number of OU students in 2006–07 was 224 000, which gives $p = 224$, since p is measured in thousands. Substituting this value of p into the formula above gives

$$r = \tfrac{1}{60} \times 224 = 3.73 \text{ (to 3 s.f.).}$$

So approximately 3.73 kg of rice is needed.

Here is a similar example for you to try.

Activity 13 *Finding a constant of proportionality*

Epilepsy in children is sometimes treated with anti-epileptic drugs. The amount of an anti-epileptic drug needed by a child each day is directly proportional to the child's weight. For a particular drug, the daily dose for a child of weight 20 kg is 400 mg.

(a) Find a formula for the amount of this drug needed each day, in terms of the weight of the child treated. Use d to represent the weight in milligrams of the drug needed each day, and c to represent the weight of the child in kilograms.

(b) How much of the drug is needed each day for a child of weight 35 kg?

You have seen that if two quantities x and y are directly proportional, then their relationship is expressed by an equation of the form $y = kx$, where k is a non-zero constant. So the graph illustrating the relationship is a straight line through the origin with gradient k.

This means that if you have a graph of the relationship between two quantities, then you can immediately recognise whether the quantities are directly proportional. If the graph is a straight line through the origin, then the quantities are directly proportional and the constant of proportionality is the gradient of the graph. If the graph has any other form, then the quantities are not directly proportional.

Activity 14 *Recognising graphs of direct proportion relationships*

(a) Which of the following graphs represent direct proportion relationships?

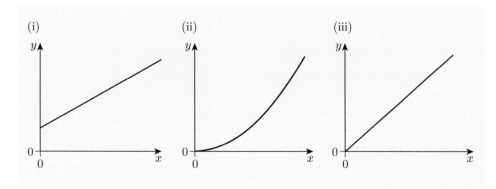

(b) Look back at graph (a) in Example 6 on page 83. Is temperature in degrees Fahrenheit directly proportional to temperature in degrees Celsius?

3.3   The general equation of a straight line

In this subsection you will see that nearly every straight line that you can draw on a graph is described by an equation of the form

$$y = mx + c,$$

where m and c are constants. (The only exceptions are vertical lines.) In the following activity you are asked to use Graphplotter to investigate the graphs of equations of this form.

 Graphplotter

Activity 15   *Investigating graphs of equations of the form $y = mx + c$*

Use Graphplotter, with the equation $y = mx + c$ selected.

(a) Click the 'Options' tab, then click 'y-intercept' to display the coordinates of the point where the graph crosses the y-axis. Click the 'Functions' tab to return to the main panel.

(b) Set $m = 2$ and $c = 0$, and check that you obtain the line through the origin with gradient 2, as expected. (To set m and c to these values, type them into the boxes and press 'Enter'.)

(c) Now set $c = 1$ and observe the effect on the graph. What is the y-intercept of the new graph?

(d) Choose some other values of c (both positive and negative) and repeat part (c) for each of these values.

(e) What is the same and what is different about all the graphs in parts (b), (c) and (d)?

(f) Use the sliders to experiment with changing the values of m and c, and observe the effect on the graph.

Here is an explanation of what you observed in Activity 15. Figure 24(a) shows the line that passes through the origin and has gradient 2. As you saw earlier in this section, the y-coordinate of every point on this line is twice the x-coordinate, so the line has equation $y = 2x$.

Now consider the equation

$$y = 2x + 1.$$

To obtain the graph of this equation, you could take every point on the graph of the equation $y = 2x$, and add 1 to the y-coordinate. This has the effect of moving the graph of $y = 2x$ up the y-axis by 1 unit. The result is the line shown in Figure 24(b). It has the same gradient as the line $y = 2x$, but it does not pass through the origin – instead, its y-intercept is 1.

A similar argument can be applied to any equation of the form $y = mx + c$. The graph of the equation $y = mx + c$ is obtained by moving the graph of the equation $y = mx$ along the y-axis by c units. You know that the graph of $y = mx$ is the straight line with gradient m through the origin, so the graph of $y = mx + c$ is the straight line with gradient m and y-intercept c. This applies whether c is positive or negative.

Figure 25 shows two more examples. Notice that the line $y = 3x - 2$ has gradient 3 and y-intercept -2, and the line $y = -x + 3$ has gradient -1 and y-intercept 3.

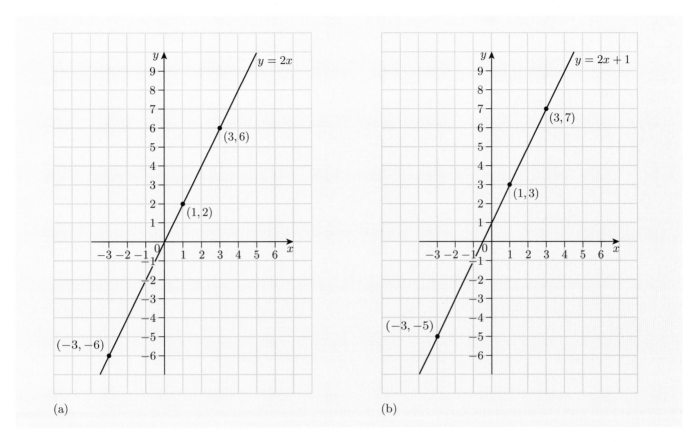

Figure 24 The lines (a) $y = 2x$ and (b) $y = 2x + 1$

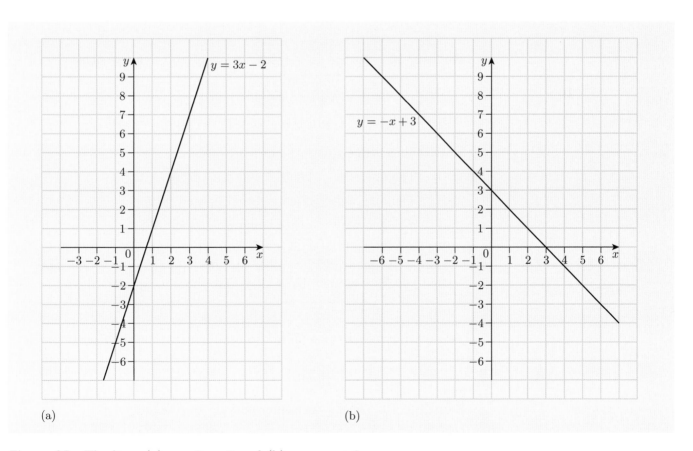

Figure 25 The lines (a) $y = 3x - 2$ and (b) $y = -x + 3$

The new fact that you have met is summarised below.

The general equation of a straight line

The line with gradient m and y-intercept c has equation

$$y = mx + c.$$

Example 9   *Writing down gradients, y-intercepts and equations of lines*

(a) Write down the gradient and y-intercept of the line $y = 4x - 3$.

(b) Write down the equation of the straight line with gradient -5 and y-intercept 2.

Solution

(a) Compare the equation with the equation $y = mx + c$ to identify the values of the gradient m and the y-intercept c. Remember that $4x - 3$ is the same as $4x + (-3)$.

The coefficient of x is 4, so the gradient is 4.

The constant term is -3, so the y-intercept is -3.

(b) The equation is $y = mx + c$, where m is the gradient and c is the y-intercept.

The equation is $y = -5x + 2$.

Activity 16   *Writing down gradients, y-intercepts and equations of lines*

(a) Write down the gradients and y-intercepts of the following lines.

   (i) $y = 2x - 1$ (ii) $y = -3x + 4$ (iii) $y = \dfrac{x}{5} - \dfrac{2}{5}$

(b) Write down the equations of the following lines.

   (i)   The line with gradient 4 and y-intercept -10

   (ii)   The line with gradient -1 and y-intercept 5

   (iii) The line with gradient 0 and y-intercept 3

(c) For each of the lines in part (b), write down the equation of the line that is parallel to the given line and has y-intercept 2. (Remember that two lines are parallel if they have the same gradient.)

The next example shows you how to use the equation of a line to find its x-intercept.

Example 10   *Finding an x-intercept from an equation*

Find the x-intercept of the line with equation $y = 4x - 3$.

Solution

💭 The x-intercept is the value of x when $y = 0$. 💭

Putting $y = 0$ gives

$$4x - 3 = 0.$$

We now solve this equation.

Add 3: $4x = 3$

Divide by 4: $x = \frac{3}{4}$

Hence the x-intercept is $\frac{3}{4}$.

> Remember that the *solution* of an equation is the value of the unknown for which the equation is true.

Activity 17 *Finding x-intercepts from equations*

Find the x-intercepts of the following lines.

(a) $y = 2x - 1$ (b) $y = -3x + 4$ (c) $y = \dfrac{x}{5} - \dfrac{2}{5}$

(These are the lines from Activity 16(a).)

The equation of a horizontal or vertical line

Figure 26(a) shows the line with gradient 0 and y-intercept 3. In Activity 16(b)(iii) you saw that the equation of this line is $y = 3$. This equation is found by substituting $m = 0$ and $c = 3$ into the general equation $y = mx + c$.

An alternative way to find the equation of this line is as follows. Every point on this line has y-coordinate 3, so the equation $y = 3$ describes each point on the line and is therefore the equation of the line.

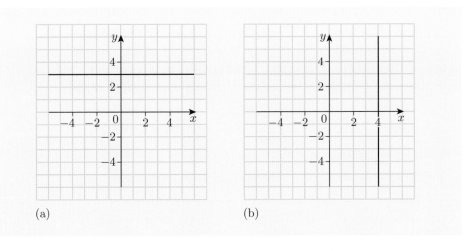

(a)   (b)

Figure 26 Graphs showing (a) a horizontal line and (b) a vertical line

What about vertical lines? You cannot use the fact that the line with gradient m and y-intercept c has equation $y = mx + c$ to find the equation of a vertical line, because the gradient of a vertical line is undefined. Vertical lines are the only lines that do not not have equations of the form $y = mx + c$.

However, you can find an equation for a vertical line by using an approach similar to the alternative approach suggested above for horizontal lines.

For example, consider the vertical line that has x-intercept 4, which is shown in Figure 26(b) on the previous page. Every point on this line has x-coordinate 4, so the equation $x = 4$ describes each point on the line and is therefore the equation of the line.

> **Equations of horizontal and vertical lines**
>
> The horizontal line with y-intercept a has equation $y = a$.
>
> The vertical line with x-intercept a has equation $x = a$.

Activity 18   *Writing down equations of horizontal and vertical lines*

(a) Write down the equations of the lines shown below.

(i)

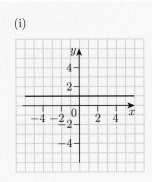

(ii)

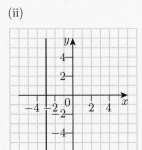

(iii)

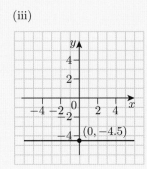

(iv)

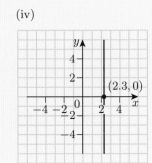

(b) Write down the equations of the x- and y-axes.

3.4 Drawing lines from their equations

When you are working on a question that involves the equation of a straight line, it often helps to draw the line on a graph. One way to do this is to use the following strategy. This strategy is particularly useful when you just want a quick sketch rather than a very accurate graph.

> **Strategy   *To draw the line $y = mx + c$ (gradient method)***
>
> Use the values of m and c.
>
> 1. Mark the point $(0, c)$ that corresponds to the y-intercept.
>
> 2. Count 1 unit right and m units up from this point, and mark the point that you reach. (If m is negative, then you count down rather than up.)
>
> 3. Draw the straight line through the two points.
>
> (If the value of m is small, then in step 2 it might be easier to count, say, 2 units right and $2m$ units up, or 3 units right and $3m$ units up, and so on – choose a convenient multiple.)

This strategy is demonstrated in the next example.

Example 11   *Drawing a line from its equation (gradient method)*

Tutorial clip

Draw the graph of the equation $y = 3x - 4$.

Solution

This equation is of the form $y = mx + c$, with $m = 3$ and $c = -4$. So the graph is a straight line with gradient 3 and y-intercept -4.

Draw the axes and mark the scales. The y-intercept is -4, so mark the point $(0, -4)$. The gradient of the line is 3, so count 1 unit right and 3 units up, and mark the point that you get to.

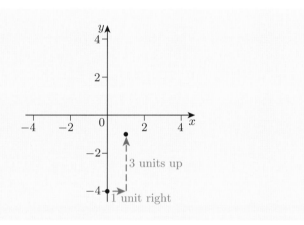

Draw the straight line through the two points and label it with the equation.

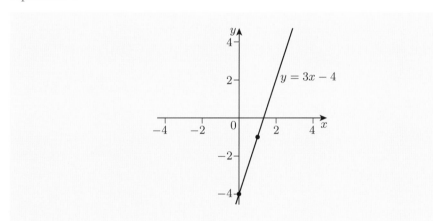

Once you have drawn a straight line from its equation, it is a good idea to check that it looks roughly as you would expect.

One check that you can do is to consider whether the slope looks reasonable. For example, you know from its equation that the line $y = 3x - 4$ has gradient 3. This is positive, so you would expect the line drawn in Example 11 to slope up, and it does. Also, this gradient is greater than 1 in size, so if the axis scales are equal then you would expect the line to make an angle of more than $45°$ with the x-axis – again, it does.

As a further check, you can work out a third point on the line. For example, substituting $x = 2$ into the equation gives

$$y = 3 \times 2 - 4 = 6 - 4 = 2.$$

So the point $(2, 2)$ should lie on the line, which it does.

Remember from Unit 2 that when you plot a graph to illustrate *data*, you should provide a title and the source of the data.

There is usually no need to provide a title for a graph that illustrates an equation. Instead, you should label the line (or curve) with the equation, as shown in Example 11.

Here is an alternative strategy for drawing a straight line from its equation. This strategy can take a little longer, but it is often preferable when accuracy is important.

> **Strategy** *To draw the line $y = mx + c$ from its equation (two-point method)*
>
> 1. Find the coordinates of two points on the line, by choosing two values of x and substituting them into the equation to find the corresponding values of y.
>
> 2. Plot the points on a graph, and draw the straight line through them.

When you use this strategy, you should also find and plot a third point on the line, as a check. The strategy is illustrated in the next example.

Tutorial clip

Example 12 Drawing a line from its equation (two-point method)

Draw the graph of the equation $y = -\frac{3}{4}x + 1$.

Solution

The equation is of the form $y = mx + c$, so the graph is a straight line.

Choose two values of x and calculate the corresponding values of y. Try to choose values of x that make the calculation simple.

An alternative way to find the point $(0, 1)$ is to observe from the equation that the y-intercept is 1.

When $x = 0$, $y = -\frac{3}{4} \times 0 + 1 = 1$.

So the point $(0, 1)$ lies on the line.

When $x = 4$, $y = -\frac{3}{4} \times 4 + 1 = -3 + 1 = -2$.

So the point $(4, -2)$ also lies on the line.

Plot the points and draw the straight line through them. Label the line with its equation.

$\cdots$n $x = -4$, $y = -\frac{3}{4} \times (-4) + 1 = 3 + 1 = 4$. So the point
$\cdots$lso lie on the line, which it does.)

The strategies above do not apply to vertical lines. However, you have seen that a vertical line has an equation of the form $x = a$, where a is the x-intercept, and a horizontal line has an equation of the form $y = a$, where a is the y-intercept. You should be able to recognise equations of these forms and hence draw their graphs.

Activity 19   *Drawing lines from their equations*

Draw the graphs of the following equations. You can use any method that you have seen in this subsection.

(a) $y = 2x + 3$ (b) $y = -2x + 4$ (c) $y = 3$

(d) $y = \frac{1}{2}x - 1$ (e) $x = \frac{5}{2}$

In this unit you have seen two different ways of producing a graph of an equation. If you are asked to *plot* a graph of an equation, then you should construct a table of values, plot the points and draw the line or curve through them in the way that you saw in Subsection 1.2. On the other hand, if you are asked to *draw* or *sketch* the graph of an equation, then you should do so using facts that you can deduce from the equation, such as the gradient and y-intercept of a straight line. You have seen how to do this for equations of the form $y = mx + c$ in this subsection, and you will find out how to draw graphs of other types of equation later in the module.

> If you are drawing a sketch of a graph for your own use, for example to help you to check an equation of a line, then you can include as much or as little detail as you like. However, if a question asks you for a sketch of a graph, then you must include all the relevant detail, such as the values of the intercepts, and the equation of the line or curve.

3.5   Finding the equations of lines

You have seen that if you know the gradient and y-intercept of a line, then you can immediately write down the equation of the line.

Sometimes you might have different information about a line, and want to determine its equation. For example, you might have a graph of the line, or you might know the coordinates of two points on the line.

In the next example, a graph of a line is used to find the gradient and the y-intercept, so that the equation can be written down. This involves using several of the skills that you developed earlier. In this example the variables on the axes are p and q instead of the usual x and y.

Example 13   *Finding the equation of a line from a graph*

Find the equation of the line shown below.

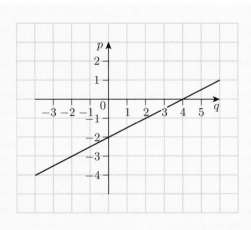

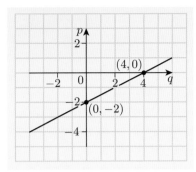

Solution

◌ Work out the gradient. To do this, choose two points on the line with coordinates that are easy to read. ◌

The points $(0, -2)$ and $(4, 0)$ lie on the line, as shown in the margin. So the gradient is

$$\frac{0 - (-2)}{4 - 0} = \frac{2}{4} = \frac{1}{2}.$$

◌ Read off the vertical intercept from the graph. ◌

The vertical intercept is -2.

◌ Substitute the gradient and vertical intercept into the general equation of a line. The variables here are not x and y, so in the general equation $y = mx + c$ replace x by the variable on the horizontal axis, q, and y by the variable on the vertical axis, p. ◌

The equation of the line is

$$p = \tfrac{1}{2}q - 2.$$

When you work out the equation of a line from its graph, remember that if the exact coordinates of points on the graph are given, then you should use these to work out the equation, rather than reading off further coordinates from the graph, as your readings may not be accurate.

Activity 20   Finding the equation of a line from a graph

Find the equations of the lines shown below.

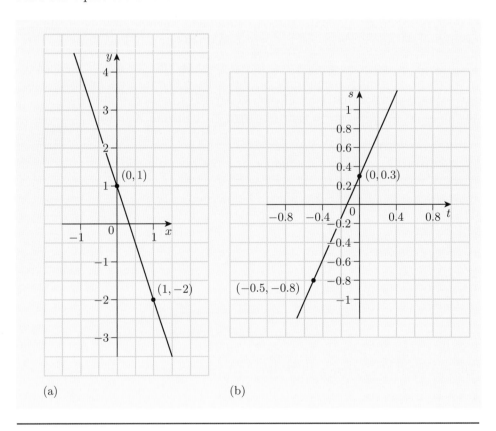

(a)   (b)

Sometimes the information that you have about a line does not include the vertical intercept. For example, you might have a graph showing a part of a line that is not near the y-axis, or you might know only the coordinates of two points on the line. In cases like these you can usually find the equation of the line by using the gradient and the coordinates of any point on the line. The method is illustrated in the next example.

When you are trying to find the equation of a line, and you do not have a graph already, it is a good idea to begin by sketching the line. Then you can use your sketch to check your answer.

Example 14 *Finding the equation of a line from the gradient and a point*

 Tutorial clip

Find the equation of the line that has gradient -2 and passes through the point $(1, 3)$.

Solution

Sketch the line – you can use the gradient method (but starting at the given point on the line rather than the y-intercept). As the sketch is just to help you to check your answer, you can save time by omitting some of the detail, such as the numbers on the axes.

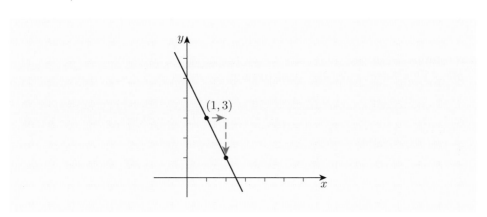

Substitute the gradient into the general equation of a line.

The equation of the line is $y = mx + c$, where m is the gradient and c is the y-intercept. The gradient is -2, so the equation is

$$y = -2x + c.$$

Substitute the coordinates of a point on the line into the equation and solve the resulting equation to find the value of the y-intercept c.

The point $(1, 3)$ lies on the line so its coordinates satisfy the equation. Substituting $x = 1$ and $y = 3$ into the equation gives

$$3 = -2 \times 1 + c; \quad \text{that is,} \quad 3 = -2 + c.$$

Adding 2 to both sides gives

$$5 = c.$$

Now the values of both m and c are known, so write down the equation of the line.

The equation of the line is

$$y = -2x + 5.$$

(Check: This is the equation of a line with y-intercept 5, and the y-intercept on the sketch does appear to be 5.)

Here is a summary of the strategy used in Example 14.

This strategy applies to *non-vertical* lines.

Strategy *To find the equation of a line when you do not know the vertical intercept*

1. Find the gradient m of the line and substitute it into the general equation $y = mx + c$.

2. Substitute the coordinates of a point on the line into the equation of the line from step 1, and solve the resulting equation to find the value of the y-intercept c.

3. Use the values of m and c to write down the equation of the line.

Here is a similar activity for you to try.

Activity 21   *Finding the equation of a line from the gradient and a point*

Find the equation of the line that has gradient 3 and passes through the point $(-2, -3)$.

You can use the strategy above to find the equation of a straight line if the only information that you have is the coordinates of two points on the line. This is illustrated in the next example.

Tutorial clip

Example 15   *Finding the equation of a line through two points*

Find the equation of the line that passes through the points $(1, 2)$ and $(3, 5)$.

Solution

A sketch of the line is shown in the margin.

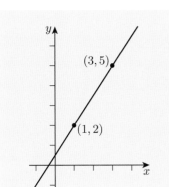

The gradient of the line is
$$\frac{5 - 2}{3 - 1} = \frac{3}{2}.$$

So the equation of the line is $y = \frac{3}{2}x + c$, where c is a constant.

Also, the line passes through the point $(1, 2)$. Substituting these coordinates into the equation gives
$$2 = \tfrac{3}{2} \times 1 + c; \quad \text{that is,} \quad 2 = \tfrac{3}{2} + c.$$

Subtracting $\frac{3}{2}$ from both sides gives
$$\tfrac{1}{2} = c.$$

So the equation of the line is
$$y = \tfrac{3}{2}x + \tfrac{1}{2}.$$

☞ Check that the coordinates of the other point satisfy the equation. ☜

(Check: Substituting $x = 3$ into the equation gives
$$y = \tfrac{3}{2} \times 3 + \tfrac{1}{2} = \tfrac{9}{2} + \tfrac{1}{2} = \tfrac{10}{2} = 5,$$
so the coordinates $(3, 5)$ satisfy the equation.)

Activity 22 *Finding the equation of a line through two points*

(a) Plot the points $(1, 4)$ and $(3, -2)$ on a graph, and draw the straight line through them.

(b) Find the equation of the line.

In the final example in this subsection, the equations of some horizontal and vertical lines are found from given information.

Example 16 *Finding the equations of horizontal and vertical lines*

Tutorial clip

Write down the equations of the following straight lines.

(a) The line that is parallel to the x-axis and passes through the point $(0, 2)$

(b) The line that is parallel to the y-axis and passes through the point $(-3, 1)$

Solution

Sketches of the lines are shown in the margin.

(a) ☁ A line parallel to the x-axis has an equation of the form $y = a$. 💭

The equation is $y = a$, where a is a constant. Since the point $(0, 2)$ satisfies the equation, the equation is $y = 2$.

(b) ☁ A line parallel to the y-axis has an equation of the form $x = a$. 💭

The equation is $x = a$, where a is a constant. Since the point $(-3, 1)$ satisfies the equation, the equation is $x = -3$.

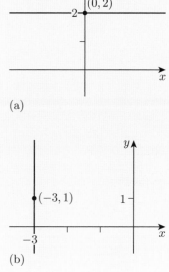

(a)

(b)

Activity 23 *Finding the equations of horizontal and vertical lines*

Write down the equations of the following straight lines.

(a) The line that is parallel to the y-axis and passes through the point $(1, 0)$

(b) The line that is parallel to the x-axis and passes through the point $(2, -4)$

In this section you have seen that an equation of the form $y = mx + c$, where m and c are constants, represents a straight line graph with gradient m and y-intercept c, and that every line (except vertical ones) can be represented by an equation of this form. This is an important result, as many situations can be modelled by using a straight line graph or a linear equation, and it can be helpful to work with both the graph and the equation. You will see some examples of this in the next section and in Unit 7.

The result stated in the paragraph above is the reason why an equation in x, each of whose terms is either a constant term or a number times x (after expanding any fractions or brackets in the equation), is called a *linear* equation. In other words, a **linear equation** in x is an equation of the form $mx + c = 0$, where m and c are constants with $m \neq 0$, or an equation that can be rearranged into this form. Similarly, any expression of the form $mx + c$ where m and c are constants with $m \neq 0$ is called a **linear expression** in x. A function with a rule of the form $y = mx + c$ where m and c are constants with $m \neq 0$ is called a **linear function**.

4 Linear models from data

In Subsection 1.3 you saw that it is sometimes possible to model a set of paired data using a straight line. In this section you will see how to find the equation of the best line to fit a set of data, and how to measure how good a fit the line is. You will see some real-life datasets modelled in this way.

4.1 Regression lines

At the time of writing, the tallest man to have had his height officially recorded was Robert Pershing Wadlow, who was born on 22 February 1918 in Alton, Illinois, USA. Mr Wadlow is pictured in Figure 27, and Table 2 gives his height in centimetres measured at various ages.

Table 2 The height of Robert Wadlow at various ages

Age (years)	5	8	9	10	12	14	16	18	20	21	22
Height (cm)	163	183	188	196	211	226	239	254	262	264	272

Source: www.altonweb.com

It is difficult to tell how quickly Mr Wadlow grew over the years from the table alone. A better impression can be obtained by plotting the data in the table on a scatterplot, as shown in Figure 28.

Figure 27 Robert Wadlow with his father, Harold Franklin Wadlow

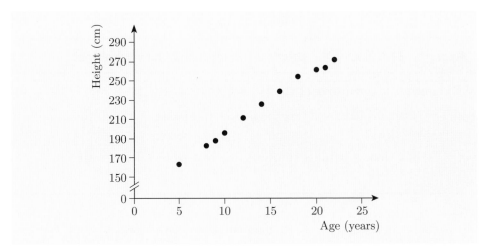

Figure 28 The height of Robert Wadlow plotted against his age

It looks as if the points in Figure 28 lie approximately in a straight line. However, it is not possible to draw a straight line that passes exactly through all the points. This may be because Mr Wadlow did not grow at a steady rate. Alternatively, it could be a consequence of how the data were collected – for example, Table 2 does not give information on the time of year when each measurement was taken. If this information were available, then a measurement taken in January, say, would be plotted at a slightly different position to a measurement taken in December, and the points might lie more closely in a straight line.

So the data on Mr Wadlow's height can be modelled approximately, but not exactly, by a straight-line graph. But what is the 'best' straight line for the data points plotted? For example, the line drawn in Figure 29(a) clearly fits the data better than the line drawn in Figure 29(b), but it may still not be the *best* line.

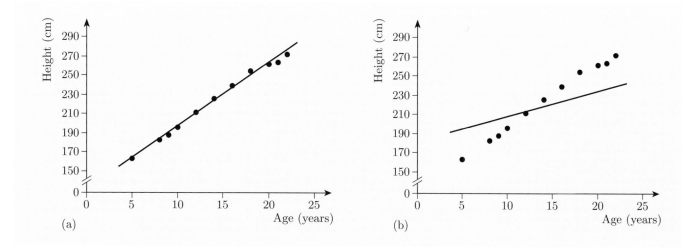

(a)

(b)

Figure 29   Straight lines drawn on the graph of Mr Wadlow's height

Roughly, a line is a good fit to data like these if the distances from the points to the line are small. Statisticians have found that the best way to measure how well a line fits the data is as follows. The vertical distances from the points to the line are measured, as illustrated in Figure 30, then each of these distances is squared, and finally the squared distances are all added up. The smaller the sum of the squared distances, the better the fit of the line. There is always just one line for which this sum is the smallest, and it is known by various names: the *regression line*, the *least squares fit line*, the *best fit line* or the *trend line*. In this module the first of these terms is used, the **regression line**.

You can learn why this is the best way to measure the fit of a line, and how this method can be turned into a formula for the equation of the best line, if you go on to study modules on statistics.

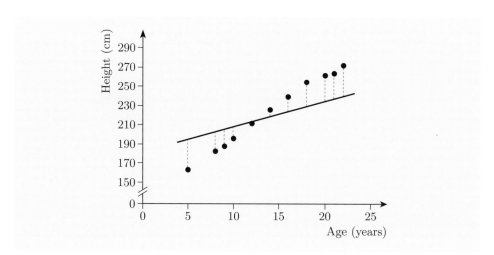

Figure 30   The distances of the points from a line

There is a formula for calculating the equation of the regression line from the data values, but it is usually easiest to use software to do the calculation. The Dataplotter software supplied with the module can calculate the equation of a regression line, as you will see in the next activity. There are instructions for using Dataplotter in the MU123 Guide.

Dataplotter

Activity 24 Finding a regression line

(a) Open Dataplotter and choose the Scatterplot tab. Use the drop-down lists to choose the datasets '# Wadlow age' and '# Wadlow ht' for the first and second column, respectively, to obtain a scatterplot.

(b) Click the 'Regression' box above the scatterplot to add the regression line to the scatterplot. Write down the equation of the regression line, which is displayed at the top of the scatterplot.

Dataplotter calculates the numbers in a regression equation to five significant figures, but it does not display trailing zeros. This means that, for example, the coefficient 6.5140 in the regression equation found in Activity 24 is displayed as 6.514.

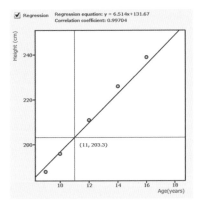

Figure 31 Using Dataplotter to obtain an estimate for Mr Wadlow's height when he was 11

In Activity 24 you should have found that the equation of the regression line for the data on Robert Wadlow's growth is

$$y = 6.5140x + 131.67,$$

where y is the height in cm and x is the age in years.

The regression line on the graph and its equation are two different ways of describing the same model for Mr Wadlow's growth, and they can both be used to make estimates about his height at different ages. For example, if you want to estimate Mr Wadlow's height when he was 11 years old, then you can read off the appropriate value from the graph. One way to do this is to move the cursor over the Dataplotter scatterplot and regression line produced in Activity 24, to find the y-coordinate of the point on the line with x-coordinate 11. This is shown in Figure 31 – zooming in increases the precision. This method gives a height of about 203 cm. Alternatively, you can substitute $x = 11$ into the equation of the regression line, which gives

$$y = 6.5140 \times 11 + 131.67 \approx 203.$$

So an estimate for Mr Wadlow's height when he was 11 is approximately 203 cm. This estimate is rounded to three significant figures because this is the level of precision of the height measurements in the data.

When you use a model to estimate a value in this way, it is important to consider how accurate the estimate is likely to be. The regression line found above for Mr Wadlow's growth is based on his height at ages from 5 to 22, and age 11 is within this range. Also, the regression line is very close to all the points plotted. So the estimate given by the model for Mr Wadlow's height at age 11 is probably reasonably accurate.

You can often use a model based on data to estimate values that are not given in the data. If the estimated value is within the *range* of the data, then this process is known as **interpolation**. As long as the model fits the data reasonably well, interpolation can provide reasonable estimates.

Dataplotter

Activity 25 Using a regression line

(a) Use the equation of the regression line for Mr Wadlow's growth to estimate his height at the age of 24 years.

(b) Use the Dataplotter graph found in Activity 24 to check your answer to part (a). You will have to move the graph within the window.

You can move the graph by dragging it or using the arrow buttons.

(c) Why might the estimate found in parts (a) and (b) be unreliable?

In Activity 25 you used a model based on a dataset to estimate a value that lies outside the range of the dataset. This is called **extrapolation**, and it can be unreliable. For example, if you read off the y-intercept of the line that models Mr Wadlow's growth (or substitute $x = 0$ into the equation of the line), then you will find that the model predicts that Mr Wadlow's height at age 0 was about 130 cm. This sounds very unlikely! In fact, although Mr Wadlow's height was not recorded at birth, his weight was a healthy 3.8 kg and his rapid growth started soon after birth.

In general it is unwise to extrapolate too far from the range of a dataset, unless you are confident that the conditions that apply to the values in the dataset also apply to values outside its range. (Sometimes there may be independent scientific evidence to suggest that this is the case.)

The gradient of a line that models a relationship tells you the rate of change of the quantity on the vertical axis with respect to the quantity on the horizontal axis. For example, the gradient of the line that models Mr Wadlow's growth is 6.5140 cm/year. So on average Mr Wadlow grew about 6 to 7 cm each year between the ages of 5 and 21.

> Because of inevitable dirt and imperfections in the disc, an audio CD player cannot successfully read every single 'bit' of data from a CD. Sophisticated mathematical error-correction techniques usually allow missing data to be reconstructed, but when too much data has been lost, the CD player may have to resort to interpolation to guess what the missing data might be.

4.2 Correlation coefficients

It is important to know how accurate a prediction provided by a regression line is likely to be, so it is useful to have some indication of how well a regression line fits its data points. To provide this, statisticians have developed a measure known as the **correlation coefficient**, which is a number calculated from the data pairs, and is often denoted by r. The value of the correlation coefficient indicates how well the regression line fits the data pairs.

There is a formula for the correlation coefficient, but, as with regression lines, it is easiest to use a calculator or computer to calculate it. The software Dataplotter supplied with the module can calculate correlation coefficients, as you will see in the next activity. In this activity you will explore how the correlation coefficient varies for different datasets. After the activity, you will see how the value of the correlation coefficient is interpreted.

> You may see the formula for the correlation coefficient if you go on to study modules on statistics.

Activity 26 *Exploring the correlation coefficient*

 Dataplotter

Use Dataplotter, with the Scatterplot tab selected. If any datasets are already selected, then first remove each of them by clicking on the 'New' button to produce a new empty dataset.

(a) Plot the four points $(0,0)$, $(1,2)$, $(3,6)$ and $(4,8)$ on the scatterplot, by entering the x-values 0, 1, 3 and 4 in the first column, and the y-values 0, 2, 6 and 8 in the second column. These points all lie in a straight line with a positive gradient.

(b) If the Regression box is not already ticked, then click it to display the regression line. The correlation coefficient is displayed at the top of the scatterplot, under the equation of the regression line. What is its value?

(c) Now plot some more points that do *not* lie on the regression line. You can do this by holding down the shift key and clicking on the graph. What happens to the regression line and the correlation coefficient?

(d) Clear each of the columns by clicking on 'Clear'. Then repeat parts (a), (b) and (c), but this time plot four points that lie on a line with a *negative* gradient, such as $(0,0)$, $(1,-2)$, $(3,-6)$ and $(4,-8)$.

The correlation coefficient described here was invented by Francis Galton (1822–1911). As well as pursuing his statistical work, Galton founded the modern system of weather-mapping (inventing the word 'anticyclone'), played a major part in the development of fingerprint classification, and invented the dog whistle, which dogs can hear but people cannot.

Figure 33   Francis Galton (1822–1911) was a pioneer in the use of regression techniques

The correlation coefficient of a set of paired data is always between −1 and 1, inclusive. If the correlation coefficient is *positive*, then the regression line for the data has a positive gradient, which means that one of the quantities tends to increase as the other increases. In this case, the quantities are said to have a **positive correlation**. On the other hand, if the correlation coefficient is *negative*, then the regression line has a negative gradient, which means that one of the quantities tends to decrease as the other increases. In this case, the quantities are said to have a **negative correlation**.

The correlation coefficient is exactly 1 or exactly −1 when all the data points lie exactly on the regression line. When this happens, the quantities are said to have a **perfect correlation**, as illustrated in Figure 32.

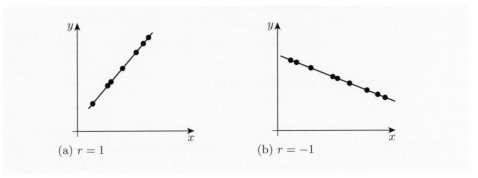

Figure 32   (a) Perfect positive correlation ($r = 1$).
(b) Perfect negative correlation ($r = −1$).

If the correlation coefficient is close to 1 or −1, then the data points lie close to the regression line, as illustrated in Figure 34, and the quantities are said to have a strong correlation.

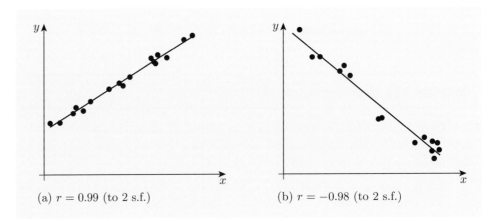

Figure 34   (a) Strong positive correlation (r close to 1).
(b) Strong negative correlation (r close to −1).

If the correlation coefficient is closer to zero, then the data points are scattered further from the regression line, as illustrated in Figure 35. In general, the closer the correlation coefficient is to zero, the weaker is the correlation between the quantities. Graphs (a) and (b) in Figure 35 illustrate **weaker correlation** than the graphs in Figure 34. In both cases, the correlation coefficient, r, is closer to zero than it is for the strong correlations shown in Figure 34. When the correlation coefficient is zero there is no correlation, as shown in graph (c).

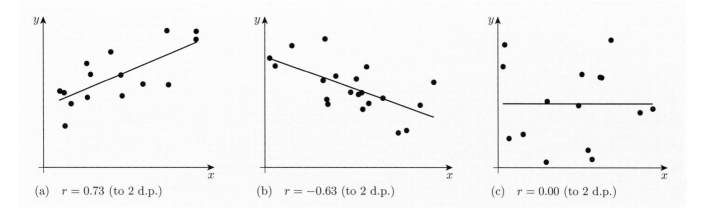

(a) $r = 0.73$ (to 2 d.p.)   (b) $r = -0.63$ (to 2 d.p.)   (c) $r = 0.00$ (to 2 d.p.)

Figure 35 (a) Weaker positive correlation (r positive but closer to 0).
(b) Weaker negative correlation (r negative but closer to 0). (c) Zero correlation ($r = 0$).

The key facts about correlation coefficients are summarised below.

> **Correlation coefficients**
>
> The correlation coefficient of a set of paired data measures how closely the regression line fits the data points.
>
> A value close to $+1$ indicates a strong positive correlation.
>
> A value close to -1 indicates a strong negative correlation.
>
> The closer the value is to 0, the weaker is the correlation.

If two data pairs in a dataset are exactly the same, then they will be plotted on top of each other in a scatterplot, but the repetition is taken into account when the regression line and correlation coefficient are calculated.

In the next activity you are asked to find the correlation coefficient for the data on Robert Wadlow's age and height.

Activity 27 *Finding the correlation coefficient for Mr Wadlow's data*

 Dataplotter

In Dataplotter, with the Scatterplot tab selected, use the drop-down lists to choose the datasets '# Wadlow age' and '# Wadlow ht' for the first and second columns, respectively. Find the correlation coefficient of these data by clicking the Regression box, if it is not already ticked. Comment on the value of the correlation coefficient.

Finding a regression line and examining the correlation coefficient are useful ways of analysing a set of paired data.

In the next activity you are asked to investigate the question: 'Is there a relationship between a mother's weight at the start and at the end of her pregnancy?' You have seen that after a question like this is posed, the next stage of the statistical modelling cycle is to collect some data. A dataset relevant to this question was introduced in Unit 4, and in the activity you are asked to use a regression line and correlation coefficient to analyse the data, and then to interpret the results that you obtain.

The relevant dataset from Unit 4 was referred to as the 'backache dataset', and you might remember that some data values were missing or clearly wrong and had to be removed from the dataset. When you plot a scatterplot using such data, you have to remember to remove data values that are not paired. Dataplotter contains adjusted versions of some of the columns from the backache dataset, with these data values removed. They are indicated with the prefix 'SP' for 'scatterplot'. Before plotting any scatterplot, you should always check that both datasets contain the same number of values and that the values are paired correctly.

Dataplotter

Activity 28   *Investigating correlation in the backache dataset*

Use Dataplotter, with the Scatterplot tab selected.

(a) Obtain a scatterplot of the mothers' weights at the end of their pregnancies against their weights at the start, by choosing the datasets '# SP Weight start' and '# SP Weight end' for the first and second columns, respectively. Make sure that the Regression box is ticked.

(b) Write down the equation of the regression line, and the correlation coefficient.

(c) Use the equation of the regression line to predict the weight of a mother at the end of her pregnancy if her weight at the start was 55 kg. How reliable do you think your prediction is?

In the next activity you are asked to use the backache dataset from Unit 4 to investigate the relationship between the weight gain of mothers during their pregnancies, and the weights of their babies.

Dataplotter

Activity 29   *Investigating correlation in the backache dataset again*

Use Dataplotter, with the Scatterplot tab selected.

(a) Obtain a scatterplot of the babies' weights against the mothers' weight gains, by choosing the datasets '# SP Weight gain' and '# SP Weight baby' for the first and second columns, respectively. Make sure that the Regression box is ticked.

(b) What is the correlation coefficient? Describe the correlation between the mothers' weight gains and their babies' weights.

In the next activity you are asked to add a rogue measurement – an outlier – to the dataset investigated in the last activity, to investigate the effect that this has on the correlation coefficient.

Dataplotter

Activity 30   *Investigating the effect of an outlier in the data*

Use Dataplotter, with the Scatterplot tab selected, and the datasets '# SP Weight gain' and '# SP Weight baby' selected for the first and second columns, respectively, as in Activity 29. Make sure that the Regression box is ticked.

In Dataplotter you cannot directly change a preloaded dataset. To edit a preloaded dataset you first need to change its name.

Change the name of the datasets '# SP Weight gain' and '# SP Weight baby' to 'SP Wt gain new' and 'SP Wt baby new', or new names of your own choice. You can do this by clicking on the blue or green dataset name above each dataset (not the dataset name in the drop-down list).

(a) Suppose that errors were made in recording one mother's data values, so that the dataset included a mother's weight gain recorded as 75 kg and her baby's weight recorded as 25 kg. Add this data pair to the data in the columns. What is the correlation coefficient of the new dataset, and how does it compare to the correlation coefficient of the original dataset, which you found in Activity 29?

(b) Would it be better to use the regression line found in part (a), instead of the one in Activity 29, to predict a baby's weight from the mother's weight? Explain your answer.

When you use a regression line to make a prediction, you should not assume that if the correlation coefficient is close to 1 or −1 then the prediction is likely to be reliable. It is important to check the scatterplot as well.

You saw a reason for this in Activity 30: an outlier in the data can cause the correlation coefficient to have a value misleadingly close to 1 or −1. You can see roughly why this happens if you compare the two scatterplots in the solutions to Activities 29 and 30. The data points are the same in each case except that an outlier has been added to the second plot. You can see that in the second plot the distances of the points from the line are much smaller in comparison to the overall range of the data, and this causes the improvement in the correlation coefficient.

Another reason why you need to check scatterplots as well as correlation coefficients is that there may be a clear relationship between two quantities that is not linear. For example, consider the data points in Figure 36. The regression line, which is shown, is a poor fit, and the correlation coefficient is also fairly poor, at 0.77. However, the data points seem to lie on a smooth curve, so it is not appropriate to model these data by a straight line – a curve would be a much better model.

You can learn about using curves to model paired data if you go on to take modules on statistics.

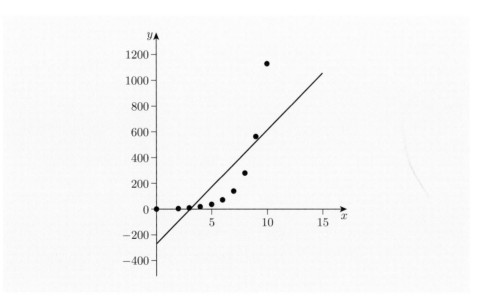

Figure 36   Data points that should not be modelled by a straight line

Correlation and causation

If there appears to be a strong correlation between two quantities, it does not necessarily mean that one has caused the other.

For example, suppose that data have been collected each year on the number of students in a particular town who are studying at least one level 1 mathematics module, and also on the number of burglaries committed in the same town. Suppose that these data give the scatterplot in Figure 37(a). Each data point corresponds to the figures for a particular year.

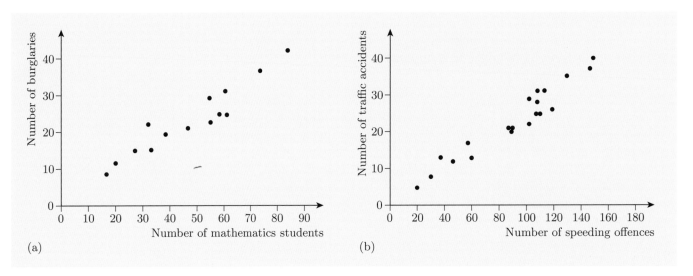

(a)   (b)

Figure 37 Two scatterplots for a fictitious town: (a) the annual number of burglaries plotted against the annual number of students studying level 1 mathematics modules; (b) the annual number of road accidents plotted against the annual number of recorded speeding offences

The graph in Figure 37(a) shows a strong correlation between the two quantities – the more mathematics students there are, the more burglaries are committed. However, you would not expect that the mathematics students are causing the burglaries! A likely explanation for the correlation is that both the number of students and the number of burglaries depend on some third quantity, such as the number of new people who are moving into the area.

Now look at the scatterplot in Figure 37(b), which shows the number of recorded speeding offences and the number of road accidents in the same town each year for several years. Again, there appears to be a strong correlation, and you might be tempted to conclude that speeding causes traffic accidents. However, just as before, the correlation does not prove a causal relationship. Again both quantities could depend on a third quantity: for example there might have been a varying number of newly-qualified drivers, and it could be that newly-qualified drivers are more likely both to exceed the speed limit and to cause road accidents. On the other hand, it *might* be true that speeding causes road accidents, but further evidence would be needed to establish this effect conclusively.

Activity 31   *Comparing mathematical ability and shoe size*

The scatterplot on the next page shows the scores achieved by some children in a mathematics test plotted against their shoe sizes.

(a) Describe the correlation between shoe size and mathematics score for these children.

(b) Can you conclude that the size of a child's feet determines his or her mathematical achievement?

(c) Give another possible explanation for the correlation observed.

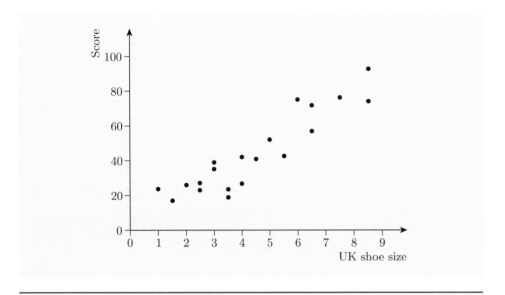

Correlations between two quantities are frequently mentioned in the media, and it is often assumed that a correlation means that one quantity has caused the other. Whenever you hear of a correlation like this, you should ask yourself whether there might be any third quantity that could explain the correlation.

For example, it has been reported that children who were breastfed for longer as babies tend to have higher IQs (intelligence quotients). This correlation does not necessarily mean that breastfeeding improves a child's IQ. It could be that the kind of mother who breastfeeds for longer tends also to be the kind of mother who does other things that might improve her child's IQ, such as spending more time reading to and playing with her child.

In 1999 the journal *Nature* published a research paper that showed that babies who slept with the light on were more likely to develop myopia (nearsightedness) later in life than babies who slept in the dark. The authors concluded that sleeping with the light on can cause myopia. However, later research showed that sleeping in the light or dark had nothing to do with developing myopia, and the following alternative explanation of the correlation was suggested. Children with myopic parents are more likely to develop myopia themselves. And if you are a myopic parent, you are more likely to leave a light on in your child's room, so that you can find your way in and out!

In this section you have seen how to find the best straight line to model a set of paired data, and how to use the correlation coefficient to measure how well the line fits the data. Many situations can be modelled by straight lines in this way, particularly if the range of the dataset is small. However some data sets are modelled better by curved graphs, as you will see in Units 10 and 13.

5 Reviewing straight-line graphs

Graphs of straight lines, their equations and models based on them are used frequently in many different contexts, and you will work with them later in the module, particularly in Unit 7. So it is important that you are confident with the ideas and techniques covered in this unit.

Some people find that a helpful way of reviewing their progress on a topic is to draw a diagram showing the main ideas and the connections between them. Writing down the key ideas and thinking about how to get from one to another can strengthen your overall understanding, help you to remember the ideas more easily and provide you with a revision guide that may be useful when you need to look something up. You can include as much or as little detail in your diagram as you like. For instance, you can include examples, or use different colours for different aspects.

The next activity invites you to complete two such diagrams for some of the ideas in this unit.

Activity 32 *Reviewing straight-line graphs*

(a) Fill in the blanks in the incomplete diagram below, starting with the equation $y = -\frac{3}{2}x + 6$ in the middle.

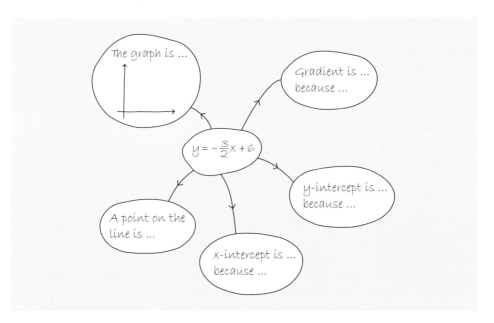

(b) Draw a diagram to summarise the ideas in Section 4. Decide what seems to be the central idea of this section – for example, regression lines – and put this idea in the centre of your diagram. Then add other ideas to this central idea as illustrated below.

What other ideas and information could you add? Use other colours or examples if you think it would help you.

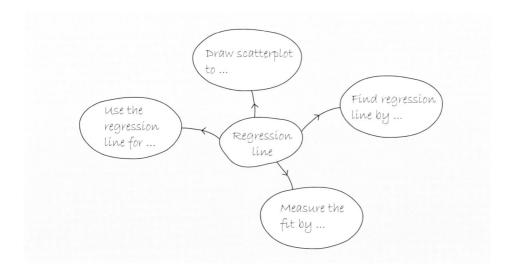

Learning checklist

After studying this unit, you should be able to:

- plot a graph by constructing a table of values for a formula and plotting points
- calculate the gradient of a straight line on a graph and interpret gradient in practical situations
- find the intercepts of a straight line on a graph and interpret them in practical situations
- recognise direct proportion relationships and their graphs, and find a formula for a direct proportion relationship
- find the intercepts and gradient of a straight line from its equation, and find the equation of a straight line from its gradient and y-intercept
- use the equation of a straight line to draw that line on a graph, either by using the y-intercept and gradient from the equation, or by plotting two points
- find the equation of a straight line from its gradient and a point on the line, or from two points on the line
- use the Scatterplot page of Dataplotter to find the regression line and correlation coefficient for a set of paired data, and interpret the results
- interpolate values sensibly and be aware of the dangers of extrapolation.

Solutions and comments on Activities

Activity 1

(a) A has coordinates $(1.5, 1)$.
B has coordinates $(-2, 3)$.
C has coordinates $(-3.5, -2)$.
D has coordinates $(2.5, -3.5)$.

(b)

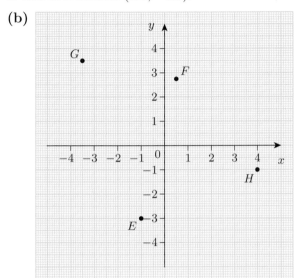

Activity 2

(a) Substituting $x = 6$ into the equation gives
$$y = \tfrac{1}{2} \times 6 + 3 = 3 + 3 = 6.$$
So the point $(6, 5)$ does not lie on the line.

(b) Substituting $x = -5$ into the equation gives
$$y = \tfrac{1}{2} \times (-5) + 3 = -2.5 + 3 = 0.5.$$
So the point $(-5, 0.5)$ lies on the line.

Activity 3

x	-2	-1	0	1	2
y	5	2	-1	-4	-7

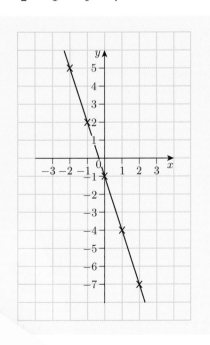

Activity 4

(a) The independent variable is c, since f is the subject of the equation.

(b)

c	-20	0	20	40
f	-4	32	68	104

(c)

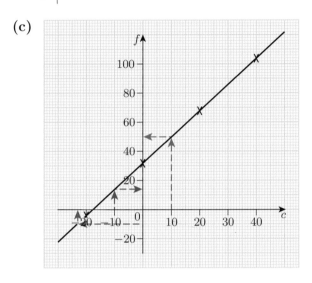

(d) (i) A temperature of $10°C$ is $50°F$. (This conversion is shown in red on the graph.)

(ii) A temperature of $-10°C$ is $14°F$. (This conversion is shown in blue on the graph.)

(iii) A temperature of $-10°F$ is approximately $-23°C$. (This conversion is shown in purple on the graph.)

(iv) A temperature of $0°F$ is approximately $-18°C$. (This is the value where the graph crosses the c-axis.)

Activity 5

(a) The line in Figure 3(b) predicts that if the greengrocer charges £3.50 per kg for tomatoes, then she should expect to sell about 770 kg.

(b) Similarly, if the greengrocer charges £4.75 per kg for tomatoes, then she should expect to sell about 600 kg.

Activity 6

(a) (i) The run is $3 - 1.5 = 1.5$. The rise is $2 - 6 = -4$. So the gradient is
$$\frac{\text{rise}}{\text{run}} = \frac{-4}{1.5} = \frac{-40}{15} = -\tfrac{8}{3}.$$
(Check: The line slopes down, so the gradient should be negative.)

(ii) The run is $1 - (-1.5) = 1 + 1.5 = 2.5$.
The rise is $2 - (-2) = 4$.

So the gradient is

$$\frac{\text{rise}}{\text{run}} = \frac{4}{2.5} = 1.6.$$

(Check: The line slopes up, so the gradient should be positive.)

(b)

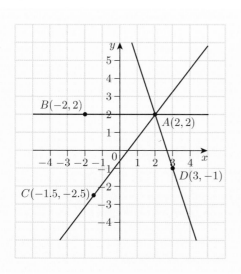

(i) The gradient of the line that passes through A and B is

$$\frac{\text{rise}}{\text{run}} = \frac{2-2}{2-(-2)} = \frac{0}{4} = 0.$$

(ii) The gradient of the line that passes through A and C is

$$\frac{\text{rise}}{\text{run}} = \frac{2-(-2.5)}{2-(-1.5)} = \frac{4.5}{3.5} = \frac{45}{35} = \frac{9}{7} = 1\tfrac{2}{7}.$$

(iii) The gradient of the line that passes through A and D is

$$\frac{\text{rise}}{\text{run}} = \frac{-1-2}{3-2} = \frac{-3}{1} = -3.$$

(c) The rise between any two points on a horizontal line is zero. Because the gradient is the rise divided by the run, it follows that the gradient of a horizontal line is zero.

Activity 7

(a) This line slopes up, so it has a positive gradient, and the angle that it makes with the x-axis is greater than $45°$, so its gradient is greater than 1.

(b) This line slopes down, so it has a negative gradient, and the angle that it makes with the x-axis seems to be about $45°$, so its gradient is about -1.

(c) This line slopes up, so it has a positive gradient, and the angle that it makes with the x-axis is less than $45°$, so its gradient is less than 1.

That is, its gradient is between 0 and 1.

(d) This line slopes down, so it has a negative gradient, and the angle that it makes with the x-axis is greater than $45°$, so its gradient is greater than 1 in size. That is, its gradient is less than -1.

Activity 8

(a) A is $(-0.6, 2)$; B is $(0.4, 1)$; C is $(-0.4, -2)$; D is $(0.2, 5)$.

(b) **(i)** The gradient of the line through A and B is

$$\frac{y_2 - y_1}{x_2 - x_1} = \frac{1-2}{0.4 - (-0.6)} = \frac{-1}{1} = -1.$$

(ii) The gradient of the line through A and D is

$$\frac{y_2 - y_1}{x_2 - x_1} = \frac{5-2}{0.2 - (-0.6)} = \frac{3}{0.8} = 3.75.$$

(iii) The gradient of the line through B and C is

$$\frac{y_2 - y_1}{x_2 - x_1} = \frac{-2-1}{-0.4 - 0.4} = \frac{-3}{-0.8} = 3.75.$$

(c) The gradients of these two lines are the same.

Activity 9

(a) The points $(0,0)$ and $(30, 600)$ lie on the line, so its gradient is

$$\frac{600 - 0}{30 - 0} = \frac{600}{30} = 20 \,\text{km/l}.$$

The gradient measures the number of kilometres travelled per litre of fuel. In other words, the gradient is the rate of fuel consumption.

(b) The points $(0,0)$ and $(2, 80)$ lie on the line, so its gradient is

$$\frac{80 - 0}{2 - 0} = \frac{80}{2} = 40 \,\text{km/h}.$$

The gradient measures the number of kilometres travelled per hour. In other words, the gradient is the speed.

Activity 10

(a) The vertical intercept is $25 \,\text{km}$.

This is the distance of the walker from the finish line at the start of the walk. In other words, it is the length of the walk.

The horizontal intercept is 5 hours.

This is the time when the distance of the walker from the finish line is zero. In other words, it is the time taken for the walker to complete the walk.

(b) The vertical intercept is $£210$.

This is the cost of hiring the venue for no people. (The total cost is this cost plus an amount that depends on the number of people using the venue.)

Activity 11

(c) The line $y = 0.5x$ makes the smallest angle with the x-axis.

Activity 12

(a) The time and the distance are directly proportional. If you multiply or divide the time by any number, then the distance changes in the same way.

(b) The number of painters and the time taken are *not* directly proportional. The more painters there are, the less time the job takes. (In theory, anyway!)

(c) The number of pounds exchanged and the number of euros received are *not* directly proportional. If you double the number of pounds, then the number of euros that you receive is not doubled, because of the transaction fee. For example, if the exchange rate is €1.20 to the pound and you exchange £100, then you receive

$$100 \times €1.20 - €10 = €110,$$

whereas if you exchange £200, then you receive

$$200 \times €1.20 - €10 = €230,$$

which is not double €110.

(d) The number of songs and the total cost are directly proportional.

(e) The number of hours worked and the gross pay are directly proportional.

Activity 13

(a) Since d is directly proportional to c, the formula expressing their relationship is of the form

$$d = kc,$$

where k is a constant.

Also, $d = 400$ when $c = 20$. Substituting these values into the equation gives

$$400 = 20k.$$

We now solve this equation to find the value of k.

Divide by 20: $\frac{400}{20} = k$

Simplify: $20 = k$

So the required formula is

$$d = 20c.$$

(b) Substituting $c = 35$ into the formula found in part (a) gives

$$d = 20 \times 35 = 700.$$

So the amount of drug needed is $700\,\text{mg}$.

Activity 14

(a) (i) This graph is a straight line but it does not pass through the origin, so it does not represent a direct proportion relationship.

(ii) This graph is not a straight line so it does not represent a direct proportion relationship.

(iii) This graph is a straight line through the origin so it represents a direct proportion relationship.

(b) Temperature in degrees Fahrenheit is not directly proportional to temperature in degrees Celsius, because the graph of this relationship does not pass through the origin.

Activity 15

(b) The line through the origin with gradient 2 is shown in Figure 21 on page 85. If you have not obtained this graph, then check that you have chosen the correct options in Graphplotter.

(c) The line moves 1 unit up the y-axis. The new graph has y-intercept 1.

(d) You should find that changing the value of c moves the graph up or down the y-axis. The y-intercept is always the value of c.

(e) The lines all have the same gradient (that is, they are all parallel to each other), but they have different y-intercepts.

(f) Changing the value of m changes the gradient, and changing the value of c changes the y-intercept.

Activity 16

(a) (i) The coefficient of x is 2, so the gradient is 2. The constant is -1, so the y-intercept is -1.

(ii) The coefficient of x is -3, so the gradient is -3. The constant is 4, so the y-intercept is 4.

(iii) The coefficient of x is $\frac{1}{5}$, so the gradient is $\frac{1}{5}$. The constant is $-\frac{2}{5}$, so the y-intercept is $-\frac{2}{5}$.

(b) (i) The equation is $y = 4x - 10$.

(ii) The equation is $y = -x + 5$.

(iii) The equation is $y = 0x + 3$; that is, $y = 3$.

(c) (i) The equation is $y = 4x + 2$.

(ii) The equation is $y = -x + 2$.

(iii) The equation is $y = 2$.

Activity 17

(a) Putting $y = 0$ gives

$$2x - 1 = 0.$$

We now solve this equation.

Add 1: $2x = 1$

Divide by 2: $x = \frac{1}{2}$

Hence the x-intercept is $\frac{1}{2}$.

(b) Putting $y = 0$ gives

$$-3x + 4 = 0.$$

We now solve this equation.

Add $3x$: $\qquad 4 = 3x$

Divide by 3: $\quad \frac{4}{3} = x$

Hence the x-intercept is $\frac{4}{3}$.

(c) Putting $y = 0$ gives

$$\frac{x}{5} - \frac{2}{5} = 0.$$

We now solve this equation.

Multiply by 5: $\quad x - 2 = 0$

Add 2: $\qquad\qquad x = 2$

Hence the x-intercept is 2.

Activity 18

(a) The equations of the lines are as follows.

(i) $y = 1$

(ii) $x = -3$

(iii) $y = -4.5$

(iv) $x = 2.3$

(b) The x-axis has equation $y = 0$, and the y-axis has equation $x = 0$.

Activity 19

(a)

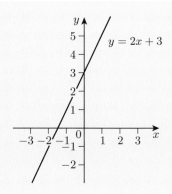

(b)

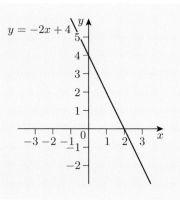

(c)

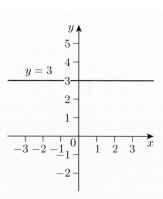

(d)

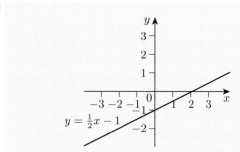

(e)

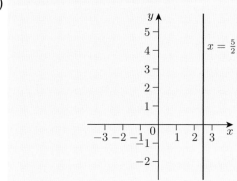

Activity 20

(a) The line passes through the points $(0, 1)$ and $(1, -2)$. So the gradient is

$$\frac{-2 - 1}{1 - 0} = \frac{-3}{1} = -3.$$

The y-intercept is 1.

Hence the equation is $y = -3x + 1$.

(b) The line passes through the points $(-0.5, -0.8)$ and $(0, 0.3)$. So the gradient is

$$\frac{0.3 - (-0.8)}{0 - (-0.5)} = \frac{1.1}{0.5} = 2.2.$$

The vertical intercept is 0.3.

Hence the equation is $s = 2.2t + 0.3$.

Activity 21

A sketch of the line is as follows.

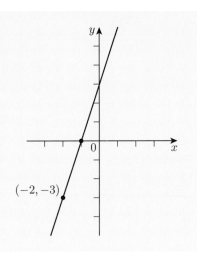

The gradient of the line is 3, so the equation is $y = 3x + c$, where c is a constant.

Also, the line passes through the point $(-2, -3)$. Substituting these coordinates into the equation gives

$$-3 = 3 \times (-2) + c; \quad \text{that is,} \quad -3 = -6 + c.$$

Adding 6 to both sides gives

$$3 = c.$$

So the equation of the line is $y = 3x + 3$.

(Check: This is the equation of a line with y-intercept 3, and the y-intercept on the sketch does appear to be 3.)

Activity 22

(a)

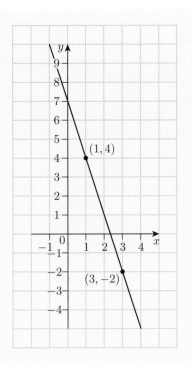

(b)   The gradient of the line is

$$\frac{-2 - 4}{3 - 1} = \frac{-6}{2} = -3.$$

So the equation of the line is $y = -3x + c$, where c is a constant.

Also, the line passes through the point $(1, 4)$. Substituting these coordinates into the equation gives

$$4 = -3 \times 1 + c; \quad \text{that is,} \quad 4 = -3 + c.$$

Adding 3 to both sides gives

$$7 = c.$$

So the equation of the line is

$$y = -3x + 7.$$

(Check: Substituting $x = 3$ into the equation gives

$$y = -3 \times 3 + 7 = -9 + 7 = -2,$$

so the coordinates $(3, -2)$ satisfy the equation.)

Activity 23

(a)   A sketch of the line is shown in the left-hand figure below. The equation is $x = a$, where a is a constant. Since the point $(1, 0)$ satisfies the equation, the equation is $x = 1$.

(b)   A sketch of the line is shown in the right-hand figure below. The equation is $y = a$, where a is a constant. Since the point $(2, -4)$ satisfies the equation, the equation is $y = -4$.

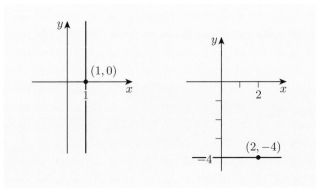

Activity 24

(a)   You should obtain a scatterplot similar to Figure 28 on page 104, as shown on the next page.

(b)   The equation of the regression line is

$$y = 6.5140x + 131.67,$$

where x and y represent Robert Wadlow's age in years and height in centimetres, respectively.

(Here the coefficient of x and the constant term are given to five significant figures. This is the default setting of the Scatterplot page of Dataplotter.)

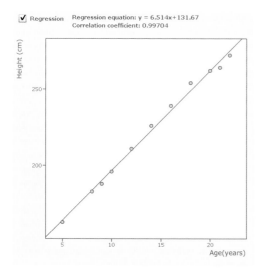

Regression equation: y = 6.514x+131.67
Correlation coefficient: 0.99704

Activity 25

(a) Substituting $x = 24$ into the equation of the line gives

$$y = 6.5140 \times 24 + 131.67 = 288.006.$$

So Mr Wadlow's height at age 24 is predicted to be about 288 cm.

(b) Moving the cursor over the Dataplotter graph to find coordinates gives a similar answer to that found in part (a).

(c) The age of 24 is outside the range of the data used to produce the model. Mr Wadlow's growth may not have continued at the same rate, so the estimate provided by the regression line for his height at age 24 may not be reliable. (In fact, sadly Mr Wadlow died when he was 22, following an infection in a blister caused by a leg brace.)

Activity 26

(b) The value of the correlation coefficient is 1.

(c) The regression line and correlation coefficient usually change each time a new point is plotted. Once there is a data point not on the regression line, the value of the correlation coefficient is not 1, but some value between -1 and 1.

(d) This time the points on the line have a correlation coefficient of -1. Again, the regression line and correlation coefficient usually change each time a new point is plotted. Once there is a data point not on the regression line, the value of the correlation coefficient is not -1, but again some value between -1 and 1.

Activity 27

The correlation coefficient for the data on Mr Wadlow's age and height is 0.99704 (to 5 s.f.). This value is close to 1, so it indicates that the regression line is a good fit to the data points.

Activity 28

(a) The scatterplot is shown below.

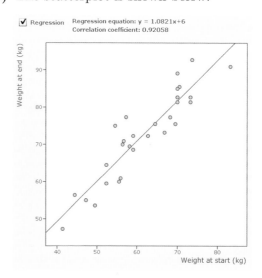

Regression equation: y = 1.0821x+6
Correlation coefficient: 0.92058

(b) The equation of the regression line is

$$y = 1.0821x + 6.0000,$$

and the correlation coefficient is 0.92058 (both to five significant figures).

(c) Substituting $x = 55$ into the equation of the regression line gives

$$y = 1.0821 \times 55 + 6.0000 = 65.5155.$$

So the model predicts that a mother weighing 55 kg at the start of her pregnancy will weigh about 66 kg at the end.

The correlation coefficient is only moderately high, at about 0.92, so the prediction is unlikely to be very accurate, though it does give some indication of the expected weight.

(However, predictions made using a regression line may not be reliable for individuals.)

Activity 29

(a) The scatterplot is shown below.

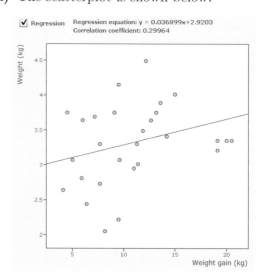

Regression equation: y = 0.036899x+2.9203
Correlation coefficient: 0.29964

(b) The correlation coefficient is only 0.29964 (to 5 s.f.), that is, about 0.30, which is fairly close to zero, so there appears to be little correlation between the mothers' weight gains and their babies' weights. This is confirmed by the scatterplot, which shows a large amount of scatter.

Activity 30

(a) The new scatterplot is shown below.

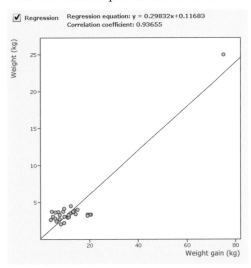

The new correlation coefficient is 0.93655 (to 5 s.f.), that is, about 0.94, which is significantly higher than the correlation coefficient for the original dataset, which is about 0.30.

(b) Despite the higher correlation coefficient in part (a), it would be better to use the regression line in Activity 29 to make a prediction, since the regression line in part (a) is based on the same data together with a misleading data pair. However, since there is little correlation shown by the data in Activity 29, it would be unwise to use either regression line to make a prediction.

(Some explanation of the effect of adding the erroneous data is given after the activity.)

Activity 31

(a) There appears to be a strong positive correlation between shoe size and mathematics score.

(b) It is not reasonable to conclude that foot size determines mathematical achievement. Correlation does not imply causation.

(c) A likely explanation for the correlation is that both foot size and mathematical achievement increase as a child gets older.

Activity 32

(a) An example of a completed diagram is shown below, but yours will probably be different to this

one – for example, you might have chosen a different point on the line, or explained your answers in slightly different ways.

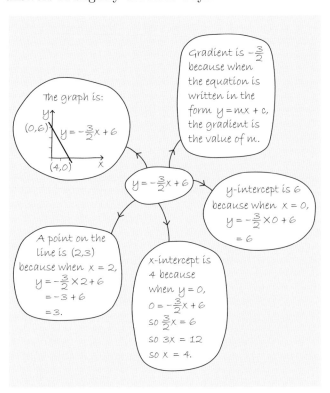

(b) One suggestion is below – notice how extra information has been added. You may wish to add other details, such as an example of how to substitute a value into the equation of a regression line, or further information on using the Scatterplot page in Dataplotter. The aim of a diagram like this is to include the main points and anything else that will help you as a revision aid.

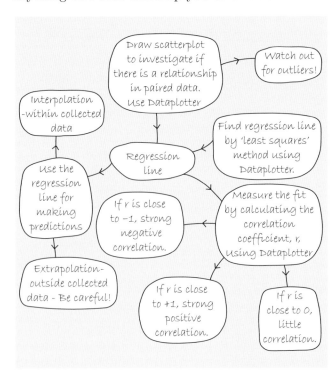

Equations and inequalities

Introduction

In this unit you will develop some more sophisticated mathematical problem-solving skills, and see how to apply them to some practical situations.

In Section 1 you will learn how you can begin with an equation involving two or more variables, choose one of the variables, and turn the equation into a *formula* with that variable as its subject. This skill is often useful when you need to work with formulas, and it is useful in many other situations where you use algebra. In particular, you will see how it allows you to express the equation of a straight line in forms other than $y = mx + c$.

Formulas were discussed in Unit 2, Subsection 3.1.

In Section 2 you will learn another basic algebraic technique: taking out common factors. This skill is helpful when you want to turn a given equation into a formula with a particular variable as its subject, and it is useful in other contexts too.

Section 3 introduces an important new algebraic skill that is based on many of the algebraic and graphical ideas that you have met throughout the module so far. You will learn how to deal with situations that involve *two* equations at once, and see how to apply this skill to some practical problems.

Finally, in Section 4, you will extend the work that you have done in Unit 2 on inequalities. You will learn how you can work with inequalities using similar techniques to those that you have used for equations, and how these ideas can be applied in practice.

1 Rearranging equations

1.1 Making a chosen variable the subject of an equation

In the previous unit you saw that one way to convert temperatures between the Celsius and Fahrenheit scales is to use a graph, like the one shown in Figure 1. You can use this graph to convert either from Celsius to Fahrenheit, or vice versa. For example, the dashed red lines on the graph show that 29°C is about 84°F, and the dashed blue lines show that 63°F is about 17°C.

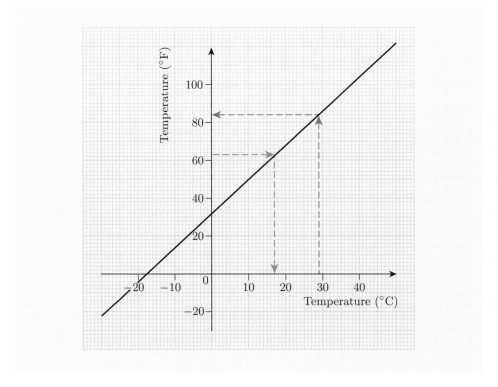

Figure I   The Celsius-Fahrenheit conversion graph

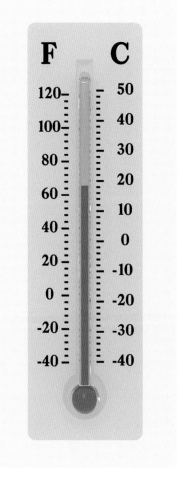

Figure 2   A thermometer with Celsius and Fahrenheit scales

If you need more accuracy than you can get from this graph, then you can use a formula instead. You have seen that if c and f denote a temperature in °C and °F, respectively, then the following formula holds:

$$f = 1.8c + 32. \tag{1}$$

For example, to find the Fahrenheit equivalent of 29°C, you substitute $c = 29$ into the formula, which gives

$$f = 1.8 \times 29 + 32 = 84.2.$$

So 29°C is the same as 84.2°F.

You can use the same formula to convert the other way, from °F to °C, but this involves solving an equation, as illustrated in the example below.

Example I   *Solving an equation obtained from a formula*

Use formula (1) to find the Celsius equivalent of 63°F.

Solution

Substitute the value of f into the formula.

Substituting $f = 63$ into the formula gives

$$63 = 1.8c + 32.$$

Solve this equation to find c.

Subtract 32: $\qquad\qquad\qquad\qquad$ $31 = 1.8c$

Divide by 1.8: $\qquad\qquad\qquad\qquad$ $\dfrac{31}{1.8} = c$

Swap the sides, and do the division: $\quad c = 17.2$ (to 1 d.p.)

So 63°F is the same as 17.2°C, to one decimal place.

Here is a similar conversion for you to try.

Activity 1 Solving an equation obtained from a formula

Use formula (1) to find the Celsius equivalent of 59°F.

So the formula above can be used to convert in either direction. But it is more suited to conversions from °C to °F, because that way you don't have to solve an equation. If you want to convert the other way, from °F to °C, then it would be more convenient to have a formula of the form

$$c = \boxed{\text{an expression containing } f}$$

– that is, a formula whose subject is c rather than f – because then you could convert from °F to °C by just substituting into the right-hand side. A formula like this is described as a formula for c in terms of f and would be especially useful if you had to make a lot of conversions from °F to °C.

This is a situation where algebra is useful! It can be used to rearrange the original formula, which has subject f, into a formula with subject c. To do this, you just 'solve' the original formula to find c in the usual way. The only difference from solving the equations in Example 1 and Activity 1 is that you don't replace f by a particular temperature – you just leave it as f. Here is what happens when you do this.

The original formula is: $f = 1.8c + 32$

Subtract 32: $f - 32 = 1.8c$

Divide by 1.8: $\dfrac{f - 32}{1.8} = c$

So a formula for c is

$$c = \frac{f - 32}{1.8}. \tag{2}$$

Remember that by convention we write the subject of a formula on the left.

Activity 2 Using the rearranged formula

Use formula (2) to find the Celsius equivalent of 85.1°F.

Any equation that contains two or more variables gives you information about how those variables are related. It's often useful to choose one of the variables and rearrange the equation to make that variable the subject. In this rest of this subsection you'll be able to practise doing that.

As you've seen, the way to do it is to use the same method that you use to solve equations, treating the variable that you want to be the subject (which we'll call the *required subject*) as the unknown. Here's a simple example for you to try.

Activity 3 Making a variable the subject of an equation

A formula for the length f cm of fabric that you need to make a square cushion with sides of length s cm and seam allowances of 1 cm is

$$f = 2s + 4.$$

This is because you need two pieces of fabric, each of which must have length s cm plus 2 cm for the seams, as shown below.

(The formula assumes that the fabric is wide enough for each piece, as shown in the diagram, but not so wide that both pieces will fit into its width.)

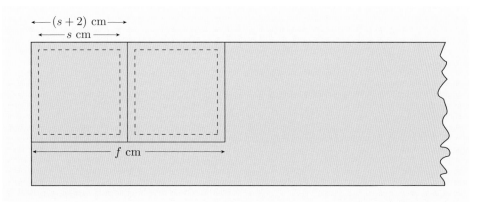

Rearrange the formula above to make s the subject. (The rearranged formula allows you to work out the side length of the largest cushion that you can make with a piece of fabric of length f cm.)

The next example illustrates how to change the subject of a slightly more complicated formula. As before, the method is the same as for solving equations.

Example 2   *Making a variable the subject of another equation*

Tutorial clip

Make R the subject of the equation

$$P = \frac{Q}{R+1}.$$

Solution

The equation is: $\qquad P = \dfrac{Q}{R+1}$

First remove any fractions and brackets. To clear the fraction, multiply both sides by $R+1$. Use brackets to show that the *whole* of each side is multiplied by the *whole* of $R+1$.

Multiply by $R+1$: $\qquad P(R+1) = \left(\dfrac{Q}{R+1}\right)(R+1)$

Simplify: $\qquad P(R+1) = Q$

Multiply out the brackets: $\qquad PR + P = Q$

Now there are no fractions or brackets. Next, find all the terms that contain the required subject, R. There is just one such term, PR. Keep this term on the left, and get all the other terms on the right.

Subtract P: $\qquad PR = Q - P$

Finally, divide by P, to get R by itself on the left-hand side.

Divide by P
(assuming that $P \neq 0$): $\qquad R = \dfrac{Q-P}{P}$

Remember that it is usually best to deal with fractions before brackets, as you often have to introduce extra brackets when clearing fractions.

The symbol '$\neq$' means (and is read as) 'is not equal to'.

Notice that a 'simplify' step is included in the working in Example 2. As you saw in Unit 5 when you were solving equations, you can shorten the working a little by doing the same thing to both sides and simplifying the resulting equation all in one step. You should do this once you've had enough practice to be confident that you can do it without making mistakes.

Another thing to notice about the working in Example 2 is that an expression was divided by P. Since you cannot divide by zero, this means that the formula obtained cannot be used when $P = 0$. But it can be used for all other values of P.

The strategy used to rearrange equations in this section is summarised in the box below. It's just the strategy that you've seen for solving equations, with the wording changed slightly so that it makes sense for equations that contain more than one letter.

You can use this strategy to rearrange many of the equations that you'll need to deal with, but it won't work for all equations. Later in the unit, and later in the module, you'll see how the strategy can be adapted to deal with a wider variety of equations.

> **Strategy** *To make a variable the subject of an equation*
>
> Carry out a sequence of steps. In each step, do one of the following:
>
> - do the same thing to both sides
> - simplify one side or both sides
> - swap the sides.
>
> Aim to do the following, in order.
>
> 1. Clear any fractions and multiply out any brackets. To clear fractions, multiply both sides by a suitable expression.
>
> 2. Add or subtract terms on both sides to get all terms containing the required subject on one side, and all the other terms on the other side. This gives an equation of the form
>
> $$\boxed{\text{expression}} \times \boxed{\text{required subject}} = \boxed{\text{expression}}.$$
>
> 3. Divide both sides by the expression that multiplies the required subject.

Remember that you have to do the same thing to the *whole* of each side.

Remember that you can do the following things to each side.

The 'something' can be any expression (since all expressions represent numbers).

- Add something.
- Subtract something.
- Multiply by something.
- Divide by something (provided that it is non-zero).

The Kelvin scale takes its name from the scientist and engineer William Thomson, 1st Baron Kelvin (1824–1907). As a scientist Thomson made major contributions to the study of heat and thermodynamics. As an engineer he worked on the installation of the first transatlantic telegraph cable.

In the next activity you're asked to rearrange a formula that is used for converting temperatures between degrees Fahrenheit and *kelvins*. As you saw in Unit 1, the kelvin is the SI unit used by scientists for measuring temperature. Temperatures measured on the Kelvin scale are in *kelvins*, not *degrees kelvin*, and the symbol used is K, not °K. The Kelvin scale uses the same increments as the Celsius scale – an increase of 1 K is the same as an increase of 1°C. The difference between the two scales is that zero on the Kelvin scale (equivalent to about -273°C) is *absolute zero*. An object with this temperature would have no heat at all.

Activity 4   *Changing the subject of a formula*

The following formula is used to convert temperatures from kelvins to degrees Fahrenheit:

$$f = 1.8(k - 273) + 32.$$

The variables f and k denote the temperatures in °F and K, respectively. (This formula is fairly accurate, but is not exact.)

(a) Make k the subject of this formula.

(b) Hence express 97.7°F in kelvins, to three significant figures.

But Sir, you said to write down the equation and change the subject!

In Unit 2 the relationship between the distance, speed and time for a journey was used in various ways. Sometimes you started with the distance and time and calculated the speed, sometimes you started with the distance and speed and calculated the time, and sometimes you started with the speed and time and calculated the distance. Now that you know how to rearrange formulas, you can remember just one formula relating the three quantities, and rearrange it into the form that you need for any particular calculation.

Activity 5   *Changing the subject of the distance–speed–time formula*

The distance d, speed s and time t for a journey are related by the formula

$$d = st.$$

(a) Make t the subject of this formula.

(b) Hence find the time that it would take to travel 96 kilometres at a speed of 80 kilometres per hour.

When you're making a variable the subject of an equation, you don't need to follow the steps of the strategy on page 128 rigidly if you can see a better way to proceed. For example, in Example 2 the equation

$$P = \frac{Q}{R+1}$$

was rearranged to make R the subject. First, both sides were multiplied by $R + 1$ to remove the fraction, which gave

$$P(R + 1) = Q.$$

At this point, instead of removing the brackets as specified by the strategy, you can proceed as follows.

Divide by P
(assuming that $P \neq 0$): $R + 1 = \dfrac{Q}{P}$

Subtract 1: $R = \dfrac{Q}{P} - 1$

The last equation above has R as its subject, and it was obtained in three steps instead of four. It's slightly different from the equation found in Example 2, which was

$$R = \frac{Q - P}{P}.$$

You saw how to expand a fraction in Unit 5.

But naturally it's equivalent, as you can check by expanding the fraction on the right-hand side of the equation found in Example 2:

$$\frac{Q - P}{P} = \frac{Q}{P} - \frac{P}{P} = \frac{Q}{P} - 1.$$

It's best to aim to follow the strategy, but if you can see a better way to proceed at any point, then go ahead with that. You just have to remember that in each step you must do the same thing to both sides, manipulate the sides or swap the sides – you must not do anything else!

The next activity gives you more practice in rearranging equations.

Activity 6   *Rearranging equations*

(a) Make x the subject of the equation $y = \dfrac{x}{2} - 3$.

(b) Make r the subject of the equation $s = \dfrac{6}{r}$.

(c) Make Z the subject of the equation $X = \dfrac{Z}{Y + 1}$.

(d) Make p the subject of the equation $q = \frac{2}{3}(p + 2)$.

(e) Make d the subject of the equation $c = \dfrac{b}{2d + 1}$.

1.2 Rearranging equations of straight lines

In this subsection you'll see that the skill of rearranging equations can be useful when you're dealing with the equations of straight lines.

In Unit 6 you saw that every non-vertical straight line has an equation of the form $y = mx + c$, where m is the gradient of the line and c is the y-intercept. For example, $y = 3x - 2$ is the equation of the line with gradient 3 and y-intercept -2, as shown in Figure 3.

The line consists of all the points (x, y) that satisfy the equation $y = 3x - 2$. (Remember that a point *satisfies* a given equation in x and y if it makes the equation correct when its coordinates are substituted in.)

If you rearrange an equation in x and y, then the points that satisfy it do not change. For example, the equations $y = 3x - 2$ and $y + 2 = 3x$ are rearrangements of each other (the second is obtained by adding 2 to each side of the first), so the same points satisfy each of them. Each of these equations represents the line in Figure 3.

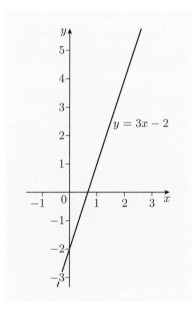

Figure 3   The line with equation $y = 3x - 2$

In the next activity you're asked to show that a particular point satisfies both of these equations.

Activity 7   *Checking that a point satisfies equations*

Show that the point $(3, 7)$ satisfies each of the following equations.

(a) $y = 3x - 2$ (b) $y + 2 = 3x$

Because rearranging an equation in x and y does not change the points that satisfy it, the following fact holds.

Any equation in x and y that can be rearranged into the form $y = mx + c$ is the equation of a straight line.

Example 3   *Rearranging the equation of a line*

 Tutorial clip

Show that the equation $-5x + 3y = 4$ can be rearranged into the form $y = mx + c$. Find the gradient and y-intercept of the line that this equation represents, and draw the line.

Solution

💭 Make y the subject of the equation, using the usual strategy. 💭

The equation is: $-5x + 3y = 4$

Add $5x$: $3y = 5x + 4$

Divide by 3: $y = \dfrac{5x + 4}{3}$ (3)

💭 This has made y the subject, but we want the form $y = mx + c$. 💭

Expand the fraction: $y = \dfrac{5x}{3} + \dfrac{4}{3}$

Simplify: $y = \tfrac{5}{3}x + \tfrac{4}{3}$

This is of the form $y = mx + c$.

💭 Read off the gradient and y-intercept. 💭

The gradient is $\tfrac{5}{3}$ and the y-intercept is $\tfrac{4}{3}$.

💭 Use the two-point method to draw the line. You can use any of the rearrangements of the equation to find the two points. 💭

The point corresponding to the y-intercept is $\left(0, \tfrac{4}{3}\right) \approx (0, 1.3)$. Another point can be found by substituting $x = 1$, say, into equation (3).

The decimal approximation $(0, 1.3)$ for $\left(0, \tfrac{4}{3}\right)$ is calculated to help with plotting this point.

This gives

$$y = \frac{5 \times 1 + 4}{3} = \frac{5 + 4}{3} = \frac{9}{3} = 3,$$

so another point on the line is $(1, 3)$.

The line is shown below.

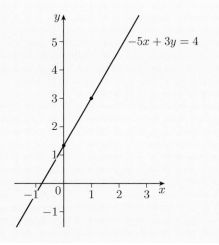

In Example 3, the equation of a line was rearranged to give

$$y = \tfrac{5}{3}x + \tfrac{4}{3}.$$

The numbers in the equation were written as fractions, not as decimal approximations.

If the numbers in an equation cannot be written exactly as finite decimals, but can be written exactly as fractions, then you should write them as fractions. This is because an exact equation is better than an approximate one. If any of the fractions in an equation are top-heavy, then you should write them in top-heavy form rather than converting them to mixed numbers. For example, if an equation contains the number $1\tfrac{1}{3}$, then you should write it as $\tfrac{4}{3}$. This makes the equation clearer to read.

If the numbers in an equation can be written exactly as either fractions or decimals, then you can use either. So, for example,

$$y = \tfrac{1}{2}x - \tfrac{7}{5} \quad \text{and} \quad y = 0.5x - 1.4$$

are both acceptable forms of the same equation.

As you have seen in earlier units, in mathematics it is usually best to work with exact numbers, unless there is a good reason to use approximations. In Example 3, a decimal approximation for a coordinate of a point was calculated to help with plotting, but exact numbers were used everywhere else.

Activity 8   Rearranging the equation of a line

Show that the equation $3x + 2y = 6$ can be rearranged into the form $y = mx + c$. Find the gradient and y-intercept of the line that this equation represents, and draw the line.

The equations in Example 3 and Activity 8 are both of the form $ax + by = d$, where a, b and d are numbers (positive or negative). Any equation of this form with $b \neq 0$ can be rearranged into the form $y = mx + c$. If b *is* zero, then provided that $a \neq 0$, the equation can be rearranged into the form $x = c$ for some number c. So we have the following fact.

> An equation of the form $ax + by = d$, where a, b and d are numbers with a and b not both zero, is the equation of a straight line.

If you're sure that an equation in x and y is the equation of a straight line, then you don't need to rearrange it into the form $y = mx + c$ before you draw the line. You can use the equation in its original form to find two points on the line, and hence draw it.

Example 4   Drawing a line from its equation

Draw the line with equation $-x + 4y = 2$.

Solution

Find two points on the line. It's often easiest to find the point with $x = 0$ and the point with $y = 0$.

Substituting $x = 0$ into the equation gives

$\qquad 4y = 2.$

Divide by 4: $\quad y = \frac{1}{2}$

So a point on the line is $(0, \frac{1}{2})$.

Substituting $y = 0$ into the equation gives

$\qquad -x = 2.$

Multiply by -1: $\quad x = -2.$

So a point on the line is $(-2, 0)$.

The line is shown below.

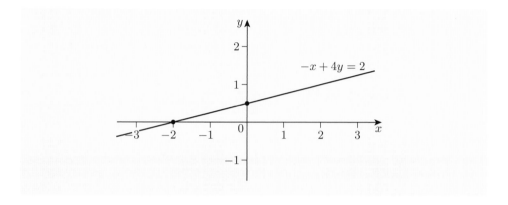

Here's a similar example for you to try.

Activity 9 *Drawing a line from its equation*

Draw the line with equation $4x - 3y = -6$.

In this section you have learned a method for rearranging equations. It was explained that although this method can be used for many equations, an improved method is needed to allow you to deal with a wider variety of equations. The next section introduces a new technique that is needed for this method.

2 Common factors

The new technique that you need for rearranging equations is called *taking out common factors*, and is the reverse of multiplying out brackets. For example, if you have the expression $x^2 + x$, then you can use the technique to write it as $x(x + 1)$.

The technique of taking out common factors is useful not only for rearranging equations, but in many other situations where algebra is used. In this section you'll learn about this technique and you'll see how you can use the skill of rearranging equations to find the answers to some practical problems.

2.1 Finding common factors

The way to reverse the process of multiplying out brackets is to consider the *factors* of the terms in the expression. A factor of a term is similar to a factor of an integer, which was discussed in Unit 3.

Remember that a positive integer that divides a given integer exactly is called a *factor* of that integer. For example, 4 and 5 are both factors of 20 because

$$20 = 4 \times 5.$$

A similar idea applies to terms. If a term can be written in the form

something $\times$ something,

then both 'somethings' are **factors** of the term.

For example, consider the term a^2b. We can write

$$a^2b = a \times ab,$$

so a and ab are factors of a^2b. Similarly,

$$a^2b = a^2 \times b \quad \text{and} \quad a^2b = 1 \times a^2b,$$

so a^2, b, 1 and a^2b are also factors of a^2b.

Example 5 *Checking a factor*

Show that $3xy$ is a factor of $3xy^3$, by writing $3xy^3$ in the form

$3xy \times$ something.

Solution

$$3xy^3 = 3xy \times y^2$$

Activity 10 *Checking factors*

(a) Write pqr in the form $q \times$ something.

(b) Write A^7 in the form $A^4 \times$ something.

(c) Write $4f^3$ in the form $2f \times$ something.

(d) Write p^3q^5 in the form $p^2q^2 \times$ something.

(e) Write $6x^5y^8$ in the form $2x^2y \times$ something.

Remember also from Unit 3 that if a positive integer is a factor of *each* of several integers, then it is a *common factor* of those integers. For example, 2 is a common factor of 8, 12 and 20, because

$$8 = 2 \times 4, \quad 12 = 2 \times 6 \quad \text{and} \quad 20 = 2 \times 10.$$

Again, a similar idea applies to terms. If something is a factor of *each* of several terms, then it is a **common factor** of those terms. For example, a is a common factor of

$$a^2b \quad \text{and} \quad abc,$$

because

$$a^2b = a \times ab \quad \text{and} \quad abc = a \times bc.$$

Example 6 *Checking a common factor*

Show that pq is a common factor of pq^2, $3p^2q^2$ and pq.

Solution

Write each term in the form $pq \times$ something.

$$pq^2 = pq \times q, \quad 3p^2q^2 = pq \times 3pq \quad \text{and} \quad pq = pq \times 1.$$

So pq is a common factor of the three terms.

Activity 11 *Checking common factors*

(a) Show that z is a common factor of $2z$ and z^2.

(b) Show that p^2 is a common factor of p^2q^2 and p^2.

(c) Show that $2AB$ is a common factor of $2A^2B^2$, $4A^2B$ and $8AB$.

In Unit 3 you saw that a collection of integers can have several common factors, and the largest of them is called the *highest* common factor. For example, the common factors of 8, 12 and 20 are 1, 2 and 4, and the highest common factor is 4.

Again, this idea also applies to terms: you can find the highest common factor of several terms. For example, consider again the terms

$$a^2b \quad \text{and} \quad abc.$$

You have seen that one common factor of these terms is a, because

$$a^2b = a \times ab \quad \text{and} \quad abc = a \times bc.$$

Another common factor is ab, because

$$a^2b = ab \times a \quad \text{and} \quad abc = ab \times c.$$

The common factor ab is a *higher* common factor than a, as it is a multiplied by another factor. In fact, ab is the **highest common factor** of the two terms, since you cannot multiply ab by any other letters or integers (except 1) and still get a common factor of the two terms.

The next example shows you how to find the highest common factor of two terms.

Tutorial clip

Example 7 *Finding a highest common factor*

Find the highest common factor of the terms

$$6ab^7c^2 \quad \text{and} \quad 9a^2b^5,$$

and write each term in the form

highest common factor $\times$ something.

Solution

First, consider the coefficients. The largest integer that divides both 6 and 9 exactly is 3.

3 is the highest common factor of 6 and 9.

Next, consider the powers of a. The largest power of a that divides both a and a^2 exactly is a.

Then consider the powers of b. The largest power of b that divides both b^7 and b^5 exactly is b^5.

Finally, consider the powers of c. The second term doesn't contain c at all.

So, the highest common factor of the two terms is

$$3ab^5.$$

The terms can be written as

$$6ab^7c^2 = 3ab^5 \times 2b^2c^2 \quad \text{and} \quad 9a^2b^5 = 3ab^5 \times 3a.$$

Activity 12   *Finding highest common factors*

In each of the following parts, find the highest common factor of the terms and write each term in the form

highest common factor $\times$ something.

(a) $2ab^2$ and $4ab$ (b) $3xy$ and $6y$

(c) $4p^3$, $9p^2$ and $2p^5$ (d) $10r$ and $15s$

2.2   Taking out common factors

Consider the expression

$$c^2d + cef.$$

The two terms in this expression, c^2d and cef, have c as a common factor. So the expression can be written as

$$c \times cd + c \times ef.$$

From your work on multiplying out brackets, you know that this is the same as

$$c(cd + ef).$$

You can now see how to reverse the process of multiplying out brackets. First, you find a common factor of the terms, and write each term in the form

common factor $\times$ something.

Then you write the common factor at the front of a pair of brackets, and inside the brackets you write what is left of each term (the 'something'). This is called taking out a common factor, or **factorising** the expression.

Tutorial clip

Example 8   *Taking out a common factor*

Factorise the expression $3rs^3 + rs$.

Solution

A common factor of the terms is rs.

$$3rs^3 + rs = rs \times 3s^2 + rs \times 1$$
$$= rs(3s^2 + 1)$$

You can take out any common factor of the terms in an expression, but it is usually best to take out the highest common factor. Do this in the next activity. Remember that you can always check a factorisation by multiplying out the brackets and checking that the expression that you get is the same as the one you factorised.

Activity 13   *Taking out common factors*

Factorise the following expressions.

(a) $ab + a^2$ (b) $x^3 y + yz$ (c) $2w^2 + w^3$ (d) $2z + 6z^4$

Expressions containing minus signs can be factorised in the same way.

Example 9   *Factorising an expression containing minus signs*

 Tutorial clip

Factorise the expression $3m^3 - 6m^2 + 3m^4$.

Solution

The highest common factor of the terms is $3m^2$.

$$3m^3 - 6m^2 + 3m^4 = 3m^2 \times m - 3m^2 \times 2 + 3m^2 \times m^2$$
$$= 3m^2(m - 2 + m^2)$$

Activity 14   *Factorising expressions containing minus signs*

Factorise the following expressions.

(a) $2ab + 2b - 6b^2$ (b) $A^5 - A^4$

As you get used to taking out common factors, you'll probably find that you can skip the step of writing each term in the form

common factor $\times$ something,

and just follow the shorter strategy below.

Strategy   *To take out a common factor from an expression*

1. Find a common factor of the terms (normally the highest common factor).

2. Write the common factor in front of a pair of brackets.

3. Write what's left of each term inside the brackets.

Tutorial clip

Example 10 *Factorising efficiently*

Factorise the expression $-8X^2 + 2X + 2XY$.

Solution

The highest common factor is $2X$.

$$-8X^2 + 2X + 2XY = 2X(-4X + 1 + Y)$$

When you use the shorter strategy above, remember that if the common factor that you're taking out is the same as one of the terms, then 'what's left' of the term is 1. In Example 10, taking the factor $2X$ out of the term $2X$ left 1.

Try the shorter strategy in the following activity.

Activity 15 *Factorising efficiently*

Factorise the following expressions.

(a) $ab - 9bc$ (b) $x^2 - x^5 + 2x^3$ (c) $-2rs + 4r^2s^2$ (d) $x\sqrt{y} - \sqrt{y}$

Once you have factorised an expression, you should check that you have taken out the *highest* common factor. To do this, check whether the terms inside the brackets have a common factor. If they do, take it out as well.

For example, suppose that you have carried out the following factorisation:

$$de^2 - d^2e^2 + de^3 = de(e - de + e^2).$$

The terms inside the brackets have the common factor e, so you did not take out the highest common factor. Your working would continue as follows.

$$= de \times e(1 - d + e)$$
$$= de^2(1 - d + e).$$

Now the terms inside the brackets have nothing in common, so de^2 is the highest common factor that can be taken out.

Many expressions cannot be factorised at all. For example, the terms in the expression

$$2de + 3ef + 4fd$$

have no common factor that can be usefully taken out.

Activity 16 *Taking out more common factors*

Factorise the following expressions, where possible.

(a) $12u + 6u^3 - 9u^2$ (b) $5r^2 - 10$

(c) $3fg - 2gh + 6fh$ (d) $-8ABC - 4AB^2 + 2AB$

If the coefficients of the terms of an expression are not integers, then you can often still factorise the expression.

Example 11   *Working with non-integer coefficients*

Factorise the following expressions.

(a) $0.2a - 0.8a^2$ (b) $\frac{1}{2} - \frac{3}{2}q$

Solution

(a) $0.2a - 0.8a^2 = 0.2a(1 - 4a)$

(b) $\frac{1}{2} - \frac{3}{2}q = \frac{1}{2}(1 - 3q)$

Activity 17   *Working with non-integer coefficients*

Factorise the following expressions.

(a) $0.3m^2 - 0.6m + 0.9$ (b) $\frac{1}{2}x - \frac{1}{2}x^2$

Earlier in the module you saw how to multiply out brackets with a minus sign in front. You just change the sign of each term in the brackets. For example,

$$-(a + 2b - 2c - d) = -a - 2b + 2c + d. \tag{4}$$

Sometimes it's useful to carry out the reverse of this process: to start with an expression without brackets and rewrite it so that it has a minus sign in front of brackets.

For example, you could start with the expression on the right-hand side of equation (4) and rewrite it as the expression on the left-hand side. As you can see, to do this you just have to change the sign of each term in the brackets. In general, remember the following.

> **To take a minus sign outside brackets**
>
> Change the sign of each term in the brackets.

Taking a minus sign outside brackets is the same as taking out a factor of -1.

For example,

$$-1 - x - x^2 + x^3 = -(1 + x + x^2 - x^3).$$

If you want to factorise an expression, and all or most of the terms have minus signs, then it's usually best to take out a minus sign as well as any other common factors. In the next example first a minus sign is taken out, and then a common factor. As you get more used to taking out common factors, you should find that you can do both these things in one step.

Example 12   *Taking out a minus sign*

Factorise the expression $-a - ab + a^2 - a^3$.

Solution

First take out a minus sign, then take out the common factor a.

$$-a - ab + a^2 - a^3 = -(a + ab - a^2 + a^3)$$
$$= -a(1 + b - a + a^2)$$

Activity 18 *Taking out minus signs*

For each of the following expressions, take out a minus sign and factorise the expression if possible.

(a) $-2u^2 - 2u^3 - 4u^4$ (b) $-1 - a + a^2$ (c) $pq - p^2q - q^2p - p^2q^2$

> When you're factorising expressions, remember that you can always check your answer. Just multiply out the brackets again and check that you get the original expression. A check is particularly useful when you've taken out a minus sign.

2.3 An improved strategy for rearranging equations

Now that you've learned how to take out common factors, you're ready to learn how to rearrange a wider variety of equations. Here is an example of an equation for which taking out common factors is useful:

$$5x = 2z + xy. \tag{5}$$

Suppose that you want to make x the subject of this equation. You can't do this by dividing each side by 5, because although that would give x by itself on the left-hand side, there would still be another occurrence of x on the right-hand side. Remember from Unit 2 what it means for a variable to be the subject of an equation – the definition can be expressed as follows.

The reason for this definition is that an equation with a subject should be of a form that allows you to substitute in for the variables other than the subject, and hence work out the value of the subject, without having to solve an equation.

> A subject of an equation is a variable that appears by itself on one side, and not at all on the other side.

Let's think about making x the subject of equation (5) by applying the strategy that you saw in Subsection 1.1, on page 128. The equation has no fractions or brackets, so the first thing to do is to make sure that all the terms containing x are on one side, and all the other terms are on the other side. You can do this by subtracting the term xy from each side, which gives

$$5x - xy = 2z.$$

In this equation, all the terms containing x are on the left, and all the other terms are on the right. According to the strategy, the next step is to divide both sides by the expression that multiplies x. But there isn't a single expression multiplying x, because x appears *twice* on the left-hand side.

You can solve this problem by taking out x as a common factor on the left-hand side. This gives

$$x(5 - y) = 2z.$$

Now there is an expression multiplying x, namely $5 - y$, and you can divide both sides by this expression to give

$$x = \frac{2z}{5 - y},$$

which is an equation with x as its subject.

(Because this equation was obtained by dividing by $5 - y$, it's not valid when $5 - y = 0$; that is, when $y = 5$. But it can be used for all other values of y.)

Here is the strategy from Subsection 1.1, amended to take account of the fact that you might need an extra step in which you take out a common factor.

Strategy *To make a variable the subject of an equation*

Carry out a sequence of steps. In each step, do one of the following:

- do the same thing to both sides
- simplify one side or both sides
- swap the sides.

Aim to do the following, in order.

1. Clear any fractions and multiply out any brackets. To clear fractions, multiply both sides by a suitable expression.

2. Add or subtract terms on both sides to get all terms containing the required subject on one side, and all the other terms on the other side.

3. If more than one term contains the required subject, then take it out as a common factor. This gives an equation of the form

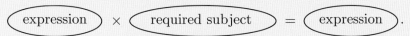

$$\boxed{\text{expression}} \times \boxed{\text{required subject}} = \boxed{\text{expression}}.$$

4. Divide both sides by the expression that multiplies the required subject.

When you use this improved strategy, you need to be especially careful when carrying out step 2. In this step it's essential to make sure that you get *all* the terms containing the required subject on one side, and *all* the terms not containing the required subject on the other side. Check carefully that you have done this before moving on to step 3. Here's an example.

Example 13 *Making a variable the subject of an equation*

 Tutorial clip

Make c the subject of the equation $2c - a = bc + 1$.

Solution

Use the strategy above.

The equation is: $2c - a = bc + 1$

There are no fractions or brackets, so step 1 isn't needed. Move on to step 2. The term $2c$ on the left and the term bc on the right both contain the required subject, c, so first get both of these terms on the left.

Subtract bc: $2c - a - bc = 1$

The term $-a$ on the left doesn't contain the required subject, c, so get it on the right.

Add a: $2c - bc = a + 1$

💭 Check that all the terms that contain the required subject, c, are on the left, and all the terms that don't contain the required subject are on the right. They are, so step 2 has been completed. Move on to step 3: take out the required subject as a common factor. 💭

Take out c as a common factor: $c(2 - b) = a + 1$

💭 Finally, do step 4: divide by the expression that multiplies the required subject. 💭

Divide by $2 - b$ (assuming that $b \neq 2$): $c = \dfrac{a + 1}{2 - b}$

💭 As a check, confirm that the subject, c, appears by itself on the left-hand side, and *not at all on the right-hand side*. 💭

The next activity will give you more practice in rearranging equations. You will need to use many of the algebraic skills that you have learned so far. Follow the strategy carefully!

Activity 19 *Making a variable the subject of an equation*

(a) Make h the subject of the equation $gh = g + h$.

(b) Make y the subject of the equation $x = \dfrac{x - y}{y}$.

(c) Make s the subject of the equation $r = \dfrac{s}{r} + 2s$.

(d) Make p the subject of the equation $2p + q = r(p + q)$.

In the next two activities you're asked to use the skills that you have learned in this section, together with skills that you learned earlier in the module, to find the answers to some practical problems.

Activity 20 *How many partygoers?*

A club is organising a party. It costs £100 to hire the venue, and £10 per person for refreshments. Five special guests will not be asked to contribute to the cost, but each other partygoer will be asked to pay an equal share of the total cost of the party.

(a) Find a formula for p, where £p is the amount paid by each paying partygoer if there are n partygoers altogether (including the special guests).

(b) Make n the subject of the formula found in part (a).

(c) Use the formula found in part (b) to find the number of partygoers who must attend if the cost for each paying partygoer is to be £12.50.

Activity 21 *How many game sales?*

A company proposes to manufacture a particular type of electronic game. There will be a fixed cost of £f to set up the production line. Thereafter each game will cost another $£c$ to manufacture, and will be sold for $£s$. Let the number of games manufactured be n.

(a) Find an expression for the total cost in $£$ of manufacturing the n games.

(b) Find an expression for the total selling price in $£$ of the n games.

(c) Use your answers to parts (a) and (b) to find a formula for p, where $£p$ is the profit made from selling n games.

(d) Make n the subject of the formula found in part (c).

(e) Use the formula from part (d) to find the number of games that must be made and sold to make a profit of $£20\,000$, if the fixed cost is $£10\,000$, the additional manufacturing cost of each game is $£15$ and the selling price of each game is $£40$.

In this section you have learned how to take out common factors, and you have used this technique to help you to rearrange equations. In the next section you'll return to the topic of *solving* equations – that is, finding the values of the unknowns in them.

3 Simultaneous linear equations

In Unit 5 you saw some situations where it was helpful to solve linear equations in one unknown, and you learned how to solve equations of this type. You'll now extend this work by learning how to solve *pairs* of linear equations, in *two* unknowns, where both equations hold at the same time. These are called **simultaneous linear equations**. You will learn algebraic and graphical methods of solving equations of this type. The algebraic methods involve the skills for rearranging equations that you have met in this unit.

We begin with an example of a situation that leads to simultaneous linear equations. You'll see some more examples of such situations later in the section.

3.1 A problem involving simultaneous equations

Suppose that a group of friends is planning to travel from one town to another town some distance away, as part of a holiday trip. One of the group, Fred, is a keen cyclist, and wants to make the trip on his bicycle. The rest of the group will travel in a car. Fred plans to set off at 10 am, and expects to be able to travel at a speed of about 30 km/h, whereas the rest of the group plan to set off an hour and a half later, at 11.30 am, and expect to be able to travel at a speed of about 90 km/h. Fred and the car will take the same route. The whole group want to meet for a picnic break, so they want to work out where and when the car will catch up with Fred.

You can tackle this problem by setting up a simple model for the progress of Fred and the car. Although in practice both Fred and the car will have to slow down and speed up according to the traffic conditions, for the purpose of the model let's assume that they travel at *constant speeds* of 30 km/h and 90 km/h, respectively.

You saw in Unit 2 that if the speed of a vehicle is constant, then its distance, speed and time are related by the formula

distance = speed × time.

So if we use t to represent the time in hours since Fred set off, and d to represent the distance in kilometres from the starting point at that time, then d and t are related by the formula

$d = 30t$.

So you can draw a graph of Fred's progress by putting the time t and the distance d on the horizontal and vertical axes, respectively, and plotting the line with equation $d = 30t$. This is the straight line through the origin with gradient 30, as shown in Figure 4.

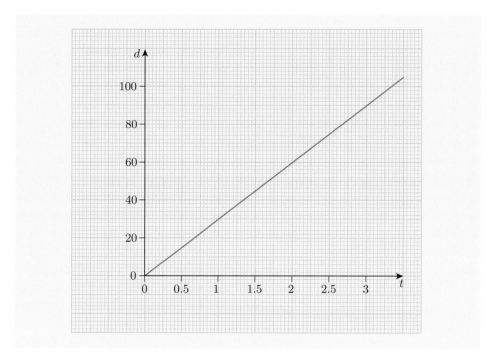

Figure 4   A graph showing the progress of the bicycle

A graph of distance against time, like that in Figure 4, is known as a distance–time graph. From the graph in Figure 4 you can read off how far Fred has travelled after any given time – for example, after 2 hours he has travelled about 60 km.

One way to try to find when and where the car will catch up with the bicycle is to draw the graph representing the progress of the car on the *same axes* as the graph of the bicycle. So we need to add the car's graph to the axes in Figure 4. Now if the variable t represented the time *since the car set off*, then the car's graph would be the straight line through the origin with gradient 90, but in fact t represents the time since *Fred* set off, which is $1\frac{1}{2}$ hours earlier, so the car's graph is shifted along the time axis by $1\frac{1}{2}$ hours (to the right).

To see why a bit more clearly, let's use the formula

distance = speed × time

again. The car sets off 1.5 hours later than Fred, and at that time it has been travelling for 0 hours. Similarly, 2 hours after Fred set off, the car has been travelling for 0.5 hours; 2.5 hours after Fred set off, the car has been travelling for 1 hour; and so on. In general, at time t the car has been travelling for $t - 1.5$ hours. So, since the car travels at $90\,\text{km/h}$, its equation is

$$d = 90(t - 1.5),$$

which is the same as

$$d = 90t - 135.$$

This is the equation of the straight line through the point $(1.5, 0)$ with gradient 90.

Figure 5 shows Fred's graph and the car's graph on the same axes.

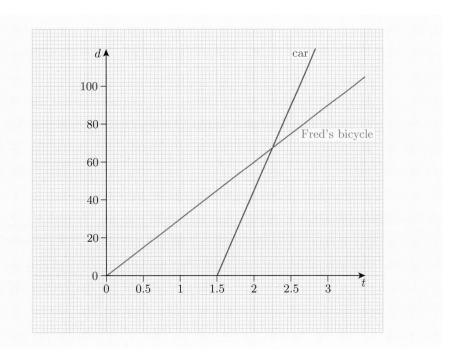

Figure 5   Graphs showing the progress of the bicycle and the car

From the distance–time graph in Figure 5 you can read off how far both Fred's bicycle and the car have travelled after any given time since Fred set off. For example, after 2 hours Fred and the car have travelled about $60\,\text{km}$ and $45\,\text{km}$, respectively, from the starting point.

Activity 22   *Using the graphs for the bicycle and the car*

Use Figure 5 to answer the following questions.

(a) Roughly how many hours and minutes after Fred sets off will the car catch up with him? What time will this be?

(b) At roughly what distance from the starting point will this happen?

In Activity 22 you used a graph to find the approximate time and distance at which the car will catch up with the bicycle. In doing this you assumed that the bicycle and the car were travelling at constant speeds, which is unlikely to happen in practice. However, an approximate answer is perfectly adequate for this situation – you just need to work out roughly when the car will catch up with the bicycle and don't need a time to the nearest second or a distance to the nearest metre!

An alternative way to find the time and distance when the car catches up is to use algebra to solve the equations directly, without using a graph. We have arrived at one of the crucial ideas in this unit: that of simultaneous linear equations and the techniques available for solving them algebraically. One advantage of using algebra is that you can find more accurate values for the solutions than you can from a graph. This is important in some situations, as you will see in some examples later in the unit.

There is evidence that the Babylonians as early as 1750 BC dealt with problems that we would nowadays consider as simultaneous equations.

Every point on the bicycle's line represents a time t and a distance d such that $d = 30t$, and every point on the car's line represents a time t and a distance d such that $d = 90t - 135$.

When the car catches up with the bicycle, they are the same distance d from the starting point at the same time t; so the equations describing the progress of the bicycle and the car are both correct for those values of t and d. That is, the values of t and d that we're looking for are the values such that $d = 30t$ *and* $d = 90t - 135$. If we can find such values, that simultaneously **satisfy** the two equations, then we have solved our problem. Mathematically, the problem is usually expressed as follows:

Solve the simultaneous equations

$$d = 30t, \tag{6}$$
$$d = 90t - 135. \tag{7}$$

The values of t and d that simultaneously satisfy both equations are together called the **solution** of the simultaneous equations, and the process of finding the solution is called **solving** the simultaneous equations. Equations (6) and (7) are called *linear* equations because each term in them is either a constant term or a number times one of the unknowns, d and t.

The problem has now been expressed in terms of two linear equations and two unknowns, d and t. Generally speaking, if there are the same number of linear equations as unknowns, then this gives you enough information to solve the problem (though there are exceptions, as you will see).

You have already seen in Unit 5 how to find the solution of *one* linear equation involving *one* unknown. The next step may be rather surprising if you haven't encountered simultaneous equations before; but it's possible to use the information from equations (6) and (7) to obtain a linear equation involving only one unknown.

The crucial thing to notice is that the left-hand sides of equations (6) and (7) are equal (they are both simply d). So the right-hand sides, being each equal to d, must be equal to each other! This gives us the equation

$$30t = 90t - 135. \tag{8}$$

Since d does not appear in this equation, we say that we have **eliminated** the unknown d from equations (6) and (7).

Activity 23   *Finding the time and distance algebraically*

(a) Solve equation (8); that is, find the value of t.

(b) Substitute the value of t into equation (6), and hence find the value of d.

(c) Hence write down the time when the car will catch up with the bicycle, and the distance from the starting point at this time.

(d) Check your answer, by checking that the LHS and RHS of equation (6) are equal when you substitute in the values of t and d that you have found, and that the LHS and RHS of equation (7) are also equal when you substitute in these values of t and d.

To reinforce your understanding of these processes (reducing two equations to one, and checking that your solution is correct), try the next activity.

Activity 24 *Solving simultaneous equations*

Solve the following pair of simultaneous equations:

$$y = 2x - 3,$$
$$y = 5x + 9.$$

So if you have to solve two simultaneous equations, and each of the equations is a formula for one of the unknowns in terms of the other (with the *same* unknown being the subject of the formula in each case), then solving them is likely to be reasonably straightforward, as the pair can be reduced to a single equation.

Or is it so straightforward? Consider again the journey of the group of friends. Suppose that instead of travelling by bicycle, Fred travels in another car. He sets off at the same time as before, 10 am, but travels at a steady 90 km/h. Then the lines representing Fred's progress and that of the original car are *parallel*, as shown in Figure 6.

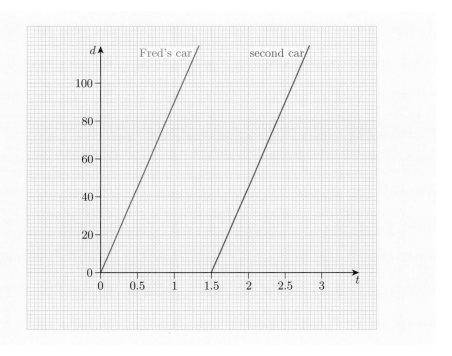

Figure 6 Graphs showing the progress of the two cars

As a matter of common sense, the second car will never catch up with Fred now (at least, not until he stops!); but there are still two simultaneous equations in two unknowns, so how does the mathematics sort this out?

The two equations are now

$$d = 90t, \tag{9}$$
$$d = 90t - 135. \tag{10}$$

Again, the two right-hand sides are equal, which gives the equation

$$90t = 90t - 135.$$

Subtracting $90t$ from each side of this equation gives the result

$$0 = -135.$$

This statement is mathematical nonsense! It says that two obviously unequal numbers are equal. Since this nonsense came from the assumption that there *is* a solution to equations (9) and (10), the conclusion that has to be drawn is that this pair of equations *has no solution*; that is, there is *no* value of t that satisfies both equations. In other words, equations (9) and (10) can't both be true at once.

So, there's a restriction on when two simultaneous equations can be solved.

How to tell whether simultaneous equations have a solution

Suppose that two simultaneous equations (in the unknowns x and y) are written in the form

These equations are the equations of straight lines with gradients a and c, respectively.

$$y = ax + b,$$
$$y = cx + d.$$

- If the constants a and c are *not equal*, then the lines representing the equations are not parallel, so the equations have one solution.

- If the constants a and c are *equal*, then the lines representing the equations are parallel, so the equations do *not* have a solution. (There is an exception to this: if the constants b and d are also equal, then the two equations are the same, so there are infinitely many solutions.)

Activity 25 *Recognising how many solutions there are*

Remember that each single solution of a pair of simultaneous equations is a *pair* of values – one value for each of the two unknowns.

State how many solutions each of the following pairs of simultaneous equations has. You are not asked to *find* any solutions.

(a) $y = -2x + 5$
   $\quad y = -2x - 1$

(b) $y = -2x + 5$
   $\quad y = 5 - 2x$

(c) $y = -2x + 5$
   $\quad y = 3x - 1$

(You might like to use Graphplotter to check your answers – you can use the 'Two graphs' tab to plot two lines on the same axes.)

In the rest of this section you'll learn how to solve pairs of simultaneous linear equations, even when they don't have the simple form of the pairs that you have seen so far. There are two methods that you can use to do this – *substitution* and *elimination*. In both methods you first find the value of one of the unknowns, because once you have such a value you can substitute it into one of the equations to find the value of the other unknown. In each method you use a different technique to find the value of the first unknown.

3.2 Substitution method for simultaneous equations

This subsection is about the substitution method for solving simultaneous linear equations. Here's an example to illustrate the idea. In this example *just one* of the equations is a formula for one of the unknowns in terms of the other.

Tutorial clip

Example 14   *Solving simultaneous equations by substitution*

Solve the simultaneous equations

$$9A - 2B = 12, \tag{11}$$
$$B = 5A - 14. \tag{12}$$

Solution

🗫 The second equation tells you that B is equal to $5A - 14$. So in the first equation, replace B by $5A - 14$. 🗩

Using equation (12) to substitute for B in equation (11) gives

$$9A - 2(5A - 14) = 12.$$

We now solve this equation.

$$9A - 2(5A - 14) = 12$$
$$9A - 10A + 28 = 12$$
$$-A + 28 = 12$$
$$-A = -16$$
$$A = 16$$

🗫 Now substitute the value of A into either of the two equations to find the value of B. Equation (12) gives the easier calculation. 🗩

Substituting $A = 16$ into equation (12) gives

$$B = 5 \times 16 - 14 = 80 - 14 = 66.$$

So the solution is

$$A = 16, \ B = 66.$$

(Check: Substituting $A = 16$, $B = 66$ into equation (11) gives

$$\text{LHS} = 9A - 2B = 9 \times 16 - 2 \times 66 = 144 - 132 = 12 = \text{RHS.})$$

🗫 There is no need to check equation (12) by substituting into it because this calculation has already been done when finding the value of B. 🗩

There is a similar activity for you to try overleaf. When you write out your answer to this activity, and whenever you solve a pair of simultaneous equations, it's helpful to begin by writing down the two equations and labelling them with numbers in brackets, as you've seen in Example 14 and earlier. Then you can use these labels to refer to the equations, to help make your working clear and concise. It's often useful to label later equations in your working too. All the equations in this unit are numbered consecutively, but when you are assigning your own labels it's fine to use the numbers (1), (2), (3), and so on, each time.

Another thing to notice about Example 14 is that the solution has been written concisely by omitting the instructions 'Multiply out the brackets', 'Subtract 28', and so on, for solving the single linear equation in the unknown A. Once you feel confident about solving linear equations, feel free to do this too!

Activity 26   *Solving simultaneous equations by substitution*

Solve the simultaneous equations

$$x = 2y - 7,$$
$$3x - y = -6.$$

You now have the means at your disposal to deal with *any* pair of simultaneous linear equations in two unknowns. Even if neither of the equations is a formula for one of the unknowns in terms of the other, you can just take one of the equations and rearrange it to give such a formula! Then you can proceed as in Example 14 and Activity 26. Here's an example.

Tutorial clip

Example 15   *Solving more simultaneous equations by substitution*

Solve the simultaneous equations

$$2x + 4y = 8, \tag{13}$$
$$-3x + 5y = -1 \tag{14}$$

by the substitution method.

Solution

💭 Choose one of the equations and rearrange it to make one of the unknowns the subject. 💭

We make x the subject of equation (13).

$$2x + 4y = 8$$
$$2x = 8 - 4y$$
$$x = \frac{8 - 4y}{2}$$
$$x = \frac{8}{2} - \frac{4y}{2}$$
$$x = 4 - 2y \tag{15}$$

💭 Use this formula to substitute for x in the *other* equation. 💭

Substituting for x in equation (14) gives

$$-3(4 - 2y) + 5y = -1.$$

We now solve this equation.

$$-3(4 - 2y) + 5y = -1$$
$$-12 + 6y + 5y = -1$$
$$-12 + 11y = -1$$
$$11y = 11$$
$$y = 1$$

✎ Substitute this value for y into one of the equations in x and y to find the value of x. Equation (15) gives the easiest calculation. 💬

Substituting $y = 1$ into equation (15) gives

$$x = 4 - 2 \times 1 = 4 - 2 = 2.$$

So the solution is

$$x = 2, \ y = 1.$$

(Check: Substituting $x = 2$, $y = 1$ into equation (13) gives

$$\text{LHS} = 2 \times 2 + 4 \times 1 = 8 = \text{RHS}.$$

Substituting the same values into equation (14) gives

$$\text{LHS} = -3 \times 2 + 5 \times 1 = -1 = \text{RHS}.)$$

One thing worth noticing about the simultaneous equations in Example 15 is that all the terms in equation (13) have a common factor of 2. So both sides of this equation can be divided by 2 to give an equivalent but slightly simpler equation, as follows:

The equation is: $\qquad 2x + 4y = 8$

Divide by 2: $\qquad \dfrac{2x + 4y}{2} = \dfrac{8}{2}$

Expand the fraction: $\qquad \dfrac{2x}{2} + \dfrac{4y}{2} = \dfrac{8}{2}$

Simplify: $\qquad x + 2y = 4$

If this had been done before the equations were solved, then some of the working would have been slightly easier.

Notice from the working above that the effect of dividing both sides of the equation by 2 is that *each term* in the equation is divided by 2.

In fact, you can see that in general the following is true.

> Multiplying or dividing both sides of an equation by a number is the same as multiplying or dividing each term in the equation by the number.

This is known as *multiplying through* or *dividing through* by a number.

It's worth looking out for numbers that are common factors of the terms in an equation, and dividing through by them before you start working with the equation. Similarly, if an equation contains numerical fractions, then it's helpful to begin by multiplying through by a suitable integer to clear them. Doing these things can be particularly helpful when you use the elimination method for solving simultaneous equations, which you'll meet in the next subsection.

You should not divide an equation through by a *letter* that is a common factor of the terms, unless you know that the letter cannot be equal to zero.

Here's a summary of the method for solving simultaneous equations that you've seen in this subsection.

> **Strategy**   *To solve simultaneous equations: substitution method*
>
> 1. Rearrange one of the equations, if necessary, to obtain a formula for one unknown in terms of the other.
> 2. Use this formula to substitute for this unknown in the other equation.
> 3. You now have an equation in one unknown. Solve it to find the value of the unknown.
> 4. Substitute this value into an equation involving both unknowns to find the value of the other unknown.
>
> (Check: Confirm that the two values satisfy the original equations.)

Try this strategy for yourself in the next activity.

Activity 27   *Solving more simultaneous equations by substitution*

Use the substitution method to solve the following pairs of simultaneous equations.

(a) $A - 2B = -3$ (b) $3S + T = 3$
      $2A + 3B = 8$ $7S + 2T = 8$

3.3   Elimination method for simultaneous equations

The method of Subsection 3.2 isn't always the simplest method. There's another method that you can use, and the idea behind it is as follows.

Suppose that you have a pair of simultaneous equations. Since the left-hand side of each equation is equal to its right-hand side, what you get by adding the two left-hand sides must be equal to what you get by adding the two right-hand sides.

For example, consider the following pair of simultaneous equations, which were solved earlier, in Example 15.

$$2x + 4y = 8,$$
$$-3x + 5y = -1.$$

If you add the left-hand sides and add the right-hand sides, then you obtain the equation

$$(2 - 3)x + (4 + 5)y = 8 - 1,$$

which simplifies to

$$-x + 9y = 7.$$

This equation must also hold for the two unknowns. We say that we have *added the two original equations*.

Adding these particular equations isn't very helpful! But adding other pairs of equations *can* be helpful, as you'll see in the next example.

Example 16   *Solving simultaneous equations by addition*

Tutorial clip

Solve the simultaneous equations

$$3A + 2B = 24, \tag{16}$$
$$3A - 2B = 36. \tag{17}$$

Solution

Notice that if you add the two equations, then the unknown B will be eliminated.

Adding equations (16) and (17) gives

$$(3 + 3)A + (2 - 2)B = 24 + 36$$
$$6A = 60$$
$$A = 10.$$

Substituting $A = 10$ into equation (16) gives

$$3 \times 10 + 2B = 24$$
$$30 + 2B = 24$$
$$2B = -6$$
$$B = -3.$$

So the solution is $A = 10$, $B = -3$.

(Check: Substituting $A = 10$, $B = -3$ into equation (16) gives

$$\text{LHS} = 3 \times 10 + 2 \times (-3) = 30 - 6 = 24 = \text{RHS}.$$

Substituting the same values into equation (17) gives

$$\text{LHS} = 3 \times 10 - 2 \times (-3) = 30 + 6 = 36 = \text{RHS}.)$$

You can also *subtract* two simultaneous equations. The reasoning behind this is the same: since the left-hand side of each equation is equal to its right-hand side, what you get by subtracting the two left-hand sides must be equal to what you get by subtracting the two right-hand sides.

In Example 16, the unknown B was eliminated by *adding* the two equations. This was possible because the coefficients of B in these equations have *the same value but with opposite signs*.

An alternative way to solve the simultaneous equations in Example 16 is to eliminate the other unknown, A, by *subtracting* the two equations. This is possible because the coefficients of A have *the same value with the same sign*. This way of solving the equations is shown in the next example.

Example 17   *Solving simultaneous equations by subtraction*

Solve the simultaneous equations

$$3A + 2B = 24, \tag{18}$$
$$3A - 2B = 36. \tag{19}$$

Solution

💭 If you subtract one equation from the other, then the unknown A will be eliminated. 💭

Subtracting equation (19) from (18) gives

$$(3 - 3)A + (2 - (-2))B = 24 - 36$$
$$4B = -12$$
$$B = -3.$$

Substituting $B = -3$ into equation (18) gives

$$3A + 2 \times (-3) = 24$$
$$3A - 6 = 24$$
$$3A = 30$$
$$A = 10.$$

So the solution is $A = 10$, $B = -3$.

(This was checked in Example 16.)

The next activity gives you examples of each of the possibilities of adding and subtracting.

Activity 28   *Solving simultaneous equations by addition and by subtraction*

Use addition or subtraction to solve the following pairs of simultaneous equations.

(a) $4x - 5y = 7$ (b) $5x + 4y = 23$
$-4x + 3y = -9$ $5x + 6y = 27$

The pairs of simultaneous equations in Examples 16 and 17 and Activity 28 are unusual because a coefficient can be eliminated straightforwardly by addition or by subtraction. This is not possible for most pairs of simultaneous equations, but you can still use addition or subtraction to solve the equations – you just need another step first! This is illustrated in the next example.

Tutorial clip

Example 18   *Solving simultaneous equations by elimination*

Solve the simultaneous equations

$$3x + 2y = 8, \tag{20}$$
$$-5x + 3y = -7. \tag{21}$$

Solution

💭 Here adding or subtracting the equations doesn't eliminate either x or y. However, you can make the coefficient of y the same in each equation by multiplying the first equation by 3 and the second equation by 2; then subtracting the new equations *will* eliminate y. 💭

Multiplying equation (20) by 3 and equation (21) by 2 gives

$$9x + 6y = 24, \tag{22}$$
$$-10x + 6y = -14. \tag{23}$$

Multiplying both sides of a true equation by the same number results in another true equation; you saw this in Unit 5.

💬 Now you can use subtraction. 💬

Subtracting equation (23) from equation (22) gives

$$(9 - (-10))x + (6 - 6)y = 24 - (-14)$$
$$19x = 38$$
$$x = 2.$$

Substituting $x = 2$ into equation (20) gives

$$3 \times 2 + 2y = 8$$
$$6 + 2y = 8$$
$$2y = 2$$
$$y = 1.$$

Hence the solution is $x = 2$, $y = 1$.

(Check: Substituting $x = 2$, $y = 1$ into equation (20) gives

$$\text{LHS} = 3 \times 2 + 2 \times 1 = 6 + 2 = 8 = \text{RHS}.$$

Substituting the same values into equation (21) gives

$$\text{LHS} = -5 \times 2 + 3 \times 1 = -10 + 3 = -7 = \text{RHS}.)$$

Here's a summary of the method for solving simultaneous equations that you've seen in this section.

> **Strategy** *To solve simultaneous equations: elimination method*
>
> 1. Multiply one or both of the equations by suitable numbers, if necessary, to obtain two equations that can be added or subtracted to eliminate one of the unknowns.
>
> 2. Add or subtract the equations to eliminate the unknown.
>
> 3. You now have an equation in one unknown. Solve it to find the value of the unknown.
>
> 4. Substitute this value into an equation involving both unknowns to find the value of the other unknown.
>
> (Check: Confirm that the two values satisfy the original equations.)

Try this strategy for yourself in the next activity.

Activity 29 *Solving simultaneous equations by elimination*

Solve the simultaneous equations

$$2x + 3y = 9,$$
$$3x - 4y = 5.$$

You've now seen two strategies for solving simultaneous linear equations. Next there is an activity that gives you several pairs of simultaneous equations, and you can choose whichever method you prefer to solve each pair. Substitution is probably easier when one of the coefficients is 1 or -1, since then you can express one of the unknowns in terms of the other without having to introduce fractions. Elimination is probably easier otherwise. The solutions show how to use each method for each pair of equations, so if you would like some extra practice, then you can try both methods on each pair.

Remember that the solutions to simultaneous equations aren't necessarily integers! It's perfectly possible for them to be fractions, and this happens in parts (b) and (d) of the activity.

Activity 30 *Putting it all together*

Solve the following pairs of simultaneous equations.

(a) $2X - Y = -1$ (b) $4X - 5Y = 1$
$\ 3X - Y = 1$ $\ 5X + 2Y = 4$

(c) $-2A + 5B = -2$ (d) $3P - 6Q = 3$
$\ -2A + 3B = 2$ $\ 7P - 4Q = 1$

Finally in this subsection, you may wonder if there's a straightforward way to tell whether a pair of equations is of the 'awkward' type that has either no solution or infinitely many solutions.

One way to tell is to rearrange both equations so that each is a formula for the same unknown in terms of the other unknown, and then use the facts in the box on page 148. You need to find out whether the equations represent parallel lines.

For example, consider the simultaneous equations

$$2X - Y = -1, \tag{24}$$
$$-4X + 2Y = 1. \tag{25}$$

Equation (24) can be rearranged to express Y in terms of X as follows:

$$2X - Y = -1$$
$$2X = -1 + Y$$
$$2X + 1 = Y$$
$$Y = 2X + 1.$$

Similarly, equation (25) can be rearranged to express Y in terms of X as follows:

$$-4X + 2Y = 1$$
$$2Y = 4X + 1$$
$$Y = 2X + \tfrac{1}{2}.$$

So the pair of equations is equivalent to the following pair:

$$Y = 2X + 1,$$
$$Y = 2X + \tfrac{1}{2}.$$

You can now see that the two equations represent lines with the same gradient, 2, but not the same line. So the equations don't have a solution.

Actually, if you use the substitution or elimination method to try to solve a pair of equations that doesn't have a solution, then the problem shows up very quickly by giving a nonsense result. For example, multiplying equation (24) by 2 and leaving equation (25) unchanged gives

$$4X - 2Y = -2,$$
$$-4X + 2Y = 1$$

and when you add these two equations, the result is

$$0 = -1.$$

This immediately tells you that (provided that *you* haven't made an arithmetical slip!) this pair of equations has no solution.

So far in this section, you have seen how to solve two simultaneous linear equations by either

- drawing the lines that represent the two equations on a graph and reading off the coordinates of the intersection point, or

- using algebra – the substitution method or the elimination method.

The advantage of using algebra is that if a solution exists, then you can calculate it exactly. It doesn't matter whether you use the substitution or elimination method – you can choose the method that you prefer or find easier. Remember, however, that not all simultaneous equations have exactly one solution: if the equations represent parallel lines, but not the same line, then they don't have a solution, and if they represent the same line, then they have infinitely many solutions.

3.4 Using simultaneous equations in real-life problems

In this subsection you'll see two scenarios where you can use simultaneous equations to solve real-life problems. Here's the first.

Choosing a venue

Suppose that a company wishes to hold an away weekend for staff development, and you've been asked to advise how to choose between two possible venues, the Sandmartin Hotel and the Swift Hotel.

The facilities offered at the two hotels are similar, so the most important factor to consider is the cost. Each hotel makes a charge for its conference rooms and a charge per person for accommodation, as shown in Table 1.

Table 1 Hotel charges

	Hire of conference rooms (£)	Accommodation per person (£)
Sandmartin Hotel	350	55
Swift Hotel	500	50

[handwritten annotations:] n = people   C = 350 + 55N ✓   C = 500 + 50N ✓

The Sandmartin charges less than the Swift for its conference rooms, but charges slightly more per person. So if there are only a few participants, then the Sandmartin will be less costly, whereas if many people attend, then it will be cheaper to book the Swift.

The boss of the company doesn't yet know how many participants there will be, but she would like some advice so that she can make a quick decision once she does know.

The first step in tackling this problem is to try to identify exactly what you need to do. As the number of participants increases, the cost of booking the Sandmartin will catch up with, and then overtake, the cost of booking the Swift. You need to find the number of participants where the overtaking happens, which is the number of participants for which the cost of the two hotels is the same. This number could turn out to be not an integer, but that doesn't matter: whatever it is, if the actual number of participants turns out to be less than that number, then the company boss should book the Sandmartin, whereas if it turns out to be more, then she should book the Swift.

The next step is to express what you know in terms of mathematics. You can use the information in Table 1 to find formulas for the cost of booking each hotel in terms of the number of participants. You need to choose letters to represent these two quantities, so let's use C to represent the cost in £ of the booking, and N to represent the number of participants.

Activity 31   *Finding the formulas*

Write down two formulas for C in terms of N, one for the Sandmartin Hotel and one for the Swift Hotel.

The formulas in the solution to Activity 31 are the equations of straight lines. To find the value of N for which each formula gives the same value of C, you need to find the point where the lines cross. You have seen two ways of doing this: a graphical method and an algebraic method. You are asked to use both methods in the next activity.

Graphplotter

Activity 32   *Solving the problem*

(a) Use the 'Two graphs' tab of Graphplotter to plot the graphs of the formulas for the costs of booking the two hotels, on the same axes. Graphplotter uses the letters x and y for the variables, so first you should rewrite the formulas that you found in Activity 31 with N replaced by x, and C replaced by y. Make sure that the axis scales extend far enough to show the crossing point – appropriate ranges are 0 to 60 for the x-axis and 0 to 3500 for the y-axis.

On Graphplotter you can zoom in to find coordinates more precisely, though this isn't necessary in this activity.

(b) Read off the coordinates of the crossing point of the two lines. What do these coordinates represent?

(c) Use algebra to solve the two simultaneous equations given by the formulas, and check that your answer agrees with your answer to part (b).

(d) How might you present the results found in this activity to the company boss?

In Activity 32 you used simultaneous equations to help with a choice between two options, each of which involves a fixed cost and a cost that depends on a variable quantity (the number of participants). This sort of choice crops up in many situations. For example, when you buy a mobile phone there's often an initial cost for the phone and a monthly cost for calls, texts and downloads. So the total cost of using a phone will be the initial cost plus the monthly cost times the number of months for which you use the phone, and the costs will be different for different phones and providers. Here the variable quantity is the number of months for which you use the phone. Similarly, when you are choosing which television to buy, you might consider not only the initial costs of the different models, but also the ongoing costs of the power that they consume.

The second scenario in this subsection involves an economic model.

Supply and demand

Most economic models assume that as the price of an item on the market goes up, the demand for the item decreases, because fewer people are willing to buy it. For example, you would expect fewer apples to be sold if the price is £3 per kg than if the price is £2 per kg. The simpler economic models assume that the relationship between price and demand is linear – that is, the graph of demand against price is a straight line.

It is also usually assumed that as the price of an item goes up, the supply increases, because there is a greater incentive for producers to make and sell the item. Again, the simple modelling assumption often made is that this relationship is linear.

Naturally, there are many other factors involved in the relationships between the price, demand and supply of a market item, such as seasonal factors in the case of foods, and political and ethical checks and balances to try to ensure general fairness. However, the simple linear models work reasonably well for items that are not particularly expensive and not central to people's lives.

The price at which the supply of an item is equal to its demand – that is, the price at which the suppliers are able to sell all that they have produced – is called the equilibrium price for the item. A person selling at below this price would probably be able to charge more and still sell all he could supply, so he would tend to increase his price; whereas a person selling at above this price would probably not be able to sell all that he could supply, so he would tend to decrease his price. The price would tend to move towards the equilibrium price, at which demand equals supply.

Suppose that data have been gathered on the supply and demand of Braeburn apples at various prices. Figure 8 shows the graph that results when the data points for supply against price, and for demand against price, are plotted on the same axes. Here P represents the price of the apples in pence per kg, and Q represents the quantity of apples supplied or demanded, in millions of kg. The regression lines for each of the two relationships have been drawn on the graph.

It has been postulated that the demand for some goods actually goes up as a direct result of price rises. These goods are known as *Veblen goods*, after the economist and sociologist Thorstein Veblen (1857–1929). Possible Veblen goods might be expensive wines and perfumes, which could be bought at least in part to demonstrate how wealthy the buyer is.

Figure 7 Braeburn apples

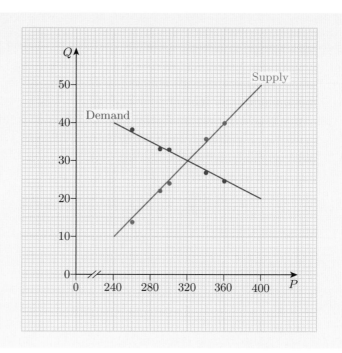

Figure 8   The supply and demand of Braeburn apples plotted against price

The equation of the regression line for the relationship between supply and price turns out to be

$$Q = \tfrac{1}{4}P - 50,$$

and the equation of the regression line for the relationship between demand and price turns out to be

$$Q = -\tfrac{1}{8}P + 70.$$

Activity 33   *Finding an equilibrium price*

In this activity you are asked to use the equations above to find the equilibrium price of Braeburn apples as follows.

(a) Multiply each of the equations

$$Q = \tfrac{1}{4}P - 50,$$
$$Q = -\tfrac{1}{8}P + 70$$

by a suitable integer to obtain two simultaneous equations that do not contain fractions.

(b) Solve the simultaneous equations that you obtained in part (a).

(c) State the equilibrium price of the apples. What is represented by the other value that you obtained as part of the solution?

In practice, an economic model like the one in Activity 33 would need to be adjusted for the effects of inflation, and other factors might need to be taken into account, as discussed earlier. The models are usually implemented using computer software, so that the calculations can be carried out automatically.

In Activity 33 you were asked to begin by multiplying the simultaneous equations by integers, to clear the fractions. As mentioned earlier, this is a useful technique to remember when you're dealing with simultaneous equations, or any other type of equations, that involve fractions.

Sometimes you can solve a practical problem by reading off an intersection point on a graph, even if you can't describe the graph using linear equations. You met an example of this in the video for Unit 2, which features a graph similar to the one shown in Figure 9. This graph shows the time that it takes to travel from Milton Keynes to Hemel Hempstead at different times of the day. One of the two curves shows the journey times for a route that uses a motorway, and the other curve shows the times for a route along main roads. By reading off the two intersection points, you can see that it is quicker to use the motorway between about 8 am and 7 pm, and quicker to use the main roads at other times.

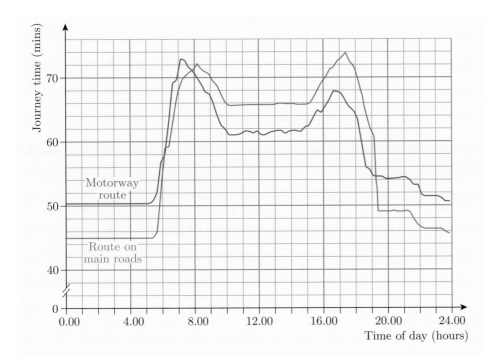

Figure 9 Journey times from Milton Keynes to Hemel Hempstead

3.5 More than two simultaneous equations

Both of the methods that you have seen for solving pairs of simultaneous equations in two unknowns involve an intermediate step of obtaining *one* equation in *one* unknown and solving that. This illustrates a very general principle, not only in mathematics, but in other branches of life.

When faced with an unfamiliar problem, see if you can turn it into a more familiar problem (so long as you know from experience that you can deal with the latter!). It's even worth turning the problem into *several* familiar problems, if that seems to be the only way forward.

So if you were faced with three equations in three unknowns, then you might expect that you could use one of the equations to reduce the other two to a pair of equations in *two* unknowns. This is indeed the case; consider, for example, the number puzzle in Figure 10 overleaf.

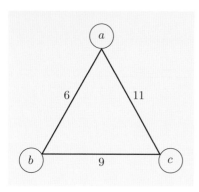

Figure 10 A number puzzle

The challenge is to replace a, b and c by three numbers in such a way that the number on each side of the triangle is the sum of the two numbers at the ends of that side. You might be able to work out the answer in your head, but using algebra definitely helps here! From the triangle, you can write down three equations in three unknowns, a, b and c:

$$a + c = 11, \tag{26}$$
$$a + b = 6, \tag{27}$$
$$b + c = 9. \tag{28}$$

If you subtract equation (27) from equation (26), you obtain

$$c - b = 5,$$

that is,

$$-b + c = 5, \tag{29}$$

You now have two equations, (28) and (29), in two unknowns, which you already know how to solve. Adding them together gives $2c = 14$, so $c = 7$. Substituting this value into equation (28) gives $b + 7 = 9$, so $b = 2$, and substituting it into equation (26) gives $a + 7 = 11$, so $a = 4$. So the puzzle is solved! This was done by reducing three equations in three unknowns to two equations in two unknowns.

It's worth knowing that being able to solve two equations in two unknowns puts you on the second step of an escalator that *in principle* allows you to deal with any number of the things!

If you continue to study mathematics, then you will probably see an efficient formalisation of this process of solving simultaneous equations in many unknowns by reducing them to equations in progressively fewer unknowns. It is known as *Gaussian elimination* after the great eighteenth-century mathematician and physicist Johann Carl Friedrich Gauss.

In practice, these days most systems of several equations in several unknowns are solved by computer. The analysis of stress patterns in bridges and buildings, for instance, often requires systems of several thousand simultaneous equations.

Figure 11 Johann Carl Friedrich Gauss (1777–1855)

4 Working with inequalities

All the examples that you have seen so far in this unit have concerned linear *equations*. Equality may not always be appropriate, though. If you need to arrive at an important interview on time, for example, then you may decide that you need to leave your house *at least* so many hours before the interview time, since you can drive on the motorway at a speed of *at most* 70 mph (if you are law-abiding). As you saw in Unit 2, facts like these can be expressed using *inequalities*.

In this section you'll see some more uses of inequalities, and how they can be manipulated in a similar way to equations.

4.1 Inequalities in one variable

In Unit 2 you saw how to express inequalities using the symbols below.

Inequality signs

$<$ is less than	$>$ is greater than
$\leq$ is less than or equal to	$\geq$ is greater than or equal to

In each of the next two activities you are asked to find an equality involving a variable, and write it down using one of the inequality signs above.

Activity 34 *Driving to an interview*

Suppose that you have to drive to an interview. It takes half an hour for you to reach the nearest motorway junction by car, and you must then drive 105 miles up the motorway. It's another quarter hour's drive from the motorway exit to where the interview takes place. Find an inequality for the length of time, t (in hours), that you must leave before the interview, assuming that you will obey the 70 mph motorway speed limit.

Since speed limits in the UK are given in miles per hour, and UK road maps normally give distances in miles, this activity uses miles rather than kilometres.

Activity 35 *Ordering CDs*

Suppose that you wish to order some CDs on the internet. You have up to £75 to spend, and the CDs are advertised at £6.50 each, with postage of £4 on an order of 15 or fewer CDs. Find an inequality concerning the number, n, of CDs that you may order.

Later in this section you'll see how to rearrange the inequality found in Activity 35 to help you work out the number of CDs that you can order.

Some of the examples that you saw in Section 2 have inequalities lurking under the surface. For instance, consider again the case of the group of friends travelling from one town to another, with Fred on his bicycle and the others in a car, which was discussed on page 143. Fred's equation, $d = 30t$, is valid only after the time $t = 0$ when he sets out, while the car's equation, $d = 90t - 135$, is valid only after the time $t = 1.5$ when *it* sets out. That is, Fred's equation is valid only when t is at least 0, and the car's equation is valid only when t is at least 1.5. These facts can be expressed as follows:

$t \geq 0$ for Fred's equation,

$t \geq 1.5$ for the car's equation.

Also, assuming that both the car and Fred stop when the car catches up, neither equation is valid after the time $t = 2.25$ when that happens. So t is at most 2.25 for each equation, and this fact can be expressed as

$t \leq 2.25$ for each equation.

To sum up, for Fred's equation the variable t can take values only between 0 and 2.25, and for the car's equation the variable t can take values only between 1.5 and 2.25. As you saw in Unit 2, these facts can be expressed as *double inequalities*:

$0 \leq t \leq 2.25$ for Fred's equation,

$1.5 \leq t \leq 2.25$ for the car's equation.

4.2 Rearranging inequalities

In Activity 35, you should have found that the number n of CDs that you could buy must satisfy the inequality $6.5n + 4 \leq 75$. If you want to know how many CDs you can buy, then you need to rearrange this inequality into the form

$$n \leq \boxed{\text{a number}}.$$

This form tells you all the numbers that satisfy the inequality. Finding all the numbers that satisfy an inequality is known as **solving** the inequality.

Let's consider how you could rearrange inequalities. Once you have learned how to do this, you'll be asked to rearrange the CD inequality into the form above.

You've already learned how to rearrange *equations*: as you know, you can do any of the following things to a correct equation to obtain another correct equation:

- do the same thing to both sides
- simplify one or both sides
- swap the sides.

The things that you can do to both sides are: adding a number, subtracting a number, multiplying by a number and dividing by a non-zero number.

An inequality can be rearranged in much the same way; but there are differences.

In the first place, if you swap the sides of an inequality, then the sense of the inequality sign reverses. That is, $<$ becomes $>$, and $>$ becomes $<$. Similarly, $\leq$ becomes $\geq$, and $\geq$ becomes $\leq$. Of course, this is to be expected: since $1 < 2$, it follows automatically that $2 > 1$.

Simplifying one or both sides of an inequality is just as valid as simplifying one or both sides of an equation; for example, $4 > 1 + 2$ is correct, and its simplified form $4 > 3$ is also correct.

What about doing the same thing to both sides of an inequality, such as adding the same number to both sides, or multiplying both sides by the same number? The next activity lets you explore these possibilities.

Activity 36 *Doing the same thing to both sides of an inequality*

(a) Consider the correct inequality $-2 < 1$.

    (i)   Does it remain correct if you add 3 to both sides?

    (ii) Does it remain correct if you subtract 4 from both sides?

(b) Consider the correct inequality $-3 \geq -5$.

    (i)   Does it remain correct if you multiply both sides by 3?

    (ii) Does it remain correct if you multiply both sides by -2?

(c) Does each of the following correct inequalities remain correct if you multiply both sides by 0?

    (i) $2 \leq 3$ (ii) $2 < 3$

The rearranged inequalities in Activity 36 illustrate the following facts.

Rearranging inequalities

You can do any of the following things to a correct inequality to obtain another correct inequality.

- Do any of the following to *both sides*.
  - Add or subtract a number.
  - Multiply or divide by a *positive* number.
  - Multiply or divide by a *negative* number, *if you reverse the inequality sign.*
- Simplify one side or both sides.
- Swap the sides, *if you reverse the inequality sign.*

You also saw in Activity 36 that if you multiply both sides of an inequality by zero, then both sides become 0, so if it was a '$\leq$' or a '$\geq$' inequality, then it remains correct, but if it was a '$<$' or a '$>$' inequality, it becomes wrong.

The next example illustrates how to rearrange inequalities. It's just like rearranging equations, except that sometimes you need to reverse the inequality sign, according to the rules in the box above.

Example 19   *Rearranging inequalities*

For each of the following inequalities, rearrange it to obtain an inequality with the variable by itself on the left-hand side and a number on the right-hand side, and illustrate the numbers that satisfy the original inequality on a number line.

(a) $3x + 2 < 1$ (b) $-3 - 2x \leq 1$

Solution

Use the usual method for solving a linear equation, remembering that sometimes you may need to reverse the inequality sign.

(a) The inequality is: $3x + 2 < 1$

Subtract 2: $3x < -1$

Divide by 3: $x < -\frac{1}{3}$

So the numbers that satisfy the original inequality can be illustrated on a number line as follows.

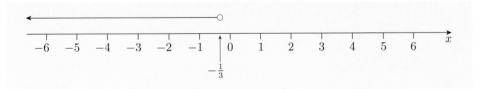

(b) The inequality is: $-3 - 2x \leq 1$

Add 3: $-2x \leq 4$

Divide by -2: $x \geq -2$

The inequality sign was reversed because -2 is negative.

Alternatively, you could proceed as follows.

The inequality is: $-3 - 2x \leq 1$

Add $2x$: $-3 \leq 1 + 2x$

Subtract 1: $-4 \leq 2x$

Divide by 2: $-2 \leq x$

Swap the sides: $x \geq -2$

So the numbers that satisfy the original inequality can be illustrated on a number line as follows.

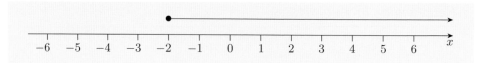

When you rearrange an inequality, as when you rearrange an equation, there are often different but equally valid approaches that you can take. The approach that you choose will be valid as long as in each step you do the same thing to both sides, simplify one or both sides, or swap the sides, and you reverse the inequality sign when appropriate.

Activity 37   *Rearranging inequalities*

Rearrange each of the following inequalities to obtain an inequality with the variable by itself on the left-hand side and a number on the right-hand side, and illustrate the numbers that satisfy the inequality on a number line.

(a) $2z - 1 \geq 5$ (b) $7 - 3a < 1$ (c) $3 < -2p$

(d) $2 - 3t > t + 1$ (e) $\frac{1}{2}c - 1 \geq c$ (f) $m > 2(1 - m)$

Activity 38   *Rearranging another inequality*

In the solution to Activity 35, the inequality

$$6.5n + 4 \leq 75$$

was found for the number n of CDs that can be bought. Rearrange this inequality to obtain n by itself on the left-hand side and a number on the right-hand side. Hence state the maximum number of CDs that can be bought.

When you multiply or divide both sides of an inequality by a *variable*, or by an expression containing a variable, you have to be careful about the sense of the inequality sign. For example, consider the inequality

$$a < \frac{b}{c}.$$

If you know that c is positive, then you can clear the fraction by multiplying both sides by c and leaving the inequality sign unchanged. Similarly, if you know that c is negative, then you can multiply both sides by c and reverse the inequality sign. If you don't know whether c is positive or negative, then all you can do is to split into cases, like this:

If c is positive then $ac < b$, whereas if c is negative then $ac > b$.

However, inequalities like this don't arise often in practice, and you won't meet any more in this module.

4.3   Inequalities in two variables

In Unit 6 you saw that some equations in two variables can be represented by straight lines on graphs. In this section you'll see that some *inequalities* in two variables can also be represented on graphs, and how it can be useful to do so.

Let's consider an inequality that arises from a practical situation. Suppose that you are organising a party, and you have £60 to spend on the soft drinks for it. You plan to buy some cartons of juice, which cost £1 each, and some bottles of lemonade, which cost £1.50 each. Let's use J and L to represent the numbers of cartons of juice and bottles of lemonade, respectively, that you buy. The total cost, in pounds, will be

$$J \times 1 + L \times 1.5 = J + 1.5L.$$

Since you have only £60 to spend,

$$J + 1.5L \leq 60.$$

So the numbers J and L of cartons of juice and bottles of lemonade that you buy must satisfy this inequality. It can be slightly easier to deal with whole numbers, so let's multiply both sides of this inequality by the positive number 2 to obtain the equivalent inequality

$$2J + 3L \leq 120.$$

Now let's look at how this inequality can be represented graphically.

First, consider the pairs of values of J and L such that $2J + 3L$ is not just *less than or equal* to 120, but actually *equal* to 120. That is, consider the pairs that satisfy the equation

$$2J + 3L = 120. \tag{30}$$

These pairs correspond to spending *all* of the £60. You know how to draw the graph of equation (30) – it will be a straight line – so let's do that. We'll put J on the horizontal axis and L on the vertical axis. As you have seen, one way to draw a line is to find two points on it. Here, if $J = 0$, then

$$3L = 120, \quad \text{so} \quad L = 40,$$

so one point on the line is $(0, 40)$. This corresponds to buying no cartons of juice and 40 bottles of lemonade. Similarly, if $L = 0$, then

$$2J = 120, \quad \text{so} \quad J = 60,$$

so another point on the line is $(60, 0)$. This corresponds to buying 60 cartons of juice and no bottles of lemonade. So the line is as shown in Figure 12.

You saw on page 132 that any equation of the form $ax + by = d$, where x and y are variables and a, b and d are numbers, is the equation of a straight line.

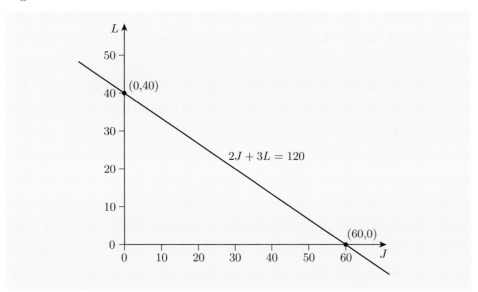

Figure 12   The straight line with equation $2J + 3L = 120$

Now consider a point somewhere on the line with equation $2J + 3L = 120$, say the point $(30, 20)$. The values $J = 30$, $L = 20$ also satisfy the inequality $2J + 3L \leq 120$, since 'less than or equal to' includes 'equal to'. Moreover, if either of the values $J = 30$ or $L = 20$ is *decreased* slightly, then the inequality will still hold. On the other hand, if either of the values is *increased*, to a value above 30 or 20, respectively, then $2J + 3L$ will exceed 120, and so the inequality will not be satisfied.

So the area below and to the left of the line $2J + 3L = 120$, *including* the line itself, represents the points that satisfy the inequality $2J + 3L \leq 120$, while the area above and to the right of the line, *but not including* the line, represents the points that do not satisfy the inequality. In Figure 13, the points that satisfy the inequality are those in the blue area or on the line, while the points that don't satisfy the inequality are those in the pink area.

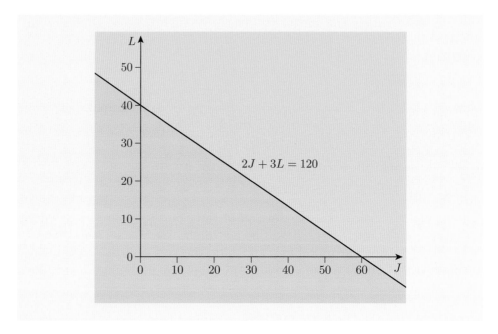

Figure 13   Points satisfying and not satisfying the inequality $2J + 3L \leq 120$

However, Figure 13 is not a particularly useful representation of the possibilities for buying drinks for the party, because it includes areas where one or both of J and L are *negative*. You can't buy negative quantities of cartons of juice or bottles of lemonade, so in order to model the choices for the party, it's necessary to consider only the area where J and L are positive. So the area of the graph that represents the practical choices for J and L is the blue triangle in Figure 14. More specifically, the practical choices are the points within this area that have *integer coordinates*.

For example, you could buy 10 cartons of juice and 30 bottles of lemonade; this comes well within the blue triangle in Figure 14. Or you could spend up to your £60 limit with 15 cartons of juice and 30 bottles of lemonade; the point on the graph that represents this expenditure is on the boundary of the blue triangle.

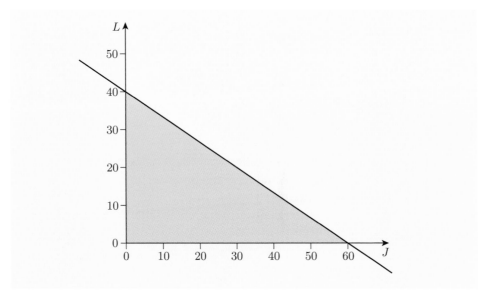

Figure 14   The area of practical choice

Activity 39   *Representing an inequality on a graph*

Now suppose that you wish to ensure that there is at least a litre of soft drink available to each party guest, of whom there will be 90. The juice cartons contain one litre each and the lemonade bottles contain three litres.

(a) Find an inequality in terms of J and L that expresses this wish.

(b) Draw a graph and shade in the area of practical choice for the inequality in part (a).

Finally, suppose that you want to choose values of J and L that satisfy *both* the original wish and the one in Activity 39. That is, you want to spend no more than £60 *and* you want to buy at least 90 litres of soft drink. Then the area of practical choice is the *overlap* of the two areas of practical choice drawn already, namely the area in Figure 14 and the area in the solution to Activity 39. This overlap is shown in Figure 15.

Graphs like the one in Figure 15 play a part in *operational research*. This is a branch of applied mathematics that is concerned with finding the best solutions to complicated practical situations.

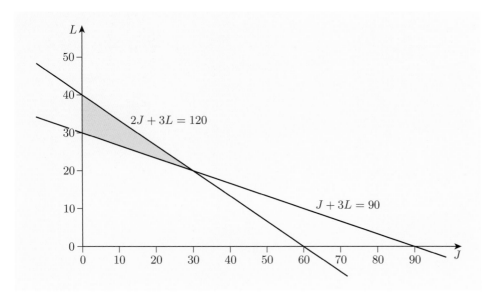

Figure 15   The area of practical choice for both inequalities together

Activity 40 *Choosing a suitable pair of values*

Use Figure 15 to find a suitable number of cartons of juice and a suitable number of bottles of lemonade that you could buy to ensure that you spend no more than £60 and buy at least 90 litres of soft drink.

In this unit you have seen various different situations in which algebra is helpful, and you have learned some new algebraic techniques that allow you to deal with situations of these types. In particular, you have learned to rearrange equations and inequalities, take out common factors and solve simultaneous linear equations.

Learning checklist

After studying this unit, you should be able to:

- rearrange a simple equation to make a chosen variable the subject
- recognise the equation of a straight line in different forms
- draw the graph of an equation of a straight line that is given in any form
- take common factors out of expressions, including highest common factors
- rearrange an equation to make a chosen variable the subject, where this involves taking out a common factor
- solve a pair of simultaneous linear equations in two unknowns
- understand how a pair of simultaneous linear equations in two unknowns is represented on a graph
- recognise when a pair of simultaneous equations in two unknowns has no solution or infinitely many solutions
- solve some practical problems involving simultaneous linear equations
- express information from a practical situation as an inequality
- rearrange an inequality
- interpret some inequalities in two unknowns as areas on graphs.

Solutions and comments on Activities

Activity 1

Substituting $f = 59$ into the formula

$$f = 1.8c + 32$$

gives

$$59 = 1.8c + 32.$$

Subtract 32: $27 = 1.8c$

Divide by 1.8: $15 = c$

So $59°F$ is the same as $15°C$.

Activity 2

Substituting $f = 85.1$ into the formula

$$c = \frac{f - 32}{1.8}$$

gives

$$c = \frac{85.1 - 32}{1.8} = 29.5.$$

So $85.1°F$ is the same as $29.5°C$.

Activity 3

The equation is: $f = 2s + 4$

Subtract 4: $f - 4 = 2s$

Divide by 2: $\dfrac{f - 4}{2} = s$

Swap the sides: $s = \dfrac{f - 4}{2}$

Activity 4

(a) The original formula is: $f = 1.8(k - 273) + 32$

Multiply out: $f = 1.8k - 491.4 + 32$

Simplify: $f = 1.8k - 459.4$

(This completes Step 1 of the strategy.)

Add 459.4: $f + 459.4 = 1.8k$

(This completes Step 2.)

Divide by 1.8: $\dfrac{f + 459.4}{1.8} = k$

(This completes Step 3.)

Hence a formula for k is

$$k = \frac{f + 459.4}{1.8}.$$

(You can obtain an alternative formula that does not contain the rather unmemorable number 459.4, by proceeding as follows.

The original formula is: $f = 1.8(k - 273) + 32$

Subtract 32: $f - 32 = 1.8(k - 273)$

Divide by 1.8: $\dfrac{f - 32}{1.8} = k - 273$

Add 273: $\dfrac{f - 32}{1.8} + 273 = k$

Hence a formula for k is

$$k = \frac{f - 32}{1.8} + 273.$$

In this second manipulation, the strategy was not followed exactly, but at each step the same thing was done to each side, the sides were simplified or the sides were swapped, so the manipulation is valid. Later in the subsection there is a discussion about the fact that you do not need to follow the strategy exactly.)

(b) Substituting $f = 97.7$ into the formula found in part (a) gives

$$k = \frac{97.7 + 459.4}{1.8} = \frac{557.1}{1.8} = 310 \text{ (to 3 s.f.)}.$$

So $97.7°F$ is about the same as $310\,K$.

Activity 5

(a) The original formula is: $d = st$

Divide by s: $\dfrac{d}{s} = t$

Hence a formula for t is

$$t = \frac{d}{s}.$$

(b) Substituting $d = 96$ and $s = 80$ into the formula found in part (a) gives

$$t = \frac{96}{80} = 1.2.$$

Hence the time taken is 1.2 hours; that is, 1 hour and 12 minutes.

(0.2 of an hour is the same as 0.2×60 minutes, that is, 12 minutes.)

Activity 6

(a) The equation is: $y = \dfrac{x}{2} - 3$

Multiply by 2: $2y = 2\left(\dfrac{x}{2} - 3\right)$

Multiply out: $2y = x - 6$

Add 6: $2y + 6 = x$

Swap the sides: $x = 2y + 6$

(The sides were swapped because it is usual to write the subject on the left-hand side.)

(b) The equation is: $s = \dfrac{6}{r}$

Multiply by r: $rs = 6$

Divide by s (assuming that $s \neq 0$): $r = \dfrac{6}{s}$

(c) The equation is: $X = \dfrac{Z}{Y+1}$

Multiply by $Y + 1$: $X(Y + 1) = Z$

Swap the sides: $Z = X(Y + 1)$

(There's no need to multiply out the brackets, but it is okay to do so.)

(d) The equation is: $q = \frac{2}{3}(p + 2)$

Multiply by 3: $3q = 2(p + 2)$

Multiply out: $3q = 2p + 4$

Subtract 4: $3q - 4 = 2p$

Divide by 2: $\dfrac{3q - 4}{2} = p$

Swap the sides: $p = \dfrac{3q - 4}{2}$

(Instead of multiplying out the brackets above, you could have proceeded as follows.

$$3q = 2(p + 2)$$

Divide by 2: $\frac{3}{2}q = p + 2$

Subtract 2: $\frac{3}{2}q - 2 = p$

Swap the sides: $p = \frac{3}{2}q - 2$

As you can see, this is slightly more efficient, and it leads to a slightly different, but equivalent, formula.)

(e) The equation is: $c = \dfrac{b}{2d + 1}$

Multiply by $2d + 1$: $c(2d + 1) = b$

Multiply out: $2cd + c = b$

Subtract c: $2cd = b - c$

Divide by $2c$
(assuming that $c \neq 0$): $d = \dfrac{b - c}{2c}$

(Instead of multiplying out the brackets above, you could have proceeded as follows.

$$c(2d + 1) = b$$

Divide by c
(assuming that $c \neq 0$): $2d + 1 = \dfrac{b}{c}$

Subtract 1: $2d = \dfrac{b}{c} - 1$

Divide by 2: $d = \dfrac{\frac{b}{c} - 1}{2}$

Expand the fraction: $d = \dfrac{\left(\frac{b}{c}\right)}{2} - \dfrac{1}{2}$

Simplify: $d = \dfrac{b}{c} \times \dfrac{1}{2} - \dfrac{1}{2}$

Simplify more: $d = \dfrac{b}{2c} - \dfrac{1}{2}$

This leads to a slightly different, but equivalent, formula.)

Activity 7

(a) Substituting $x = 3$ into the equation $y = 3x - 2$ gives

$$y = 3 \times 3 - 2 = 9 - 2 = 7.$$

So the point $(3, 7)$ satisfies the equation.

(b) Substituting $x = 3$ and $y = 7$ into the equation $y + 2 = 3x$ gives

$$\text{LHS} = 7 + 2 = 9$$

and

$$\text{RHS} = 3 \times 3 = 9.$$

Since LHS = RHS, the point $(3, 7)$ satisfies the equation.

(When you check whether an equation is satisfied, it is usually best to substitute into each side separately, as in the solution to part (b). However, as you have seen, if one side of the equation is very simple, such as a number or letter by itself, then you can just substitute into the other side and confirm that you get the expected answer, as in part (a).)

Activity 8

The equation is: $3x + 2y = 6$

Subtract $3x$: $2y = -3x + 6$

Divide by 2: $y = \dfrac{-3x + 6}{2}$

Expand the fraction: $y = \dfrac{-3x}{2} + \dfrac{6}{2}$

Simplify: $y = -\frac{3}{2}x + 3$

The gradient is $-\frac{3}{2}$ and the y-intercept is 3.

One point on the line is $(0, 3)$ (the point corresponding to the y-intercept). Another point can be found by substituting $x = 1$, for example, into the equation

$$y = -\tfrac{3}{2}x + 3.$$

This gives

$$y = -\tfrac{3}{2} \times 1 + 3 = -\tfrac{3}{2} + 3 = \tfrac{3}{2}.$$

So another point is $(1, \frac{3}{2}) = (1, 1.5)$.

The line is shown on the next page.

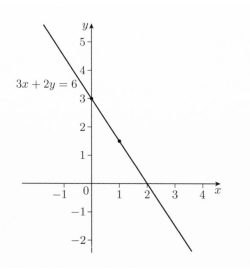

Activity 9

Substituting $x = 0$ into the equation gives $-3y = -6$.

Divide by -3: $\quad y = 2$

So a point on the line is $(0, 2)$.

Substituting $y = 0$ into the equation gives $4x = -6$.

Divide by 4: $\quad x = -\frac{3}{2}$.

So another point on the line is $\left(-\frac{3}{2}, 0\right) = (-1.5, 0)$.

The line is shown below.

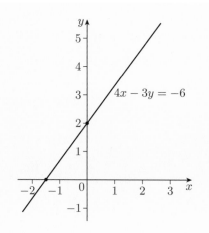

Activity 10

(a) $pqr = q \times pr$

(b) $A^7 = A^4 \times A^3$

(c) $4f^3 = 2f \times 2f^2$

(d) $p^3 q^5 = p^2 q^2 \times pq^3$

(e) $6x^5 y^8 = 2x^2 y \times 3x^3 y^7$

Activity 11

(a) $2z = z \times 2$ $\quad$ and $\quad z^2 = z \times z$.

So z is a common factor of the two terms.

(b) $p^2 q^2 = p^2 \times q^2$ $\quad$ and $\quad p^2 = p^2 \times 1$.

So p^2 is a common factor of the two terms.

(c) $2A^2 B^2 = 2AB \times AB$, $4A^2 B = 2AB \times 2A$ and $\quad 8AB = 2AB \times 4$.

So $2AB$ is a common factor of the three terms.

Activity 12

(a) The highest common factor of $2ab^2$ and $4ab$ is $2ab$.

$2ab^2 = 2ab \times b$ $\quad$ and $\quad 4ab = 2ab \times 2$.

(b) The highest common factor of $3xy$ and $6y$ is $3y$.

$3xy = 3y \times x$ $\quad$ and $\quad 6y = 3y \times 2$.

(c) The highest common factor of $4p^3$, $9p^2$ and $2p^5$ is p^2.

$4p^3 = p^2 \times 4p$, $\quad 9p^2 = p^2 \times 9$ $\quad$ and $\quad 2p^5 = p^2 \times 2p^3$.

(d) The highest common factor of $10r$ and $15s$ is 5.

$10r = 5 \times 2r$ $\quad$ and $\quad 15s = 5 \times 3s$.

Activity 13

(a) $ab + a^2 = a \times b + a \times a = a(b + a)$

(b) $x^3 y + yz = y \times x^3 + y \times z = y(x^3 + z)$

(c) $2w^2 + w^3 = w^2 \times 2 + w^2 \times w = w^2(2 + w)$

(d) $2z + 6z^4 = 2z \times 1 + 2z \times 3z^3 = 2z(1 + 3z^3)$

Activity 14

(a) $2ab + 2b - 6b^2 = 2b \times a + 2b \times 1 - 2b \times 3b$
$$= 2b(a + 1 - 3b)$$

(b) $A^5 - A^4 = A^4 \times A - A^4 \times 1 = A^4(A - 1)$

Activity 15

(a) $ab - 9bc = b(a - 9c)$

(b) $x^2 - x^5 + 2x^3 = x^2(1 - x^3 + 2x)$

(c) $-2rs + 4r^2 s^2 = 2rs(-1 + 2rs)$

(d) $x\sqrt{y} - \sqrt{y} = \sqrt{y}(x - 1)$

Activity 16

(a) $12u + 6u^3 - 9u^2 = 3u(4 + 2u^2 - 3u)$

(b) $5r^2 - 10 = 5(r^2 - 2)$

(c) The terms of the expression $3fg - 2gh + 6fh$ have no common factors.

(d) $-8ABC - 4AB^2 + 2AB$
$= 2AB(-4C - 2B + 1)$

Activity 17

(a) $0.3m^2 - 0.6m + 0.9 = 0.3(m^2 - 2m + 3)$

(b) $\frac{1}{2}x - \frac{1}{2}x^2 = \frac{1}{2}x(1 - x)$

Activity 18

(a) $-2u^2 - 2u^3 - 4u^4 = -(2u^2 + 2u^3 + 4u^4)$
$$= -2u^2(1 + u + 2u^2)$$

(b) $-1 - a + a^2 = -(1 + a - a^2)$

(c) $pq - p^2q - q^2p - p^2q^2$
$$= -(-pq + p^2q + q^2p + p^2q^2)$$
$$= -pq(-1 + p + q + pq)$$
$$= -pq(p + q + pq - 1)$$

(In the final step of part (c), the order of the terms inside the brackets has been changed, so that the term with a minus sign is not first. This is not essential, but it makes the expression slightly shorter and tidier.)

Activity 19

(a) The equation is: $gh = g + h$

Subtract h: $gh - h = g$

Take out h as a
common factor: $h(g - 1) = g$

Divide by $g - 1$
(assuming that $g \neq 1$): $h = \dfrac{g}{g - 1}$

(b) The equation is: $x = \dfrac{x - y}{y}$

Multiply by y: $xy = x - y$

Add y: $xy + y = x$

Take out y as a
common factor: $y(x + 1) = x$

Divide by $x + 1$
(assuming that $x \neq -1$): $y = \dfrac{x}{x + 1}$

(c) The equation is: $r = \dfrac{s}{r} + 2s$

Multiply by r: $r^2 = r\left(\dfrac{s}{r} + 2s\right)$

Multiply out the brackets: $r^2 = s + 2rs$

Take out s as a
common factor: $r^2 = s(1 + 2r)$

Divide by $1 + 2r$
(assuming that $r \neq -\frac{1}{2}$): $\dfrac{r^2}{1 + 2r} = s$

Swap the sides: $s = \dfrac{r^2}{1 + 2r}$

(d) The equation is: $2p + q = r(p + q)$

Multiply out the brackets: $2p + q = rp + rq$

Subtract rp: $2p + q - rp = rq$

Subtract q: $2p - rp = rq - q$

Take out p as a
common factor: $p(2 - r) = rq - q$

Divide by $2 - r$
(assuming that $r \neq 2$): $p = \dfrac{rq - q}{2 - r}$

This equation can be expressed slightly more simply if you take out the common factor in the numerator:

$$p = \frac{q(r - 1)}{2 - r}.$$

Activity 20

(a) The cost of hiring the venue is £100, and the cost of refreshments is £$10n$, so the total cost of the party, in pounds, is

$$100 + 10n.$$

The number of paying partygoers is $n - 5$. Hence the amount £p paid by each paying partygoer is given by the formula

$$p = \frac{100 + 10n}{n - 5}.$$

(b) The equation is: $p = \dfrac{100 + 10n}{n - 5}$

Multiply by $n - 5$: $p(n - 5) = 100 + 10n$
(This removes the fraction.)

Multiply out the brackets: $np - 5p = 100 + 10n$

Subtract $10n$: $np - 5p - 10n = 100$

Add $5p$: $np - 10n = 100 + 5p$

Take out n as a
common factor: $n(p - 10) = 100 + 5p$

Divide by $p - 10$
(assuming that $p \neq 10$): $n = \dfrac{100 + 5p}{p - 10}$

(c) We substitute $p = 12.5$ into the formula. This gives

$$n = \frac{100 + 5 \times 12.5}{12.5 - 10}$$
$$= \frac{100 + 62.5}{2.5}$$
$$= \frac{162.5}{2.5}$$
$$= 65.$$

The number of partygoers who must attend is 65.

Activity 21

(a) The total cost of manufacturing the n games, in pounds, is $f + nc$.

(b) The total selling price of the n games, in pounds, is ns.

(c) The profit is given by

$$p = ns - (f + nc),$$

that is,

$$p = ns - f - nc.$$

(d) The equation is: $p = ns - f - nc$

Add f: $\qquad\qquad\quad p + f = ns - nc$

Swap the sides: $\qquad\; ns - nc = p + f$

Take out n as a
common factor: $\qquad n(s - c) = p + f$

Divide by $s - c$
(valid if $s \neq c$): $\qquad n = \dfrac{p + f}{s - c}$

(e) Substituting $p = 20\,000$, $f = 10\,000$, $s = 40$ and $c = 15$ into the formula gives

$$n = \frac{20\,000 + 10\,000}{40 - 15} = \frac{30\,000}{25} = 1200.$$

So the number of games required is 1200.

Activity 22

(a) From the graph it looks as if the car will catch up with Fred about 2.25 hours after Fred sets off, which is 2 hours and 15 minutes after he sets off. Since Fred will set off at 10 am, this will be at about quarter past 12.

(b) From the graph it looks as if the car will catch up with the bicycle after about 68 km.

Activity 23

(a) The equation is: $30t = 90t - 135$

Subtract $30t$: $\qquad\quad 0 = 60t - 135$

Add 135: $\qquad\qquad\; 135 = 60t$

Divide by 60: $\qquad\;\; 2.25 = t$

Thus the solution is $t = 2.25$.

(b) Equation (6) is

$$d = 30t.$$

Substituting $t = 2.25$ into this equation gives

$$d = 30 \times 2.25 = 67.5.$$

(c) The car will catch up with the bicycle after 2.25 hours, which is 2 hours and 15 minutes. This will be at 12.15 pm. At this time the car and the bicycle will be 67.5 km from the start point.

(Notice that these values are close to the approximate values obtained from the graph.)

(d) Substituting $t = 2.25$ and $d = 67.5$ into equation (6) gives

LHS $= 67.5$,

RHS $= 30 \times 2.25 = 67.5$.

Substituting the same values into equation (7) gives

LHS $= 67.5$,

RHS $= 90 \times 2.25 - 135 = 202.5 - 135 = 67.5$.

Thus both equations are satisfied.

Activity 24

The equations are

$$y = 2x - 3, \qquad\qquad\qquad\qquad (31)$$
$$y = 5x + 9. \qquad\qquad\qquad\qquad (32)$$

The right-hand sides must be equal to each other; that is,

$$2x - 3 = 5x + 9.$$

This equation can be solved as follows.

The equation is: $\qquad 2x - 3 = 5x + 9$

Subtract $2x$: $\qquad\qquad -3 = 3x + 9$

Subtract 9: $\qquad\qquad\; -12 = 3x$

Divide by 3: $\qquad\qquad\;\; -4 = x$

So $x = -4$. Substituting this value of x into equation (31) gives

$$y = 2 \times (-4) - 3 = -8 - 3 = -11.$$

(Check: Substituting $x = -4$, $y = -11$ into equation (31) gives

LHS $= -11$,

RHS $= 2 \times (-4) - 3 = -11$.

Substituting the same values into equation (32) gives

LHS $= -11$,

RHS $= 5 \times (-4) + 9 = -11$.)

Activity 25

(a) The equations

$$y = -2x + 5,$$
$$y = -2x - 1$$

represent parallel lines, so they do not have a solution.

(b) The equations can be arranged to give

$$y = -2x + 5,$$
$$y = -2x + 5.$$

As they represent the same line, they have infinitely many solutions.

(c) The equations

$$y = -2x + 5,$$
$$y = 3x - 1$$

represent lines that are not parallel, so they have exactly one solution.

Activity 26

The equations are

$$x = 2y - 7, \tag{33}$$
$$3x - y = -6. \tag{34}$$

Using equation (33) to substitute for x in equation (34) gives

$$3(2y - 7) - y = -6.$$

We now solve this equation.

$$3(2y - 7) - y = -6$$
$$6y - 21 - y = -6$$
$$5y - 21 = -6$$
$$5y = 15$$
$$y = 3$$

Substituting $y = 3$ into equation (33) gives

$$x = 2 \times 3 - 7 = 6 - 7 = -1.$$

So the solution is

$$x = -1, \ y = 3.$$

(Check: Substituting $x = -1$, $y = 3$ into equation (34) gives

$$\text{LHS} = 3 \times (-1) - 3 = -3 - 3 = -6 = \text{RHS.})$$

Activity 27

(a) The equations are

$$A - 2B = -3, \tag{35}$$
$$2A + 3B = 8. \tag{36}$$

Making A the subject of equation (35) gives

$$A = 2B - 3. \tag{37}$$

Substituting for A in equation (36) gives

$$2(2B - 3) + 3B = 8$$
$$4B - 6 + 3B = 8$$
$$7B - 6 = 8$$
$$7B = 14$$
$$B = 2.$$

Substituting for B in equation (37) gives

$$A = 2 \times 2 - 3 = 4 - 3 = 1.$$

Thus the solution is

$$A = 1, \ B = 2.$$

(Check: Substituting $A = 1$, $B = 2$ into equation (35) gives

$$\text{LHS} = 1 - 2 \times 2 = 1 - 4 = -3 = \text{RHS.}$$

Substituting the same values into equation (36) gives

$$\text{LHS} = 2 \times 1 + 3 \times 2 = 2 + 6 = 8 = \text{RHS.})$$

(b) The equations are

$$3S + T = 3, \tag{38}$$
$$7S + 2T = 8. \tag{39}$$

Making T the subject of equation (38) gives

$$T = 3 - 3S. \tag{40}$$

Substituting for T in equation (39) gives

$$7S + 2(3 - 3S) = 8$$
$$7S + 6 - 6S = 8$$
$$S + 6 = 8$$
$$S = 2.$$

Substituting for S in equation (40) gives

$$T = 3 - 3 \times 2 = 3 - 6 = -3.$$

Thus the solution is

$$S = 2, \ T = -3.$$

(Check: Substituting $S = 2$, $T = -3$ into equation (38) gives

$$\text{LHS} = 3 \times 2 + (-3) = 6 - 3 = 3 = \text{RHS.}$$

Substituting the same values into equation (39) gives

$$\text{LHS} = 7 \times 2 + 2 \times (-3) = 14 - 6 = 8 = \text{RHS.})$$

Activity 28

(a) The equations are

$$4x - 5y = 7, \tag{41}$$
$$-4x + 3y = -9. \tag{42}$$

Adding equations (41) and (42) gives

$$(4 - 4)x + (-5 + 3)y = 7 - 9$$
$$-2y = -2$$
$$y = 1.$$

Substituting this value of y into equation (41) gives

$$4x - 5 \times 1 = 7$$
$$4x - 5 = 7$$
$$4x = 12$$
$$x = 3.$$

Thus the solution is $x = 3$, $y = 1$.

(Check: Substituting $x = 3$, $y = 1$ into equation (41) gives

$$\text{LHS} = 4 \times 3 - 5 \times 1 = 12 - 5 = 7 = \text{RHS.}$$

Substituting the same values into equation (42) gives

$$\text{LHS} = -4 \times 3 + 3 \times 1 = -12 + 3 = -9 = \text{RHS.})$$

(b) The equations are

$$5x + 4y = 23, \tag{43}$$
$$5x + 6y = 27. \tag{44}$$

Subtracting equation (44) from equation (43) gives

$$(5 - 5)x + (4 - 6)y = 23 - 27$$
$$-2y = -4$$
$$y = 2.$$

(Instead of subtracting equation (44) from equation (43) you could have subtracted equation (43) from equation (44), which gives

$$2y = 4$$
$$y = 2.)$$

Substituting this value of y into equation (43) gives

$$5x + 4 \times 2 = 23$$
$$5x + 8 = 23$$
$$5x = 15$$
$$x = 3.$$

Thus the solution is $x = 3$, $y = 2$.

(Check: Substituting $x = 3$, $y = 2$ into equation (43) gives

$$\text{LHS} = 5 \times 3 + 4 \times 2 = 15 + 8 = 23 = \text{RHS}.$$

Substituting the same values into equation (44) gives

$$\text{LHS} = 5 \times 3 + 6 \times 2 = 15 + 12 = 27 = \text{RHS}.)$$

Activity 29

The equations are

$$2x + 3y = 9, \tag{45}$$
$$3x - 4y = 5. \tag{46}$$

Probably the simplest choice is to multiply equation (45) by 3 and equation (46) by 2 to obtain

$$6x + 9y = 27, \tag{47}$$
$$6x - 8y = 10. \tag{48}$$

Subtracting equation (48) from equation (47) gives

$$17y = 17$$
$$y = 1.$$

Substituting $y = 1$ into equation (45) gives

$$2x + 3 \times 1 = 9$$
$$2x + 3 = 9$$
$$2x = 6$$
$$x = 3.$$

Thus the solution to equations (45) and (46) is $x = 3$, $y = 1$.

(Check: Substituting $x = 3$, $y = 1$ into equation (45) gives

$$\text{LHS} = 2 \times 3 + 3 \times 1 = 6 + 3 = 9 = \text{RHS}.$$

Substituting the same values into equation (46) gives

$$\text{LHS} = 3 \times 3 - 4 \times 1 = 9 - 4 = 5 = \text{RHS}.)$$

Activity 30

(a) The equations are

$$2X - Y = -1, \tag{49}$$
$$3X - Y = 1. \tag{50}$$

Substitution method

Equation (49) can be rearranged as

$$Y = 2X + 1. \tag{51}$$

Substituting into equation (50) gives

$$3X - (2X + 1) = 1$$
$$3X - 2X - 1 = 1$$
$$X - 1 = 1$$
$$X = 2.$$

Substituting into equation (51) gives

$$Y = 2 \times 2 + 1 = 5$$

So the solution is $X = 2$, $Y = 5$.

Elimination method

Subtracting equation (49) from equation (50) gives

$$X = 2.$$

Substituting into equation (49) gives

$$2 \times 2 - Y = -1$$
$$4 - Y = -1$$
$$-Y = -5$$
$$Y = 5.$$

So the solution is $X = 2$, $Y = 5$.

(Check: Substituting $X = 2$, $Y = 5$ into equation (49) gives

$$\text{LHS} = 2 \times 2 - 5 = -1 = \text{RHS}.$$

Substituting the same values into equation (50) gives

$$\text{LHS} = 3 \times 2 - 5 = 1 = \text{RHS}.)$$

(b) The equations are

$$4X - 5Y = 1, \tag{52}$$
$$5X + 2Y = 4. \tag{53}$$

Substitution method

Rearranging equation (53) gives

$$5X + 2Y = 4$$
$$2Y = 4 - 5X$$
$$Y = 2 - \tfrac{5}{2}X. \tag{54}$$

Substituting into equation (52) gives

$$4X - 5\left(2 - \tfrac{5}{2}X\right) = 1$$
$$4X - 10 + \tfrac{25}{2}X = 1$$
$$\tfrac{33}{2}X = 11$$
$$X = \tfrac{2}{3}.$$

Substituting into equation (54) gives

$$Y = 2 - \tfrac{5}{2} \times \tfrac{2}{3} = \tfrac{12}{6} - \tfrac{10}{6} = \tfrac{2}{6} = \tfrac{1}{3}.$$

So the solution is $X = \tfrac{2}{3}$, $Y = \tfrac{1}{3}$.

Elimination method

Multiplying equation (52) by 2 and equation (53) by 5 gives

$$8X - 10Y = 2,$$
$$25X + 10Y = 20.$$

Adding the two equations gives

$$33X = 22$$
$$X = \tfrac{2}{3}.$$

Substituting into equation (52) gives

$$4 \times \tfrac{2}{3} - 5Y = 1$$
$$\tfrac{8}{3} - 5Y = 1$$
$$\tfrac{8}{3} = 1 + 5Y$$
$$\tfrac{5}{3} = 5Y$$
$$\tfrac{1}{3} = Y.$$

So the solution is $X = \tfrac{2}{3}$, $Y = \tfrac{1}{3}$.

(Check: Substituting $X = \tfrac{2}{3}, Y = \tfrac{1}{3}$ into equation (52) gives

$$\text{LHS} = 4 \times \tfrac{2}{3} - 5 \times \tfrac{1}{3} = \tfrac{8}{3} - \tfrac{5}{3} = \tfrac{3}{3} = 1 = \text{RHS.}$$

Substituting the same values into equation (53) gives

$$\text{LHS} = 5 \times \tfrac{2}{3} + 2 \times \tfrac{1}{3} = \tfrac{10}{3} + \tfrac{2}{3} = \tfrac{12}{3} = 4 = \text{RHS.})$$

(c) The equations are

$$-2A + 5B = -2, \tag{55}$$
$$-2A + 3B = 2. \tag{56}$$

Substitution method

Rearranging equation (56) gives

$$-2A + 3B = 2$$
$$-2A = -3B + 2$$
$$A = \tfrac{3}{2}B - 1. \tag{57}$$

Substituting into equation (55) gives

$$-2\left(\tfrac{3}{2}B - 1\right) + 5B = -2$$
$$-3B + 2 + 5B = -2$$
$$2B + 2 = -2$$
$$2B = -4$$
$$B = -2.$$

Substituting into equation (57) gives

$$A = \tfrac{3}{2} \times (-2) - 1 = -3 - 1 = -4.$$

So the solution is $A = -4$, $B = -2$.

Elimination method

Subtracting equation (56) from equation (55) gives

$$2B = -4$$
$$B = -2.$$

Substituting into equation (55) gives

$$-2A + 5 \times (-2) = -2$$
$$-2A - 10 = -2$$
$$-2A = 8$$
$$A = -4.$$

So the solution is $A = -4$, $B = -2$.

(Check: Substituting $A = -4$, $B = -2$ into equation (55) gives

$$\text{LHS} = -2 \times (-4) + 5 \times (-2) = 8 - 10 = -2$$
$$= \text{RHS.}$$

Substituting the same values into equation (56) gives

$$\text{LHS} = -2 \times (-4) + 3 \times (-2) = 8 - 6 = 2$$
$$= \text{RHS.})$$

(d) The equations are

$$3P - 6Q = 3,$$
$$7P - 4Q = 1.$$

Dividing the first equation by the common factor 3 gives the equations

$$P - 2Q = 1, \tag{58}$$
$$7P - 4Q = 1. \tag{59}$$

Substitution method

Equation (58) can be rearranged as

$$P = 2Q + 1. \tag{60}$$

Substituting into equation (59) gives

$$7(2Q + 1) - 4Q = 1$$
$$14Q + 7 - 4Q = 1$$
$$10Q + 7 = 1$$
$$10Q = -6$$
$$Q = -\tfrac{3}{5}.$$

Substituting into equation (60) gives

$$P = 2 \times \left(-\tfrac{3}{5}\right) + 1 = -\tfrac{6}{5} + \tfrac{5}{5} = -\tfrac{1}{5}.$$

So the solution is $P = -\tfrac{1}{5}$, $Q = -\tfrac{3}{5}$.

Elimination method

Multiplying equation (58) by 2 and leaving equation (59) unchanged gives

$$2P - 4Q = 2,$$
$$7P - 4Q = 1.$$

Subtracting the first of these equations from the second gives

$$5P = -1$$
$$P = -\tfrac{1}{5}.$$

Substituting into equation (58) gives

$-\frac{1}{5} - 2Q = 1$

$-2Q = \frac{1}{5} + 1$

$-2Q = \frac{6}{5}$

$Q = -\frac{3}{5}.$

So the solution is $P = -\frac{1}{5}$, $Q = -\frac{3}{5}$.

(Check: Substituting $P = -\frac{1}{5}$, $Q = -\frac{3}{5}$ into equation (58) gives

LHS $= -\frac{1}{5} - 2 \times \left(-\frac{3}{5}\right) = -\frac{1}{5} + \frac{6}{5} = 1 =$ RHS.

Substituting the same values into equation (59) gives

LHS $= 7 \times \left(-\frac{1}{5}\right) - 4 \times \left(-\frac{3}{5}\right) = -\frac{7}{5} + \frac{12}{5} = 1$

$=$ RHS.)

Activity 31

The Sandmartin Hotel charges £350 plus £55 for each person, so its formula is

$C = 350 + 55N.$

The Swift Hotel charges £500 plus £50 for each person, so its formula is

$C = 500 + 50N.$

Activity 32

(a) Replacing N by x and C by y in the formula found in Activity 31 gives

$y = 350 + 55x$, that is, $y = 55x + 350$,

for the Sandmartin Hotel and

$y = 500 + 50x$, that is, $y = 50x + 500$,

for the Swift Hotel.

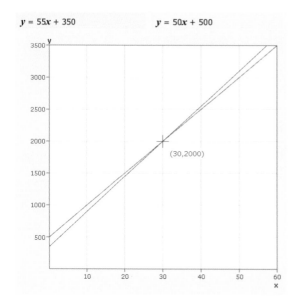

(b) The coordinates of the crossing point seem to be about $(30, 2000)$. The x-coordinate of this point represents the number of participants for which the costs of the two hotels are the same. The y-coordinate represents the cost of holding the event for this number of people at either hotel.

(c) The equations are

$C = 350 + 55N$,

$C = 500 + 50N$.

The easiest way to solve them is to subtract the first from the second. This gives

$0 = 150 - 5N$

$5N = 150$

$N = 30.$

Substituting $N = 30$ into the first equation (the Sandmartin's) gives

$C = 350 + 55 \times 30 = 350 + 1650 = 2000.$

(Check: Substituting $N = 30$ into the second equation (the Swift's) gives

$C = 500 + 50 \times 30 = 500 + 1500 = 2000.$)

So, as expected, for 30 people the cost is the same for the two hotels; it is £2000 in each case.

This agrees with the answer found in part (b).

(d) The boss would probably like to see the graph; that way, when you give her the information she wants, she will be able to check your answer against the graph, and it will be a useful thing to flash around at meetings!

You should also give her a clear statement explaining how she can make her decision, such as the following:

> If there are 30 participants, then each hotel will charge £2000. If there are fewer than 30 participants, then the Sandmartin should be booked; if more, then the Swift should be booked.

Activity 33

(a) The equations are

$Q = \frac{1}{4}P - 50$, (61)

$Q = -\frac{1}{8}P + 70$. (62)

Multiplying equation (61) by 4 and equation (62) by 8 gives

$4Q = P - 200$, (63)

$8Q = -P + 560$. (64)

(b) Adding the two equations gives

$12Q = 360$

$Q = 30.$

Substituting this value of Q into equation (63) gives

$$4 \times 30 = P - 200$$
$$120 = P - 200$$
$$320 = P.$$

So the solution is

$$P = 320, \quad Q = 30.$$

(c) The equilibrium price of the apples is £3.20 per kg.

The value of Q obtained in part (b) is the quantity of apples supplied and demanded at the equilibrium price, in millions of kilograms.

Activity 34

If you drive at the maximum speed of 70 mph during the motorway part of the journey, then the time for that part is

$$\frac{\text{distance}}{\text{speed}} = \frac{105}{70} = 1\tfrac{1}{2} \text{ hours.}$$

So you will take at least $1\tfrac{1}{2}$ hours on the motorway. With half an hour to get to the junction, and a quarter of an hour at the other end, you need to leave at least $2\tfrac{1}{4}$ hours in total. That is, $t \geq 2\tfrac{1}{4}$, or $t \geq \tfrac{9}{4}$.

Activity 35

You certainly can't order as many as 15 CDs, as that would cost over £90 even without considering postage. So your postage will definitely cost £4. So if you order n CDs, you must pay $6.5n + 4$ pounds. Thus an inequality concerning the number of CDs that you can order is

$$6.5n + 4 \leq 75.$$

Activity 36

(a) (i) Yes. Adding 3 to both sides of the inequality $-2 < 1$ gives $1 < 4$, which is correct.

(ii) Yes. Subtracting 4 from both sides of the inequality $-2 < 1$ gives $-6 < -3$, which is correct.

(b) (i) Yes. Multiplying both sides of the inequality $-3 \geq -5$ by 3 gives $-9 \geq -15$, which is correct.

(ii) *No!* Multiplying both sides of the inequality $-3 \geq -5$ by -2 gives $6 \geq 10$, which is wrong.

(c) (i) Yes. Multiplying both sides of the inequality $2 \leq 3$ by 0 gives $0 \leq 0$, which is correct.

(ii) *No!* Multiplying both sides of the inequality $2 < 3$ by 0 gives $0 < 0$, which is wrong.

Activity 37

(a) The inequality is: $2z - 1 \geq 5$

Add 1: $\qquad\qquad 2z \geq 6$

Divide by 2: $\qquad\quad z \geq 3$

The numbers that satisfy the original inequality can be illustrated on a number line as follows.

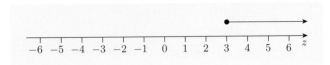

(b) The inequality is: $7 - 3a < 1$

Subtract 7: $\qquad\qquad -3a < -6$

Divide by -3: $\qquad\quad a > 2$

The numbers that satisfy the original inequality can be illustrated as follows.

(c) The inequality is: $3 < -2p$

Divide by -2: $\qquad -\tfrac{3}{2} > p$

Swap the sides: $\qquad p < -\tfrac{3}{2}$

The numbers that satisfy the original inequality can be illustrated as follows.

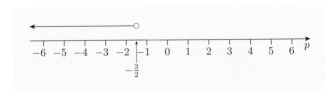

(d) The inequality is: $2 - 3t > t + 1$

Add $3t$: $\qquad\qquad 2 > 4t + 1$

Subtract 1: $\qquad\qquad 1 > 4t$

Divide by 4: $\qquad\qquad \tfrac{1}{4} > t$

Swap the sides: $\qquad\; t < \tfrac{1}{4}$

The numbers that satisfy the original inequality can be illustrated as follows.

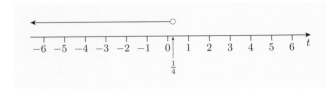

(e) The inequality is: $\frac{1}{2}c - 1 \geq c$

Multiply by 2: $\qquad c - 2 \geq 2c$

Subtract c: $\qquad -2 \geq c$

Swap the sides: $\qquad c \leq -2$

The numbers that satisfy the original inequality can be illustrated as follows.

(f) The inequality is: $m > 2(1 - m)$

Multiply out: $\qquad m > 2 - 2m$

Add $2m$: $\qquad 3m > 2$

Divide by 3: $\qquad m > \frac{2}{3}$

The numbers that satisfy the original inequality can be illustrated as follows.

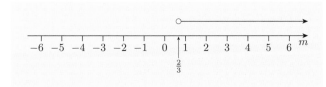

Activity 38

The inequality is: $\qquad 6.5n + 4 \leq 75$

Subtract 4: $\qquad 6.5n \leq 71$

Divide by 6.5: $\qquad n \leq \dfrac{71}{6.5}$

Simplify: $\qquad n \leq \dfrac{142}{13}$

Since
$$\frac{142}{13} \approx 10.9,$$

the maximum number of CDs that can be bought is 10.

Activity 39

(a) The total quantity of soft drink, in litres, will be

$$J \times 1 + L \times 3 = J + 3L,$$

and you need at least 90 litres, so the inequality is

$$J + 3L \geq 90.$$

(b) The area of practical choice is shown below. It is infinite! This is because you could buy any large numbers of cartons of juice and bottles of lemonade, and the total quantity of drink would always be at least 90 litres.

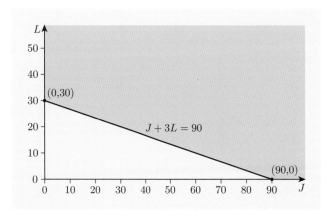

Activity 40

The point $(10, 30)$ lies within the blue triangle in Figure 15, so one possibility is to buy 10 cartons of juice and 30 bottles of lemonade.

(Check: The cost of these numbers of cartons of juice and bottles of lemonade is

$$\text{£}(10 \times 1 + 30 \times 1.50) = \text{£}55,$$

which is less than £60, and the quantity of drink that they provide is

$$(10 \times 1 + 30 \times 3) \text{ litres} = 100 \text{ litres},$$

which is more than 90 litres, so both wishes are satisfied.)

Of course, your choice of point could have been slightly different!

Acknowledgements

Grateful acknowledgement is made to the following sources for permission to reproduce material in this book.

Unit 5

Figure 1 © Bettmann/CORBIS; Figure 5: From www.wikipedia.org; Figure 6 © The Trustees of the British Museum; Figure 7: Yale Babylonian Collection.

Unit 6

Figure 16 © Dolas/iStockphoto; Figure 23 © Karen Stafford from the show 'Of all the people in all the world' by *Stan's Café* (www.stanscafe.co.uk); Figure 27: From www.maniacworld.com; Figure 33: From www-history.mcs.st-andrews.ac.uk.

Unit 7

Figure 2 © Theasis/iStockphoto; Figure 11: From www.wikipedia.org.

INDEX